Before enlisting in the army at age twenty-six, Colby Buzzell lived in the San Francisco Bay area. He served for two years, including about a year in Iraq, and now lives in Los Angeles.

www.booksattransworld.co.uk

MY WAR

Killing Time in Iraq

Colby Buzzell

CORGI BOOKS

MY WAR
A CORGI BOOK : 0552154377
9780552154376

Originally published in Great Britain by Doubleday,
a division of Transworld Publishers

First publication in Great Britain
Originally published in the US by G.P. Putnam's Sons,
a division of the Penguin Group

PRINTING HISTORY
Corgi edition published 2006

1 3 5 7 9 10 8 6 4 2

Permissions appear on pages 411-412

Some names and identifying characteristics have been changed
to protect the privacy of the individuals involved.

While the author has made every effort to provide accurate telephone
numbers and internet addresses at the time of publication, neither the
publisher nor the author assumes any responsibility for errors, or for
changes that occur after publication. Further, the publisher does not have any
control over and does not assume any responsibility for author or
third-party websites or their content.

Set in 11/13pt Minion by
Falcon Oast Graphic Art Ltd.

Corgi Books are published by Transworld Publishers,
61–63 Uxbridge Road, London W5 5SA,
a division of The Random House Group Ltd,
in Australia by Random House Australia (Pty) Ltd,
20 Alfred Street, Milsons Point, Sydney, NSW 2061, Australia,
in New Zealand by Random House New Zealand Ltd,
18 Poland Road, Glenfield, Auckland 10, New Zealand
and in South Africa by Random House (Pty) Ltd, Isle of Houghton,
Corner of Boundary Road & Carse O'Gowrie, Houghton 2198, South Africa.

Printed and bound in Great Britain by
Cox & Wyman Ltd, Reading, Berkshire.

Papers used by Transworld Publishers are natural, recyclable
products made from wood grown in sustainable forests. The
manufacturing processes conform to the environmental
regulations of the country of origin

This book is dedicated
to all those who served in
Operation Iraqi Freedom

Part One

Help Wanted

Kids from the suburbs don't really join the military. At least not where I'm from. After high school you do one of two things, you either get your education on at some big-name university or college, or you live at your parents' and smoke pot and work a shit job, like telemarketing. Maybe even pretend to go to college by taking one or two remedial classes at the JC, just to get Mom and Pops off your back while you figure out exactly what you want to do with yourself.

The only guys I knew who joined the armed forces were guys who came from families who had fathers who served in the military at some point in their lives. When you grow up with a parent who was in the military, you don't really look down on the military, you just look at it as an acceptable path to take, an option. The only guys I knew from high school who joined the military didn't join up right after the graduation ceremony, either, they joined several years after, once they dropped out of school and/or realized living at their parents' house kinda sucked.

There's this bar over by my parents' house in the Bay Area that I fucking hate going to, just because it's like a bad high school reunion every time I walk into it. You can't even enjoy a drink without bumping into somebody you went to high school with, either somebody you knew or somebody you barely knew. They'd all act super excited to see you. "Oh my God!" they'd say. "Is that you? Oh my God it is! Do you remember me? We had third-period U.S. history together. How are you?! What have you been up to?!"

I'd always say one of two things, "Oh, same old shit," or if I had a couple drinks in me already, I'd tell them some phony-baloney story that I was working part-time programming digital orbital satellite missions for NASA down in San Jose. Either way, whether I told them I was working for NASA or that I wasn't doing jack shit with my life, it didn't really matter, they would *all* say the same thing in return—"Wow, that's really cool." And then, without me even asking for it, they would give me a sit rep (situation report) on what they'd done since high school. They'd start talking about how college was so great (I'm sure it was), how they, like, *love* their job (yeah right), or they'd talk about all the horizon-expanding places that they'd traveled to (a trip to New York does not count as traveling), and how they're only living at home right now temporarily, for whatever reason (maybe because once they graduated from college they realized that they couldn't find a job with that diploma that they spent the last four years of their life on and they have no idea what to do now).

All my friends and almost everybody that I knew were barely making it and were always one or two paychecks away from moving back home. The only guys I knew from high school (keep in mind I didn't really hang out with Model UN or Academic Decathlon kids) who were actually making some kind of a decent living were guys who went off and got action-hero jobs—cops, firemen, soldiers.

Right before I moved to San Francisco I was in that bar that I hate, over by my parents' house, and I bumped into an old friend of mine from high school whom I hadn't seen in years.

We knew each other from playing football together. Both of our fathers fought in the jungles of Nam, his in the Marines, mine in the Army. For as long as I can remember, my father never once advised me or encouraged me to join the military. He also never tried to talk me out of it whenever I flirted with the idea. He always suggested and strongly encouraged that I go to college instead, or art school, or some kind of tech school. Which I never did, except for a couple wank community-college classes here and there, like photography and computers 101, just so my parents would get off my back and stop fucking asking me, "So when are you going back to school?"

My friend went off and joined the Marine Corps a couple years after high school, and now he was back living at his parents' temporarily while he was working at a local recruiting station. At the bar, we got drunk together and he told me all about the Marines and the friends he'd made there. It sounded pretty cool. I was twenty-five at the time, and I asked him if that was too old to join, and he said hell no. He told me about another guy I had graduated with who wasn't doing shit with his life either, who had just enlisted in the Corps.

As we got more and more drunk and the night went on and the stories about the Marines got wilder and wilder, so did my enthusiasm about signing up. He made it sound like joining the Marines was like joining a party frat with weapons that gave out paychecks, which of course sounded good to me, and maybe the globe-and-eagle Marine Corps tattoo with the words "Semper Fi" over it might look kinda cool on my forearm. So at the end of the night I slammed an empty Guinness glass down on the bar and told him, "Fuck it, I'll do it!" and we exchanged numbers (our parents' digits of course).

The next morning, when I woke up and started sobering up, the idea of being a jarhead didn't seem quite so appealing. So when my friend called and told me how I got home (it was one of those nights) and asked me when I wanted to stop by the recruiting office, I told him, "Sorry dude, that was the beers talking last night."

And I didn't hear from him again until I was in Mosul. He sent me this e-mail:

Hey Bro
How are things going long time no talk. Its Sturg. Well I am glad you joined the service even if it is the wrong one. Your mom gave my mom your email adress. I hope you are having a good stay in the holy land I have already been there done that. My company led the march to Baghdad we caused a lot of hate and discontent. Anyways hopefully your time is short over there I know it gets old. Well email me back and let me know how you are doing. Take care of yourself.
Sturg

I e-mailed him back, telling him that when I got back home, I'd buy him a couple beers at that bar that I hate going to by our parents' house, and we could exchange war stories and maybe even debate about which branch of the service was kicking the most ass in Iraq (Army). He wrote back to me:

Glad to hear back from you. Glad to see you are doing well. I will take you up on the beers when you get home. Anyways those Hajjis are pretty dam funny huh. How many kills have you had I know you must have had a few. My confirmed count was in the thirties but I know there was more than that being a gunner on a tank you tend to blow shit up to no recognition so you cant really tell. I bet it is already hot as shit over there. I know you are busy shoot me a line when you get a chance.
Later
Sturg

I had a job interview in the Potrero Hill district of San Francisco. Data entry, $10.50 an hour. The interview was at 9:00 a.m.

My job experience previous to this was: flower-delivery guy, valet-parker guy, mailroom guy, bike-messenger guy, busboy guy, carpet-cutter guy, cash-register-at-Orchard-Supply guy, car-washer guy, gift-shop sales guy, telemarketing guy, Kinko's guy, 7-Eleven guy, record-store guy, towel-guy-at-the-gym guy, and I worked seasonally at Toys "R" Us. The longest I'd ever held on to a job was like three to six months, then I would quit or get myself fired. I hate jobs. If it wasn't for something called "money" and/or "rent," I probably would have never worked one.

When I lived in Los Angeles a couple years back, I took a generic computer 101 class at Los Angeles Community College and taught myself data entry. I figured it was time for me to get with the times and learn a computer skill, so that way I could move on up and get myself a cubicle job someday and make something more than ten bucks an hour.

I arrived to the job interview an hour early, so I went over to this convenience store on a nearby corner to get a cup of coffee and a pack of Marlboro Lights. Potrero Hill kinda reminds me of Los Angeles, very industrial with a lot of working-class Mexicans. Outside the store they had some plastic chairs set up, so I sat down, lit up a smoke, and drank my coffee and waited for nine o'clock to come around.

A clean-cut older guy with a flattop came out of the liquor store with a paper bag and asked if it was okay to sit next to me and I said sure. Inside the paper bag was a red-and-white twenty-four-ounce can of Budweiser, which he cracked open and started drinking like it was morning coffee.

Anybody who starts a day off with a beer is A-OK in my book. We exchanged some small talk and I told him I had a job interview; he told me that he had an interview as well, some packing job for Federal Express, where he said they were really good about hiring veterans. I was curious so I asked him what branch he served in, and very proudly he said Marines, and I told him the story about how I got drunk a couple nights ago and briefly thought about becoming a marine. He got all excited and asked why I changed my mind. I told him that I felt I was too old. He said that was a bunch of bullshit. He then asked me how old I was, so I told him, and he flipped out. "Holy shit boy, if I was your fucking age right now I'd be joining the fucking Marines, you're not too old, no way, fuck, if the Marines didn't have rules on age, I'd go back to boot camp right fucking now, even at my old age." He then went on and on about his glory days, telling me how great the Marines were, how tough they were, how much of a killer they made him, and how once a marine, always a marine. He even physically stood up one time and excitedly said, "Fuckin A, man! I've been out of the fucking Corps for over twenty something years and I can still put a bullet in some fucker's skull at three hundred meters!"

He then sat down and took an enormous chug of his beer.

I then realized that even though this guy had been out of the Marines for over twenty something years, it was like he never really left the Marines, if you know what I mean. He then went on and on about how easy it was to get a city job if you were a veteran, especially one of those city jobs that require you to wear one of those bright-orange vests. He said the city of San Francisco was always hiring military vets and they were always the first applicants picked for jobs. And they paid pretty good, like sixteen to eighteen bucks an hour, some jobs with benefits, which was a hell of a lot more than I've ever made. It didn't occur to me at the time to ask him, if it's so easy to get a city job, what's he doing trying to land a job at FedEx, but whatever.

I listened to all his Marine Corps glory stories up until it got close to nine o'clock, and then we wished each other luck and went our separate ways.

I didn't get the data-entry job because they wanted somebody with more experience, somebody who was able to hold a job longer than a couple months, and somebody who didn't move all over the country.

I spent the rest of that day looking for another job and wondering if that marine got his.

San Francisco Daze

For a while, I did temp assignments doing brainless data entry for financial companies down on Market Street. The problem with doing temp work is you work a job for like a week or two, and then they let you go, and you're fucking right back to being jobless again. And it's always right about the time you run out of money, and you're right about to step out the door to go down to the welfare agency to register for government assistance when you receive a phone call from the temp agency for your next remedial job assignment.

At the time, I was begging everybody for a full-time job, and the only place that would hire me to do data entry was this pre-employment screening company located in Walnut Creek, about a forty-five-minute BART ride from the city (but fifteen minutes away from my parents' house). It was like God was playing a sick joke on me, no matter how hard I tried to get the hell away from the house where I grew up, I always ended up right back, or near it.

Nobody in San Francisco wanted to hire me, so I took the job in Walnut Creek because I was sick and tired of running around working temp assignments, and this gig in Walnut

Creek was full time. Since it was a full-time job, I was able to say "later" to my night job as a valet parker.

The Math:
JOB: $12 an hour (no benefits)
$12 an hour × 40 hours a week = $480 a week
4 weeks in a month × $480 = $1,920 a month
Subtract 15 percent for taxes ($288)
Subtract round-trip BART fare—Civic Center to Walnut Creek is $8 a day (that's $160 a month)
Subtract $45 for a monthly Muni bus pass (no car)
Subtract $45 for phone/Internet service
Subtract $124 for nicotine addiction ($4 a pack per day)
Subtract $675 for rent
Subtract $20 for utilities
Subtract $155 for food (which at $5 a day is a shitload of Top Ramen)
TOTAL Subtractions: $1,512 (conservative estimate)

$1,920 – $1,512 = $408

GRAND TOTAL: $408 (that's $102 a week, or $13.16 a day extra)
Not living at my parents' house: Priceless

Four hundred and eight dollars is how much I had extra at the end of the month to save up for my retirement, and for my nonprescription medication that I was taking at the time in very heavy doses (booze).

I finally decided to join the military after almost a year of living like this.

Tell It to the Marines

I dialed the 411 and got the digits to the parents of my friend from high school who was in the Marines, to see if he was still on recruiting duty. His sister answered the phone and she told me that he was done with his recruiting assignment and back with his Marine unit, doing some training somewhere and getting ready for war in Iraq.

There was a Marine recruiting station by this independent record store I used to work at in Pleasant Hill, so one day I took a half day from work and went over to sign up. This time, I made sure I was sober when I decided.

Marines always had the cool commercials with their "the few, the proud" warrior-image thing going on. The Army always had these lame-ass commercials that stressed getting money for college, as if I gave a fuck about that. It wasn't until about the time I joined the Army that they came up with a cool campaign, the "every generation has its heroes, this one is no different" ads. Those are kinda cool.

The Pleasant Hill Marine recruiting office is conveniently located right next to an Army recruiting station, and as I walked from the parking lot, I looked over at the Army office and saw a wide-eyed Army recruiter staring back at me through the big plate-glass windows. I thought nothing of him as I continued walking into the Marine recruiting station, and there was this Marine Corps sergeant in uniform sitting behind the desk who looked like he had the attitude that he didn't want to be at work today. The office was decorated with tough red-and-gold Marine Corps recruiting posters of every kind. I walked up to the desk and my exact words were, "I want to be a marine."

The guy didn't even get up from his seat, he just sorta looked me up and down and he said, "Really, huh? You want to be a marine?" This was a strange question coming from a recruiter and I wondered if it was because of how I looked. At the time I was going through a Social Distortion/rockabilly phase. I had on a vintage cowboy shirt and my long hair was slicked back like a switchblade-packing greaser. I said, "Yeah really, I came here because I want to enlist in the Marine Corps."

He looked at me again and asked me how old I was. I said, "I'm twenty-six, but my friend who's a marine said I'm not too old to enlist." He smiled and said, "Well, to be honest with you we like to recruit eighteen-year-olds straight out of high school, but if you're interested, I can have you fill out this little card and we'll call you."

Jesus fucking Christ. I'm thinking to myself that I didn't take no fucking half day from work to fill out some goddamn postcard. What the shit? I could see that this was turning into one of my many "Don't call us, we'll call you" job interviews.

For years the Marines had been calling my parents' house trying to get me to join, and the one time I walk in and say, "Take me, I'm all yours," they don't want me?

I looked into the Marine recruiter's eyes and said, "Look dude, you don't understand, I want to be a marine, like right now. I swear to God, I'll sign the fucking papers right now."

He then just kinda smirked and said, "Sure you do, but we're way over our quota this month, we have more people than we know what to do with right now. Just fill the card out and we'll call you in a couple."

Fine. So I filled the card out, gave him a half-assed thank-you, and walked out. And no shit, waiting patiently for me right outside the Marine Corps door was the Army recruiter with a handful of green pamphlets. As soon as I stepped outside, he extended his hand and said, "Hello, I'm a recruiter with the United States Army. Have you put any thought toward joining the United States Army?" I chuckled at his boldness. But I was also kinda shocked that he had the balls to wait right outside the Marine recruiting office for me. I told him, "Sorry dude, I'm not interested in the Army, I already made up my mind that I'm joining the Marine Corps." And as I was walking away from him I heard him say, "That's cool, good luck with the Marines." And then in a lower tone just loud enough for me to hear, he said, "Just so you know, the Army offers two-year enlistments right now and up to a four-thousand-dollar signing bonus."

Right when I heard him say that, the weirdest thing happened. I immediately envisioned myself in an Army uniform singing Airborne Ranger cadences. I felt like the Samuel L. Jackson character in *Pulp Fiction* when he says, "Well shit, Negro, that's all you had to say!"

I turned around and said, "What? Did you say two-year enlistments and a signing bonus?"

With a huge smile he said, "Sure did, and the GI Bill, medical, dental, two weeks paid leave every year, meal card . . ."

I was back at his side by then and he guided me inside the Army recruiting office and I sat and listened to everything he had to say, which began with a whole lot of bad-mouthing of the Corps: "Oh, their budget is nothing, they're part of the Navy, their posts suck, their equipment sucks, their training sucks, their tactics suck, their chow sucks . . ."

So far nothing he was saying was news to me—it was the same shit my father had been telling me about them for years. The only thing positive about the Marines, that both my recruiter and my father said, was that they had cooler uniforms. But other than that, they sucked.

But the most shocking thing my recruiter said was that the Marines don't guarantee what kind of job you'll get. A marine is a marine is a marine. He gave me an example: "Say you want to be infantry; the Army can legally guarantee that you'll get infantry. The Marines don't do that. You go to their boot camp, you're a marine, and when you're done they put you where they need you, like maybe in the supply or the finance." I said, "You mean I can join the Marines and after their boot camp they could make me, say . . ." me thinking to myself what would be the lowest, most degrading job for anybody in the Army with a pair of balls between their legs, "a cook?! . . . You mean they could make me a cook?" I said.

I thought about that for a second and said, "Hell, if I wanted to be a cook I'd go out and be a housewife."

There was this pause, and then my recruiter said, "I was a cook." Then me, red with embarrassment, I said, "Oh shit, I didn't mean it like that, I meant like I don't want to be a cook kind of thing . . . shit . . . sorry, man."

I was concerned about maybe being too old to join, so I brought that up with my recruiter. He answered me like I was a retard for even asking. He said, "You're not too old, no way. You're the perfect age, we get plenty of guys way older than you." Which was an attitude that was a 180-degree turn from the Marines. The Marines wanted the eighteen-year-old virgin meat, to fuck the hell out of young recruits and build them back into killers. The Army, like a lot of the people in the Army didn't give a flying fuck who they stuck their green dicks inside of. As long as it was warm, and a body, the Army would fuck the shit outta it. The Marines wanted virgins, and the Army wanted quantity, not quality. They didn't give a fuck how old I was, what shape I was in, or what kind of past I'd had, they'd take me.

On his desk were a bunch of papers from guys going in, and he started flipping through them for me. "This guy's twenty-eight, this guy's thirty-four, this guy's your age, this guy's thirty-one . . . " And then I asked him, "Why are all these older guys joining the Army?"

My recruiter told me the Bay Area was going through a recession and a lot of guys were having a hard time finding a job, and a lot of them were also looking for some excitement and adventure, which, with all the stuff going down in the Middle East, was something the Army was guaranteed to provide. He proudly pointed to a newspaper article up on the wall about Pat Tillman, an Arizona Cardinal safety who gave up his multimillion-dollar football contract to join the Army. He pointed out to me that Tillman was the same age as me when he joined. Of course this was before Tillman was killed by friendly fire serving in Afghanistan while I was in Iraq. I bet you a million bucks that newspaper article ain't up on that recruiter's wall now.

I liked this Army recruiter way more than the Marine Corps guy, probably because the Army guy was completely selling me the Army like it was some fucking Club Med vacation. But the big thing was that the Marines made you sign up for four years, the Army only wanted to take away two years of your life. He then went on and on, handing me brochure after brochure, and started talking again about all the perks and benefits that the Army offers. It got to where I finally had to tell him, "Look man, that's cool and all, but all I care about is signing up and joining the infantry. Just get to the part where I sign on the dotted line."

He got out the paperwork and he started asking me some questions: "Do you have a criminal record and, if so, in which counties?" He even wanted to know about the stuff on my juvenile record. I told him my rap sheet (a couple of assault-and-battery charges, drunk in public, shoplifting, open containers, that kinda crap), and he said, "No problem, tomorrow I'll go to the courthouses and take care of them. Next question, Did you graduate high school and what high school?" I told him that I had and he said, "No problem, I'll go down to the school tomorrow and get a transcript."

"Are your tattoos gang related?"

I told him no.

"Cool, I can get an officer to sign a waiver for those tats on your arms. Are you a U.S. citizen and do you have a Social Security card?"

I told him yes, but I wasn't sure where my SS card was.

He said, "No problem, I'll take care of that."

I was amazed by how fast the process was going.

He asked me if I ever did drugs.

With me, the question's not *if* I've ever done any drugs, it's more like "How much drugs are you on right now?"

I kind of hesitated with that one. And he looked over to his superior, who was in the same room doing paperwork at his desk, and gave me this look like "Don't say anything more" and motioned for me to walk with him to the back of the office.

In the back, out of hearing range of the other guy, I started spilling my guts. "Dude, I've done like hella drugs, man." He said that wasn't a problem. So long as I could pass the initial drug test, I'd be golden. He wanted to know when was the last time I got stoned. I honestly couldn't fucking remember, maybe a couple weeks ago, I don't know, I guess at the annual Haight Street Fair, me and a couple of my friends pigged out on these pot brownies, you know, the ones that these runaway tweaker hippie girls were selling out of woven baskets for three dollars a pop. That was several weeks before, so I told him, "I don't know, I guess like a couple weeks ago."

My recruiter then walked over to his metal desk and brought back a little drug-test kit in a small cardboard box that he'd probably bought at a Walgreens. He told me to take it into the bathroom and piss in this test-tube thing, which I did.

When I came out of the pisser with the test tube of my own piss, my recruiter already had the rubber gloves on, and when I handed it to him he inserted a litmus-paper thing into the tube and his eyes got all big and he said, "Holy shit! Did you just get high in the parking lot before you came in here?" He held up the little strip, which was bright red. Shaking his head he kept saying, "This ain't good."

Shit, that's right. I completely forgot about that one party the other weekend . . .

The disappointment showed on his face. Now we had to wait. Recruiters know that a lot of people change their minds, wimp out, jump ship, talk to their parents right when they're about to join, so they want to hurry up and get you to sign the dotted line as fast as possible so that there's no backing out. Once you sign that dotted line and raise your hand and swear that you'll uphold the Constitution against enemies both foreign and domestic, you're fucked if you want to back out.

My recruiter couldn't send me to MEPS right away with my piss turning shit all bright red. MEPS (Military Entrance Processing Station) is the place the Army sends you to get all the initial paperwork and medical bullshit needed to enlist done. The Army even pays for you to spend the night at a hotel the night before to make sure your ass doesn't flake. So he told me he could reschedule the physical and the drug test. He told me he could give me a solution for this problem—this drink, he said it was really expensive—that would make my piss come out clean.

So we rescheduled and he told me again to stay away from the drugs and he gave me a reservation for a hotel room I could stay in the night before.

So for two weeks I drank a lot of beer and stayed away from the illegal shit and the night before the physical I drank the miracle drink that my recruiter gave me earlier, which was concealed inside an old Powerade bottle, and a gallon of water.

I drank everything like I was told and the next day I passed the drug test with flying colors.

I scored well on the Armed Forces version of the SAT test, the ASVAB (Armed Services Vocational Aptitude Battery). You're eligible for two-year enlistments if you score above 70. I completely bombed on the math part of the test, like I'm at a seventh-grade dum-dum level, but my written and word comprehension was okay, so it kinda jacked my score up a lot. My recruiter told me with my GT (General Technical) score being what it was, I could choose any job in the Army. The only job I wanted was the infantry.

At this point, my recruiter pulled me aside and said, "Look, you could learn a skill and get out of the Army with a good job if you choose something different; there's no jobs out there for infantry guys." I didn't care about all that, my heart was dead set on being a trigger puller, and so I told him there's nothing else that interests me in the Army besides the infantry.

At Fort Benning, Georgia, I had a drill sergeant in basic who immediately yelled "*He lied!*" whenever a private would start a sentence off with, "But drill sergeant, my recruiter told me . . . "

When I signed the dotted line on my contract, it said something about how I was obligated to spend eight years in the inactive reserve. When I asked my recruiter about this, he was like, "Hey, don't worry, every contract says that." He explained that this would kick in only if World War III broke out and the North Koreans were lobbing nukes at us.

He lied.

Mi Vida Loca

I grew up about a forty-five-minute drive outside San Francisco in the suburbs, in a medium-size town, where most kids on their sixteenth birthday got cars that were way more expensive and newer than the ones that my parents drove.

My aunt and uncle lived in "the city," which is what we folks in the suburbs refer to San Francisco as, and when I was younger, they used to kidnap me and my brother all the time and take us to the city to do these way-cool San Francisco things with them, like go see Will Clark at Candlestick, explore Golden Gate Park, check out the seals down at Fisherman's Wharf, walk the Golden Gate Bridge, etc., etc. So I fell in love with San Francisco at a very early age. It was the complete opposite of the suburban doldrums that I grew up in. I loved the whole vibe and everything about the city, the homeless dudes, the fog, the hole-in-the-wall shops, the old Victorian houses, the Tenderloin, North Beach, etc.

When I first wanted to move to San Francisco, I couldn't because it was the Gold Rush redux over there thanks to the dot-com boom, and I couldn't afford to live there. Insurgent dot-com geeks from all over the country were migrating to San Francisco, gentrifying it by renting all the apartments, which sent rent prices to astronomical levels, and the cost of living also skyrocketed because these people had way too much money in their pockets. So I couldn't afford to live in S.F. at the time, and I also didn't really feel like living in a city that was overly polluted with yuppie scum dot-commers, so I decided to move to Los Angeles for a couple years instead, where I heard the cost of living was a little bit more reasonable.

My dad wasn't really a big fan of me moving down south to Los Angeles. My dad has some kind of a computer job in Silicon Valley, and he told me that there were computer-industry jobs up the ass in the Bay Area and companies were hiring like crazy; in fact they couldn't find enough people for a lot of these entry-level computer jobs. He insisted that I go to school, like a voc-tech, take some generic computer-science classes, and stay in the Bay Area. Maybe even learn HTML or Web design. But being a computer geek sounded about as exciting to me as a hand job.

It wasn't something I really wanted to do with myself, and I wasn't too jazzed about going back to school, I hated school and always had a hard time concentrating during class.

So I ignored my father's advice and packed all my personal belongings (records, skateboard, clothes) into the enormous *Goodfellas* trunk of my '65 Chevy Impala (a friend of mine once referred to the trunk of my '65 as a *Goodfellas* trunk because it could fit as least three dead bodies), and I drove all the way down to L.A. via I-5, and that's where I spent the next couple years of my life.

I bought that Impala with money I saved up working three jobs: file clerk for a mortgage company during the workweek, a Toys "R" Us job at night, and on the weekends I drove a passenger van for some real estate company.

Before I got my job as a file clerk, I was working at a car-rental place washing and cleaning cars. One day at work, this nice lady came in with her little son to reserve a couple passenger vans for the weekend. Her son immediately recognized me and said hello and then pointed out to his mother that he knew who I was from his church youth group, where I had been a volunteer a while back. I played with the kids, that sort of shit. His mom, thinking that I was probably a good Christian boy who liked to play with kids and volunteer his free time at local churches, offered me a weekend job driving people around to see these properties that her company sells. She said the job would pay $150 a day and it was a weekend position.

So I took the job, and I never told her that I was only a volunteer at her kid's church because it was part of my court-ordered community service for an assault-and-battery charge.

I lived in Los Angeles for a couple years, and then moved to Cleveland, Ohio, where my girlfriend at the time, Julia, grew up. I'd met her several years before in New York, where I spent the summer after high school. We kept in touch, and when I moved to L.A., she moved down there with me, but she hated everything about Los Angeles and wanted to move to New York, so we spent a winter in Cleveland, where we lived at her father's pad rent-free, saved up some money, and then we moved to Brooklyn.

Then September 11 happened.

I had lost my job a week before, and it was pretty much impossible for me to find a job in N.Y.C. after that. Absolutely nobody was hiring. So Julia and I decided that it would be better for both of us to split up and take a break from each other. I moved back home, to my parents' house, and lived there for about a month until I found myself an apartment in San Francisco.

My father actually refers to my generation as the "Boomerang Generation," because it seems like every time one of the kids leaves the house and the world kicks his ass, it's not long before he comes right back home.

The dot-com boom was now all dead and gone, and after all the dot-commers left, the only thing that was left in San Francisco were vacant apartments. In fact if you drove around town, it seemed like every single Victorian had a For Rent sign posted on the outside of it, which to me was a good sign.

In 2003, I was living in a little room in the Richmond district of S.F. in a renovated Victorian house over by Golden Gate Park. It wasn't much. Like, it wasn't anything that *MTV Cribs* would do a show on, but I was extremely cool with it. My room consisted of just a mattress that sat on the ground, next to a cableless TV that also sat on the ground, next to a couple stolen plastic milk crates set up as a makeshift bookshelf, and in the corner I had a Macintosh computer up on a stylin' Ikea desk that I bought for like sixty bucks.

Momma Tried

Right after I signed on the dotted line and raised my hand at MEPS and took the oath that I would defend the Constitution of the United States against enemies both foreign and domestic, I ended the lease on my apartment, quit my job, and moved back home to my parents' house for a couple of months, where rent was free, the food was free, and they had cable television, a luxury I'd never had on my own. Actually, I take that back, I had cable once when I lived in Los Angeles, but they disconnected it after about two months when I stopped paying my bill due to laziness.

Another added perk about staying at my parents' house was of course the skate park that the city had built at the exact moment that I finally moved out, which was a couple pathetic years after I graduated high school. The whole time I was growing up there, there was no legal place to skate, so most of the skating I did was at places that had signs that said No Skateboarding Allowed.

Story of my life.

Seeing me skating that park deeply embarrassed my mom. She thought twenty-six was way too old to be keeping it real on a skateboard, though all the guys that I idolized—Jay Adams, Mark Gonzales, and Duane Peters just to name a few—were all way older than I was and they were all still skating. But my mom would have none of that. Her rebuttal to that was that they were pros and I was just a wannabe and a bum without a job or a future.

After seeing all of the neighborhood kids move on to college and listening to their parents' proud boastings for years, my mom wasn't interested at all in my ability to shred. But she did like the idea of me joining the Army. In fact she liked the idea a lot, and couldn't wait for me to go to basic training. I think it was because she thought it would be great payback for all the years of headaches I caused her growing up, and that the drill sergeants at basic would have a field day with me and drill me with some much-needed discipline, and that the Army would kick my ass into shape. And hopefully after that I would finally get my shit together and "grow up" and evolve beyond the skate park, and maybe even eventually turn into a responsible adult, kinda like my father. Something that my mother, no matter how hard she tried, could never get me to become.

You Joined Because of Why??

I didn't necessarily enlist in the military because I was a product of the suburbs and was afflicted with self-induced poverty or anything dumb like that, and I didn't join the military because I was all traumatized over September 11. I joined because, like they say in the old recruiting commercials, I wanted to "Be all that you can be," and more importantly, "It's not just a job, it's an adventure."

I was sick of living my life in oblivion where every fucking day was the same fucking thing as the day before, and the same fucking routine day in and day out. Eat, shit, work, sleep, repeat.

At the time, I saw no escape from this. I was in my mid-twenties and I still had no fucking idea what the hell I wanted to do with myself. I was too old for college, and even if I wanted to go back to college, there was nothing that they were teaching that I was really interested in, and I was afraid that if

I didn't do something fast, I'd probably be spending the rest of my life doing data entry.

I figured if I joined the military it might be a quick-fix solution to my problems, it would add some excitement to my life, and at the same time give me the sense that I had finally done something with myself. And who knows? A trip to the Middle East could be one hell of an adventure.

You're in the Army Now

DEPARTMENT OF THE ARMY
Bravo Company, 1st Battalion, 50th Infantry Regiment
United States Army Infantry Training Brigade
Fort Benning, Georgia 31905-5710

15 NOV 02
LETTER TO: The Parents of the Soldiers of Bravo Company 1-50th IN
SUBJECT: Family Information

To the parents of ____________
On Behalf of the Commander of the 1st Battalion, 50th Infantry Regiment, and the Cadre of Bravo Company, I would like to inform you that your soldier has arrived safely at Fort Benning. He is currently training to be a United States Army infantryman in the best Army in the World. I would also like to thank you for the support that you will give your loved one during the next 14 weeks of tough demanding training.

The next couple of weeks your soldier will be introduced to SOLDIERIZATION process. This is a transformation from civilian to infantry soldier, ready to fight and win our nation's wars. Your soldier will find the next 14 weeks quite different

from anything he has done before. My cadre is extremely professional and the safety of your loved one is paramount. You can rest assured that he is being taken care of 24 hours a day, 7 days a week.

During the next 14 weeks of training, your loved one will undergo some stressful times. The best cure for this is to receive positive and cheerful letters from home. If for any reason, if you need to inform your loved one of an accident, please contact your local Red Cross Chapter and they will inform my Cadre.

There are only two times that I can think of that I've had second thoughts about the Army. One was the time in Iraq when I definitely thought I was going to get killed, and the other time was my first day of basic training.

On the first day of basic training, they marched us all over to our barracks from the in-processing center at 30th AG (Adjunct General), where we were all told to form up in a formation. In front of us was a huge pile of duffel bags, each one belonging to a different private. Then the drill sergeants, all of them wearing the round and brown Smokey the Bear hat, all came out and told us all that we had something like four minutes to go find our duffel bags, which was an impossible task, but we all ran around and tried to accomplish this task. It was total chaos. The whole time, the drill sergeants were running around, yelling in all our ears, and in the chaos to find my duffel bag, I accidentally bumped into a drill sergeant and inadvertently knocked his hat off of his head. This is quite possibly the worst sin that a private at basic training can commit.

I'm kind of a big guy, drink milk, lift weights, about six one, 210 pounds, and this drill sergeant grabbed me by the chest with both hands, lifted me off the ground, and started yelling at me as loud as he possibly could about how wrong I was for knocking his hat off of his head. Besides maybe my mom, I've never seen anybody mad at me like that before. He then tossed me backward, and I landed flat on my back, which knocked the wind out of me. As I was struggling to get back up, he continued to get in my face, yelling all sorts of things, and I remember being on the ground, trying to get my breath back, and looking over at the chaplain, who was just walking around, watching all this go on with a smirk on his face, and I knew right there and then that even God couldn't help me now.

After we made several attempts to gather up all our duffel bags in less than four minutes, they then sent us to our barracks bays, where the drill sergeants then spent the next several hours smoking the shit out of us. (In the Army, "smoking" is a form of corrective training executed by physical torture—push-ups, sit-ups, flutter kicks, low crawl, etc.—to the point of muscle failure and/or physical exhaustion, when one becomes "smoked.") A couple of the privates in my platoon actually couldn't take it anymore and started breaking down in tears on the first day.

Finally the drill sergeant made us all toe the line in front of our bunk beds. I remember looking at all the guys that were standing in line in front of me and every single one of them had this scared look on his face like he just realized that he just made the biggest mistake of his life. I had the same face on me as well. Our drill sergeant then wanted to know why we joined *his* be-lov-ed Army. He asked us all to raise our hands if we joined the Army to serve our country. I didn't raise my hand. Only several privates in my platoon raised their hands for that one. I was hoping the next question was going to be "Who joined the Army to be a killer?" so I could raise my hand and get to do the let-me-see-your-war-face thing, but instead the drill sergeant calmly asked us all how many of us enlisted for the college money. I kept my hand down for this one as well, but surprisingly a handful of people raised their hands to that one.

Dude, that was the wrong fucking answer.

This poll resulted in the drill sergeant going into this crazed all-out 'roid fit. Cursing and yelling, he screamed for all of us to get down on our faces and start pushing. As the sweat was dripping down our faces while we were knocking out the push-ups, he yelled in our ears about how disgusted he was at how unpatriotic this generation is and how every single one of us should have raised our hands when asked if we joined to serve our country.

You don't even want to know what the drill sergeant did to us later on that day when he asked us all to sing "The Star Spangled Banner," and there were people (the guys from East L.A.) who didn't know a single word to that song and had no idea what the hell "The Star Spangled Banner" was.

Orders

Because my enlistment was only for twenty-four months, my recruiter couldn't guarantee me in writing a slot with the 101st Airborne Division (For a guarantee, you have to enlist on a three- or four-year contract.) But he assured me that getting into the 101st was easy, all I had to do when I got to Fort Benning was request the 101st on this dream-sheet thing that they hand you at the in-processing center, which asks you what units you want to be in. At the in-processing station, we were all handed this dream sheet, and I of course listed the 101st as my number one choice in duty station.

He lied.

When my drill sergeant called off my name and handed me my orders to join the Stryker Brigade based out of Fort Lewis,

Washington, I was beyond heartbroken. I was like, *What the fuck is this? Fort fucking Lewis?* At the time, I had my heart dead set on being in the same unit that my main man Jimi Hendrix was once in, the legendary 101st Airborne Division. A unit that's rich with combat history and experience, and, most importantly, deployable. Which means that there was a very high probability that the Screaming Eagles were going to have another rendezvous with destiny in the near future.

Almost everybody in my platoon at basic got orders for Korea, and every single soldier who enlisted on the two-year contract (me) got orders for Fort Lewis. At the time, the guys in my platoon were telling me that the Stryker Brigade at Fort Lewis was an experimental unit that was nondeployable. So my chances of going overseas and telling my grandkids one day that I spent the war kicking terrorist ass with an open-bolt weapon were next to nothing, which most rational people might consider a good thing. I wanted absolutely nothing to do with that—half the reason I joined the United States Army was I wanted it to be an escape from the temp work, cubicles, and data entry, and the other was I wanted to experience the sting of battle and experience up close and personal an overseas combat deployment.

I didn't want to get all old and have my bratty grandkids ask me, "Grandpa, where were you during the Iraq war?" and me going, "Oh, I was busy doing temp work and data entry for twelve bucks an hour."

The day after I received my deployment orders for Fort Lewis, I utilized my drill sergeant's open-door policy, and with orders in hand I banged on his door. He looked pissed but he growled for me to come in, which I did.

With that unenthused drill-sergeant stare, he asked me, "What the hell do you want, Private?" I was standing at parade rest, this was my last hope. "Drill sergeant, my orders are for the Stryker Brigade at Fort Lewis, Washington. This is a nondeployable unit and I am asking if I could have my orders changed to a deployable unit that's going to Iraq, like maybe the 101st Airborne Division."

My drill sergeant, who was a Desert Storm vet, looked at me all confused, like I was crazy or some shit, and he said, "You want to be deployed, huh?"

"Roger, drill sergeant, that's why I joined the Army."

He thought about that for a second and said, "Look, there's nothing I can do right now to get your orders changed, it's too late, it's all set in stone, but just because Fort Lewis is a nondeployable unit right now doesn't mean it's going to be a nondeployable unit forever. Shit can change at any time. I wouldn't be too sure about them being a nondeployable unit for long. In fact, I bet you anything that'll change."

He didn't lie.

Home Sweet Home

After graduation from basic training I flew back to California and stayed at my parents' house for the two weeks I had off. One of the first things I did when I got back home was grab my skateboard and go down to the skate park.

My mom actually wanted to write a letter to my drill sergeants saying that she thought that they didn't do a good enough job on me, and that as far as she could see, I hadn't changed at all. On the second or third day home, I was sleeping on the sofa in the living room while my mom was in the kitchen cooking, when my younger brother stopped by the house to see how I was doing. I was sleeping on the sofa because I got so wasted the night before that when I came home I didn't feel like walking up the stairs to my room, so I just parked it on the sofa in the living room and crashed there.

He asked me how basic training was, and began to ask a bunch of questions about what that experience was like, when my mom couldn't take it anymore, and she completely lost her top and started yelling at me from the kitchen, "Look at him!! He's still a bum!!! The Army didn't teach him anything!!! It's twelve o'clock and he's still sleeping!!" And she went on and on, complaining how my room's a mess, how my attitude sucks, how I leave the toilet seat up, how I drink too much, how I don't do any chores around the house, and on and on . . . and I just looked over at my brother and said, "You see how Mom's yelling at me right now, that is exactly what basic training was like."

Hometown Recruiting

Even though I don't remember volunteering for the Hometown Recruiting Assistance Program, I was ordered to do so. Hometown recruiting is when you go back to your recruiter and try to recruit all your friends into the Army, and you hang out at the recruiting office for a couple days in your Class A uniform and talk to prospective privates about how great Army life is. Most guys who do hometown recruiting just show up for a couple hours, say hello, and then pop smoke, but my recruiter actually expected me to go out to the nearby shopping mall and junior college every day and bust my ass trying to recruit people.

Keep in mind this is Northern California, a place where "Guess what? I'm following the hippie band Phish for the next year!" receives by far a lesser reaction of shock than "Guess what? I joined the military for the next two years of my life!"

Totally and completely embarrassed, I had to walk around a nearby junior college in my ugly-ass Class A pickle-green uniform, decorated with two freebie ribbons (Army Service and National Defense), with a stack of "Army of One" postcards and try to get phone numbers and contact info of possible recruits.

I actually had a quota I had to meet every day if I wanted to go home; he wanted me to get five phone numbers per day.

What an asshole.

So the first day what I did was I wrote down a bunch of bogus numbers—I had some skaters that I met at the Diablo Valley Junior College parking lot help me out and fill them in with bogus info. I went up to them and told them my deal, that my recruiter was making me do this, and they helped me out and filled out the cards with false intel.

The next day, my recruiter asked, "Hey, all those numbers you gave me were bogus. Did you fill those out yourself?" I then explained to him that the kids I got the numbers from didn't sound too serious about joining, so they might have put down fake numbers.

I hated walking around that junior college, which was located kinda close to the town I grew up in. I was scared to death of bumping into somebody I went to high school with. Like this one time in L.A., when I was a flower-delivery guy, I had to deliver these arrangements of flowers to a sorority at UCLA, and the sorority girl that opened the door was a chick that I went to high school with. I felt like I immediately had a big L on my forehead, like I could tell exactly what she was thinking when she saw me—"Oh my God! Aren't you, like, Colby Buzzell? Wow, cool, so you're like a flower-delivery guy now! Cool!"

So not cool.

So I tried to keep a low pro while I walked around that campus.

At the time, America had just got done kicking Taliban ass in

Afghanistan, and we were now getting ready to shift fire over toward Iraq, and right now the entire campus looked like UC Berkeley in the sixties, completely decorated with a whole bunch of pep-rally-esque antiwar banners and posters, stuff that read, "No More Racist War for Oil" and "No Blood for Oil" in rainbow colors with a bunch of flowers and peace symbols drawn around it.

And a lot of the JC students that walked past me on their way to class had fashionable antiwar pins on their shirt lapels. And I realized that all these decorative posters and pins that were made to maybe do something, like, I don't know, end the war, were absolutely pointless and about as dumb as me walking around that campus in my Army uniform trying to recruit these people.

Vegas, Baby, Vegas!

As they say in the Army, if you came in married, you won't be when you get out, and if you came in single, you won't be when you get out, either. I never really envisioned myself ever getting married, but I guess that all changed when I joined the Army.

BAH (Basic Allowance for Housing) is money that the Army gives you that allows you and your wife to live in an apartment off post if you choose not to live in the swank free housing (that's a joke) that the Army has available on post. Go to any military post and you'll see the same thing—the married officers and generals live in the nice houses in the nice neighborhoods, and the enlisted personnel live in the shitty housing that makes any Section 8 neighborhood look like Beverly Hills.

Pay for an E-2 private with less than two years in the military is $1,337.70 a month. Which is far less than what I was making when I was a civilian, but if you figure all the benefits, and no rent and free food, it's $1,337.70 of straight profit, thus it was a lot more than what I was making before Army life.

At least, $1,337.70 was what my recruiter told me I'd be making a month. The first couple paychecks I received from the military when I was in basic training were less than a hundred dollars, in fact the first paycheck I got was less than fifty dollars. To this day I have no idea why the first couple paychecks at basic were so tiny.

If it weren't for BAH, my wife and I probably wouldn't be married right now.

Julia and I were pretty much broken up prior to me joining the Army, but we still kept in touch even though we were apart and living on opposite sides of the country. When I told her that I was enlisting in the Army, she was surprisingly supportive of my decision. I think she liked the idea that I would have a steady job for the next couple of years, something I was never really able to do when I lived with her. We had been talking about getting back together for good, so I told her all about BAH and how it worked and hinted to her that if we were going to be together for the long haul, we might as well get married and I'd save up all the BAH money for us, so that when I got out of the Army, we'd have a nice chunk of change for us to start over with.

So she agreed to get married.

I even offered to split the BAH money as a thank-you, which she surprisingly declined. She had a good job that paid her pretty well, and she was going through this financially independent phase that women who move to New York all seem to want to go through, so she told me that she didn't need any of the extra money.

After my stint with hometown recruiting came to an end (thank God), I had my brother give me a ride to the Oakland airport. I told my brother and my parents that I was spending the weekend in Los Angeles to hang with some old friends, when in fact I was flying to Vegas to get married. I had to keep the whole marriage thing OPSEC, because I didn't want to explain it to them. (My parents still don't know that I'm married.) We both landed at the Vegas airport at around the same time and took a cab to Caesars Palace, where Julia had a room reserved for us. We gambled and hung out and the next day we went to the courthouse and waited in line with all the other losers who were getting married and needed a marriage license. Right before we got the marriage license I looked over at Julia and said, "Are you sure you want to do this?" And she said, "Sure, why not." So we paid the twenty-five bucks for the marriage license and drove around Vegas looking for a cool chapel to get married in.

Julia had this very sexy fifties-style white sundress on, and I was kickin' it old-school with the Dickies, Vans, and *Thrasher*-magazine hooded sweatshirt.

I was all for the Elvis marriage, but Julia wanted to just get done with it, so we picked out a drive-thru wedding chapel in downtown Las Vegas, and pulled up to the drive-thru window in our twenty-dollar-a-day rental car, and ordered a number-one wedding with a side order of postcards of the drive-thru chapel, and a garter belt. To go.

The rental car had a CD player in it, and since I had a couple CDs on me, I asked her if she wanted to get married to Guns N' Roses *Appetite for Destruction or Slayer's Reign in Blood.* She rolled her eyes at me and chose Slayer. (She hates GN'R, and she knows that I love Slayer.) I said fine, but I get to choose the song, so I put it on track one, "Angel of Death."

We didn't have the time or money (at least I didn't) to get real wedding rings, so instead we used my basic-training ring, and an old silver antique ring that Julia owned, to get married with. A basic-training ring is a ring you can buy for like a hundred bucks at basic training that's kind of like a class ring from high school.

The priest, an older man with wire-rimmed glasses, stuck his head out of the drive-thru window, did his whole holy-matrimony speech to us, and the next thing you know, on 15 March 2003, we were married.

Julia had to go back to the airport almost immediately after we got married because the flight back to N.Y.C. was leaving in a couple hours and she had work the next morning, so after we said our "I do's" and made out in the rental car, I dropped her off at the airport and we said our good-byes. I'm probably the only guy on this planet who didn't get laid on his wedding night, but whatever, it didn't matter to me. I was now married, and to a girl that I loved. Hopefully, things would work out for us this second time around.

The next day I took the Greyhound bus back to my parents' house in Northern California, and a couple days after that I took a plane to Seattle, and from there I took a shuttle bus to Fort Lewis, Washington.

Welcome to Fort Lewis

The first thing I noticed about Fort Lewis on my first day was not the spectacular view of Mount Rainier, but of the on-post skateboard park. When I first saw that, I remember thinking, "Hell, yeah! A skate park on a military post?!" How bad could Army life be? Maybe my recruiter was right when he made the Army out to be some Club Med vacation with all kinds of fun extracurricular activities and benefits.

I didn't skate the skate park as much as I wanted to, because Fort Lewis is located pretty much in the middle of a rain forest and it rained almost every single day I was there. It rained on my first day there, and it rained the day I left, and it rained pretty much every day in between. And it didn't help that the skate park was outdoors. Thus, it was kinda pointless.

Beltway Mortarmen

The only thing that I really knew about Fort Lewis prior to joining the Army was that the Beltway sniper guy, John Muhammad, was stationed there a long time ago when he was in the Army, before he got all trigger-happy postal and started capping Americans around the suburbs of D.C. I knew this because I watched that whole thing go down moment by moment on my parents' television set when I stayed at their house right before I took off for basic training.

I remember watching the Columbine High School horror live on the tube when I lived in Los Angeles as it was happening, but the Beltway-sniper episode was way more engaging to watch. Columbine lasted for a couple hours and it was over and out and done with just as soon as it started. This Beltway-sniper thing lasted for several weeks and had all the elements of a movie: suspense, horror, comedy, murder, the whole media sideshow thing, the whodunit thing, and the million-dollar question—*How the fuck do we catch this guy?*

Every day my dad would drive home from his Silicon Valley engineering job, business-casual dress, and at the dinner table we would discuss the details and analyze what had transpired that day with the sniper. That was how me and my dad bonded, watching the news together at the dinner table and discussing the current events of the day. This sniper was nailing at least one person a day for a while. The whole thing was completely insane to me; I couldn't understand how this guy, who had *everybody* trying to catch him, was getting away with this shit. Every single police force in the area was called up to try to catch this guy, the FBI, even the fucking red-beret-wearing Guardian Angels. Some of the best minds in the business were hard at work trying to crack this case and capture this guy. All the major news networks were following this story in real time, and they had on all these crazy psychics and profilers, and all sorts of people who thought they knew who the guy was and how to catch him. I would sit there on my parents' Ethan Allen sofa, buzzing through the news channels with the remote, looking for new developments.

If they didn't have news, the networks would trot out some jobless ex-FBI criminal profiler to say that the guy was probably some highly trained military sniper at one time, that he probably received his training from sniper school at Fort Benning, the best school on the planet for shooters. I even heard that they had Pentagon reconnaissance planes flying up above to catch him; every single asset and cutting-edge top-of-the-line technology available was activated in trying to catch this guy, and they still couldn't get him. He sent them all on a crazy-ass goose chase. I remember the cops at one point giving a hysterical press conference saying the sniper was firing from a white van and to be on the lookout for one. A white van? How many thousands of fucking white vans are there in Virginia?

They finally caught the guys, and it turned out they were just a couple of thugs armed with an AR15, and one of the guys, John Muhammad, didn't have all this fancy sniper-school experience after all, in fact he had limited military experience and no sniper-school training whatsoever.

Kinda like the mortarmen in Mosul, impossible to catch.

One Strap, Not Two, Stupid

When I showed up at Fort Lewis, I reported to Waller Hall, where I signed in and was then sent to the 525 Replacement Detachment, where I would undergo in-processing. The very next morning we had a bright-and-early formation in the parking lot, and the NCO that was in charge of us came out and informed us that "it's not a question of *if* you're going to the Middle East, it's a question of *when* you're going."

This was good news to me. So much for the Stryker Brigade being an experimental nondeployable unit.

At this initial formation we were also informed of all the on-post dos and don'ts. For instance, black backpacks are the only authorized backpacks that a soldier could wear on post at Fort Lewis, and if you were going to wear a black backpack, you were not authorized to use both shoulder straps that every backpack on this planet comes equipped with.

You were to *only* use *one* of the two shoulder straps.

When a soldier in the formation asked why only one shoulder strap was authorized and not both, which I thought was a very good question, the NCO looked at him like he'd just asked the dumbest question in the world, and said, "Because it's on-post policy."

Nothing further.

Till the day I left the main gate of Fort Lewis for good, I always saw new guys walking to the PX wearing their black backpacks using only one shoulder strap, and I always wondered why.

Looking back on this now, I can only speculate that this policy is just there to indoctrinate the new soldiers right away to Army life, and to get them all numb and used to the fact that the Army has a bunch of stupid rules, and your job is to *not* think or question these stupid rules, but to just follow them blindly instead.

At least that's what I think.

Fuck

I bumped into a friend of mine from basic training. He was from a small Midwestern farm town, and I remembered him telling me that he joined the Army because he didn't want to work at the factory like everybody that he grew up with did after high school, and he was bored with junior college, so he joined the Army for the adventure and to see the world.

He asked me where my orders were taking me and I told him 3rd Brigade, and he said I was lucky because the rumor that he was hearing was that 3rd Brigade was headed to Afghanistan or Iraq.

I asked him where his orders were taking him and he told me 1st Brigade, which at the time wasn't going anywhere. I told him, "Man, that sucks." We then started talking, and I was telling him all about a crazy drunken night I had in San Francisco prior to showing up to Lewis, when out of nowhere a disgusted E-6 sergeant came up to me and said, "Hey, Private, I've been standing over there trying to smoke a cigarette, and in the last thirty seconds or so, I've heard you use the F-word over a dozen times."

I then snapped to the position of parade rest and out of nervousness I said, "Fuck, I'm sorry Sergeant, I didn't realize I was swearing so much."

"What did you say? Are you messing with me, Private?!"

I told him no, that I wasn't messing with him, which was true, I really did accidentally slip up when I used the F-word again, and then he briefed me that if a female officer was outside right now and heard me talking like that, I would have gotten my ass chewed out, and he said something to me about always having military bearing while in uniform and to watch my language at all times.

And I told him sorry and told him I'd watch my language from here on out. While he walked away to continue smoking his cigarette I looked over to my friend and quietly said, "Fuck that guy," and continued my story.

B.CO 1/23

The in-processing took about a week and after I was done with that I was assigned to Bravo Company 2nd Platoon (the Tomahawk Battalion), 23rd Infantry Regiment, 3rd (Arrowhead) Brigade, 2nd Infantry Division. Which was the Army's first-ever Stryker Brigade Combat Team.

When I first showed up to the unit, all the guys in my platoon were at the NTC (National Training Center) down at Fort Irwin, California. So I was put on Rear D (Rear Detachment) until they returned. What they had me do on Rear D was "gate guard," where me and a couple of the other new guys to the unit had to check the ID cards of people trying to drive onto post.

Since I don't own a car, I couldn't really explore or go anywhere off post, and since I was a new guy, I didn't know anybody or have any friends yet. So I spent most of my time alone, hanging out at the gym lifting weights, and whenever I was bored with that I'd walk down to the PX and just hang out.

Geographical Bachelor

"Geographical bachelors" is what the Army calls married soldiers who live in the barracks.

My wife had no interest in moving to Fort Lewis with all the rumors flying around about 3rd Brigade being deployed to the Middle East. We decided that it might be best if she stayed in New York, where her job was, while I went off and played Army for the next two years.

So I got issued a room in the barracks where all the other geographical bachelors lived, as well as the single soldiers. At first they didn't have any room for me in the barracks, so I slept on the floor of a room up on the third floor where two other soldiers were already assigned, until a room finally opened up for me on the first floor, right about when my unit all got back. That was when I first met Sgt. Vance, a blond, athletically built twenty-two-year-old surfer from Southern California. I remember walking up to him and asking, "Hey, Sergeant, do you listen to punk?" because when I was sleeping on the floor of his room, I noticed that he had a couple punk CDs (Social Distortion, Rancid, Dropkick Murphys) lying around and some books about European soccer hooligans up on his bookshelf, as well as a paperback copy of Anthony Burgess's classic *Clockwork Orange,* so he seemed like he might be a pretty cool guy with cool interests.

He told me that he was into punk, and one thing led to another and we became friends. I was a new guy to the unit and to the Army and he took it upon himself to take me under his wing and show me the ropes. I learned more from him about the Army than I did from all my team leaders and squad leaders combined. He'd tell me all about his personal Army experience, his old unit out in Germany, what to look out for and stay away from, how to do things correctly, what's expected of me, the kinds of training they did, the stuff he learned, and since I was eager to learn as much as I could from him, I hung out with him as much as possible and he helped me out by constantly handing me TMs (training manuals) and FMs (field manuals) and pointing out to me what to read and study and what to skip over, and he also gave me a copy of the *Ranger Handbook,* with sections highlighted for me to study.

One of the sections that he heavily highlighted was Urban Operations, next to which he wrote "Key on," with an arrow.

> 14-1 GENERAL Urban operations are defined as all military actions that are planned and conducted on terrain where man-made construction affects the tactical options available. Urban terrain is likely to be one of the most significant future areas of operations for American forces throughout the world. Expanding urban development affects military operations as the terrain is altered. The increasing focus on stability and support operations, urban terrorism, and civil disorder emphasizes that combat in urbanized areas is unavoidable. Urban areas are power centers, the center of gravity, and thus the future battlefield.

Welcome to Weapons Squad

Here is the breakdown of a platoon in the infantry:

> Four squads in a platoon.
> Three line squads and one weapons squad.
> Weapons squad consists of one squad leader and two team leaders.
> Each team leader is responsible for a gun team.

Two fully automatic machine guns (M240 Bravo) per platoon. A gun team consists of a gunner, an assistant gunner, and an ammo bearer.

When the rest of my platoon finally returned from NTC, I was placed in weapons squad and was introduced to my squad leader, Sgt. Baxter, who handed me an ammo bag and said "Congratulations, you're our new AB [ammo bearer]."

An AB's job is to carry ammo for the M240 Bravo machine gun. In other words, my job was basically pretty much the same as a mule's, which is to just carry heavy shit on my back. When I chose infantry, I thought my job was going to be shooting guns and blowing shit up like Rambo, not carrying around a bunch of heavy ammo on my back for a heavy machine gun. If I would have known that my job in the infantry was to just carry shit on my back, I probably would have never chosen the infantry and probably would have gone for a different assignment, maybe even signed up to be a cook instead.

The two team leaders in weapons squad at this time were Spc. Ramos and Spc. Evans. Spc. Ramos, an early-twenties Puerto Rican from Florida, was my first team leader. Spc. Evans, who was not even old enough to drink at the time and looked like an All-American high school quarterback to me, was the other team leader. He had his shit together and acted more mature than anybody I knew my age and older. He was already married with a kid.

Weapons squad at the time was filled with short-timers and guys who were in the process of getting out. I noticed that the guys who were getting out had somewhat of a "Fuck it" attitude, which I didn't really understand.

I thought the Army was the best job in the world, and by far the best job I'd ever had. I didn't have to worry about a lot of the things that I worried about when I was a civilian, like getting fired, losing my job, bills, rent, thinking up creative ways of cooking Top Ramen. Basically, if I needed it, the Army issued it to me. Everything was pretty much free, rent was free, food was free. And for the first time ever I had medical and dental, and it was also the first time ever that I wasn't bothered with the headache of being broke, and I was even able to save up a little bit of money on the side.

More importantly, it was the first job I'd ever had that I was proud to do, like I no longer had to worry about being embarrassed or not knowing what to say when somebody asked me the dreaded question, "So, what do you do?"

Being a soldier, I thought, was a pretty respectable job, and I took a lot of pride in that. Since I took a lot of pride in what I was doing, I took my job very seriously, and I tried my best to learn as much as I possibly could.

After work, I'd go to the gym, which was located right next to our barracks and was free to soldiers, and do extra PT on my own. I'd run the airfield on my own, which is about a 3.5-mile run, and for the first time ever I applied myself, I studied all the training manuals and field manuals that I borrowed from Sgt. Vance, I read them and reread them, and took down notes, and even copied an entire training manual word-for-word so I'd have it memorized in my head. For the first time ever, I was teaching myself how to learn.

And surprisingly, I *was* able to memorize the stuff by doing this.

Since I had such a positive attitude about the Army and wanted to learn as much as possible, my team leader, Spc. Ramos, started calling me "lifer," and every now and then he'd say things like, "Dude, you are *so* reenlisting it's not even funny."

Sgt. Baxter told me that being an AB was only a temporary thing, and if I wanted to, if I continued to bust ass and show improvement as a soldier, I could move on up to the gunner position someday. Which is what I told him I wanted to do from the get-go, be a machine gunner in the infantry, not some fucking jackass cargo mule.

Lessons Learned at JRTC

- Always bring at least a carton of cigarettes (or if you dip, a log of dip) on field problems.
- Spank mags are required reading amongst infantrymen on field problems (the dirtier the better).
- Everybody jerks off in the field. Masturbating is not looked down upon but instead applauded, and is an effective practice to stay awake on guard.
- Chewing tobacco is an alternative to cigarettes when and where smoking is not allowed (at night and inside of the Stryker vehicles).
- All sensitive items must be tied down.
- Anybody who is noninfantry is considered a POG (person other than a grunt).
- Don't feed the alligators.

Joint Readiness Training Center

A "field problem" is any training exercise that takes place in the field. My first field problem with my unit was a two-and-a-half-week field problem at the Joint Readiness Training Center at Fort Polk, Louisiana. JRTC is where the Army sends units before they deploy them to combat zones.

At JRTC, Sgt. Vance slept a couple bunk beds away from me and he'd always come up to my bunk to check up on me, see how I was doing, and to see if my equipment was all squared away, and if something was wrong he'd make an on-the-spot correction.

For example: my "tie-downs." Soldiers carry a lot of expensive equipment, known as "sensitive items," and to prevent these items from being lost or going missing in action while you're crawling around in the woods, each item must be tied down with 5/50 survival cord.

There's a technique to this, and certain knots have to be used so that they don't come undone. Sgt. Vance taught me the correct way to do things in the Army. Spc. St. George, on the other hand, who was an M240 Bravo gunner in my squad, taught me what *not* to do in the Army. St. George was an E-4 specialist, as well as a short-timer, and he was getting out of the Army once his rotation at JRTC was complete.

Right before we left for JRTC my entire platoon was issued an itemized packing list. A packing list is a list of items and equipment, and how many of each item we were required to pack in our duffel bags and rucksacks. Shortly after a packing list is issued to all the soldiers, what takes place next is a layout to make sure everybody has every item that's listed on the packing list packed away in our bags.

The squad leader and/or team leader usually conducts the layout.

Spc. St. George, who always referred to me not by my last name or rank but as "Cherry," told me that even though magazines were not on the packing list, I should bring a stack of magazines with me to JRTC.

Easy enough, so I told him I would.

When we got to Fort Polk, they placed us all in barracks filled with Army bunk beds. I slept on a bottom bunk, and St. George slept on a top bunk. Right next to our beds were steel wall lockers, where we stashed all our equipment.

While I was putting my stuff away in my locker, St. George came up to me and asked, "Hey dude, did you bring those magazines like I told you to?"

Like a good private, I told him that I did, and I grabbed the stack of magazines that I bought at the PX and handed it to him. He flipped through them and said, "*You fuckin' cherry!* These aren't magazines!"

The stack of magazines I handed him consisted of *National Geographic, Time, Mad, Thrasher, Rolling Stone,* etc.

All of which I thought were magazines.

"Dude, porno mags you idiot!"

He then called over a couple of other soldiers to embarrass me. "Dude, look at the magazines Cherry brought!"

Spc. Horrocks, who was sleeping on a bottom bunk next to me, came to my defense and said, "What's wrong with *National Geographic*?"

St. George reiterated that I was supposed to bring porno mags, not *National Geographic* and *Time.* He even went so far as to explain to me that the dirtier the magazine the better, like for example *Playboy* and *Penthouse* were way too G-rated by infantryman standards, but magazines like *Swank, Cherry,* and *High Society,* that depicted anal, oral, facial cum shots, group orgies, multiple penetration, bondage, etc., those were all okay. The only exception to this rule was of course *Maxim.* (Because of the articles. Duh.) He then explained to me that you can't jerk off to *National Geographic* in the field. Which was debatable, but I then made the mistake of asking, "You guys jerk off in the field?"

St. George yelled out, "Cherry doesn't think you jerk off in the field! HA HA HA!!!"

Spc. Cannon, who was now laughing at me along with everyone else, briefed me that all soldiers jerk off in the field. At first I thought that this was just another stupid joke that soldiers like to play on the FNG (fuckin' new guy).

New guys always get fucked with. Like, a common joke is to tell the new guy, "Go find a grid square, and don't come back until you find one!" and the private will run around asking everybody, "Hey, do you have a grid square?" (Note: A grid square is found where longitude and latitude lines intersect on a map.)

When I told him I didn't believe him, Cannon yelled for another soldier to come over, and he then walked over to us and asked what was up.

"Hey," Cannon said. "The new guy doesn't believe that people jerk off in the field, tell him . . ."

This soldier explained to me that everybody does it, either out of boredom or to stay awake on guard, and in fact he even boasted that he himself was a chronic masturbator in the field, and told me that he already jerked off three times that day.

Cannon looked at me and said, "See, I told you!"

I still thought that this was a trick, like, "Hey, let's see if we can get the new guy to jerk off in the field! Ha ha ha. That would be funny!" kinda thing, but the sad thing was they weren't fucking with me at all, and what they said to me was all true.

Horrocks the next day came up to me and asked to borrow the *National Geographic.* Horrocks was about my age, and seemed like a pretty cool guy. He was a new guy to the unit as well, so we both didn't really know anybody in the platoon, and since our beds were right next to each other, we talked a lot.

He told me all about his old unit up in Alaska, which he had great pride in, because they were like Arctic Warriors or something up there. He grew up in some trailer park or house in Idaho, loved hunting, loved the outdoors, and loved drinking in bars. And so we kinda bonded and we told each other that when we got back to Fort Lewis, we should go out drinking sometime. Which we did. A lot.

Dude, They Killed Buzzell! (Again)

Whatever enthusiasm I had about me going overseas to experience combat was tempered by what happened at JRTC. JRTC was just basically one huge war game. We were all issued MILES gear before going there. MILES (multiple integrated laser engagement system) is just a high-speed version of laser tag, where everybody wears these sensors on his helmet and body armor, and when one of the sensors on you gets hit with one of the lasers, it sets off the MILES gear, which makes a loud ringing noise, and then you pretend to be dead. Then an OC comes along (an OC is kinda like the referee) and pulls the casualty feeder card out from your BDU (battle dress uniform) shirt pocket. The casualty feeder card states what kind of casualty you are and how severe the casualty is so simulated first aid can be done on you.

I felt like Kenny from *South Park*, every single time we got into a simulated firefight, I was *always* the very first one killed. *Every single fucking time!*

I spent more time at the casualty-collection point than I did out in the field. When you get killed they send you there, where you hang out for a day or so before they reactivate you and you can go back in. It got to where the guys at the casualty-collection point recognized me and would say, "Back again, huh?"

It got so bad that my entire squad, squad leader, and platoon sergeant were all asking me, "Hey Buzzell, you're not *trying* to get killed every time out there are you?" The reason they were asking me this is because we were totally sucking out in the field, almost all of us were suffering from exhaustion, getting eaten alive by bugs, covered in poision oak, sick of eating MREs, and it was hot as hell out there. So they thought for a second that I was trying to get out of that, which I swear to God I wasn't.

To this day, people still come up to me and say, "Hey, didn't you get killed every time down at JRTC?"

The first time I got killed it was by one of the guys in my own platoon. On the few occasions when I wasn't killed at JRTC, all we did was just drive around the woods, riding in the back of the Strykers, reading porno mags, and every now and then we'd park the Stryker, dismount, bring both the guns out (M240s), set up a gun position, and wait.

My first team leader, Spc. Ramos, I didn't think really liked me too much at first because I had way too much of a positive attitude about the Army, which kinda irritated him.

On this one field problem, Spc. Ramos was behind the gun, I was to his side, and when I looked over at him he had this distant, expressionless look on his face. In a dreamlike state, out loud, not really to me but more to himself, he said, "This was the biggest mistake of my life."

I didn't know what to say after that, because even though I was always the first one killed once the blanks started firing, I thought that this was the best job in the world, so I kept my mouth shut.

He then said something that I will never forget:

"I should have gone to college."

Tied Down

On one of the last days in the field at JRTC we had to dig something called a Hastings fighting position, a deep hole, on the side of this road. So we all pulled out our miniature folding shovels and took turns digging.

St. George left his 9mm unsecured while digging, meaning it wasn't tied down to his vest with some 5/50 cord, it was lying on the ground, so as corrective training, my squad leader, Sgt.

Baxter, ordered him to go tie down all his equipment again and to come back to him for an inspection. St. George then angrily grabbed a huge ball of 5/50 cord out of his rucksack and started cutting the 5/50 cord into small pieces to be used as tie-downs.

We had our Hastings fighting position all dug, and I was positioned inside it, scanning the tree line for OP-FOR (opposition forces), bored out of my mind but loving every second of this, because even though I was in my mid-twenties, I was playing soldier, for real. Which I thought was kinda cool.

I then looked back over to St. George and said, "Dude, what the hell are you doing?!" St. George, in defiance, had decided to be a smartass and he literally had everything on his body tied down with 5/50 cord. His helmet to his glasses, his glasses to his BDU top, his BDU top to his BDU pants, his watch to his sleeve, his earplug container to his flak jacket, his belt to his pants, his socks to his boots. He had 5/50 cord all over him and everything from head to toe was tied down, even his wallet.

I advised him to think twice about doing this and said, "Dude, you're gonna get busted man!"

He then told me that he didn't care and was sick and tired of all the stupid "Army games," and then he said, "So what, I'm getting out anyway." Which pretty much summed up his whole attitude about everything.

I then watched him walk over to Sgt. Baxter with everything on him tied down, some items tied down multiple times, and he said, "Sergeant, all my stuff is tied down now." I couldn't help it, I was biting my tongue trying not to laugh out loud, but Sgt. Baxter didn't think this was funny at all and immediately told him to drop and start pushing. So St. George, while down in the push-up position, said, "But Sergeant, you told me to tie everything down!"

Dumb and Dumber

Even though a lot of people in the platoon didn't like St. George, and advised me to keep my distance from him, I thought he was an all-right guy because he was entertaining to be around. The day before, we had parked the Stryker in the middle of the woods, and we were bored, hanging out at our gun position, waiting for something to happen, when St. George started opening up an MRE, poking holes in the food packet with his Gerber knife, and tying it to a long string of 5/50 cord. I asked him what the hell he was doing and he told me that he was going to try to catch one of the baby alligators that he had seen earlier at this pond that we had driven past, not far away.

When I told him that I didn't think that was a good idea, because usually if there's a baby alligator, mommy alligator isn't too far behind, and more importantly we could get busted for doing this, he again called me Cherry and said to stop acting like a chickenshit, and to go along with this. So I followed him to the pond, all the while telling him over and over again that this probably wasn't a good idea.

When we got to the pond there was the baby alligator, just floating there with just its head and eyeballs sticking out of the water. St. George threw the MRE packet into the pond, but the alligator just sat there.

Then, just kidding around, I said, "Maybe we should throw a hand grenade at it instead," which he thought was a great idea. So I took a dummy grenade off my flak jacket, and we argued for a second or two about whether we should do this, when all of a sudden, "ST. GEORGE, BUZZELL, GET YOUR ASSES OVER HERE RIGHT NOW!!!" came over the radio on our iComs. (iComs are kinda like walkie-talkies.)

Busted.

I freaked out and told St. George that since I was the new guy, I didn't want to get busted for this, and he told me to stop freaking out, that he would take all the blame for this, which surprisingly he did.

When we walked back to the Stryker, our squad leader was there waiting for us, demanding to know what the hell was going on. We told him (leaving out the grenade idea), and Sgt. Baxter told us some pissed-off OC had just happened to be passing by the area and saw us trying to feed the alligators and just about lost it. We told Sgt. Baxter that we had thought about feeding the alligator but didn't because we thought it was a bad idea, which he dittoed.

Sgt. Baxter then told me that I should have known better and asked me what the hell I was doing with St. George, and I told him that Sgt. St. George needed a battle buddy, and that I tried to talk him out of it but he wouldn't listen. And after a good ass-chewing, Baxter told us to go back to our gun position and not to feed the alligators.

Shughart Gordon

Shughart Gordon is the name of the mock city at JRTC, named after the two D-Boys who lost their lives in Mogadishu. At the very end of JRTC, what they had planned for us was a simulated urban battle at Shughart Gordon, which would be jam-packed with OP-FOR. We would storm into the city on our Strykers and there would be this huge epic urban battle. I wish I could write about that experience in detail but unfortunately I can't because I was killed a couple days before that, and I had to spend the battle at the aid station, covered in pink calamine lotion for the poison oak and chigger bites that covered the majority of my body.

So far, I wasn't too good at any of this soldier business, and I left Fort Polk, Louisiana, praying to God that Iraq would be nothing like JRTC. Because if it was, I was dead.

Change-Up

Here's what happened when we got back from Fort Polk:

Sgt. Baxter got moved to snipers, and Sgt. Fisher was brought in to replace him.

Weapons squad now looked like this:

Squad leader: Sgt. Fisher.

Team leaders and gunners: Spc. Ramos and Spc. Evans.

Gun one: Spc. Horrocks, gunner; Spc. Ramos, AG; Pfc. Cortinas, AB.

Gun two: Spc. Evans, gunner; Pfc. Buzzell, AG; Spc. Scroggins, AB.

Reigensburg

One of the last training exercises that we had before we left the States was at this plywood mock city located somewhere in the backyard of Fort Lewis. It was called Reigensburg. Built almost exactly like an old beat-up low-budget Hollywood set at Universal Studios, the houses in Reigensburg were made of plywood and 2x4s, and inside, they were pretty much completely empty. On this particular training exercise the set was made to look like a fictional Iraqi village, which I guess means bringing in some raggedy Third World–looking livestock, which they did, and have them run around to make it more realistic.

Basically how this training exercise worked was a company

of soldiers dressed up in civilian attire to play the part of innocent Iraqi civilians, and a couple of those people were handed lead roles as "bad guys," and they were given weapons. Then a platoon of Strykers would roll into the mock city.

The scenario: Soldiers roll in, village is filled with combination of innocent Iraqi civilians and anti-American Iraqis, and several of the houses have weapons caches hidden inside them.

The first time we did this, my company played the part of the Iraqi village people, and another platoon got to roll into the city and play U.S. soldier. When they rolled into the city that first time, we all made it look like the L.A. riots were going on. People were running around all over the place cheering and screaming "*Fuck you, G.I.!*" throwing rocks and dirt at the soldiers, picking up the scared-to-death livestock that were running around and throwing them down the hatches of the Stryker vehicles, pelting the soldiers with water balloons from the second stories of the buildings, and climbing on top of Strykers and looting everything not strapped down. It was pure chaos, but at the same time, a whole lot of fun.

That was until, of course, some officer, who was pretty much in charge of directing this whole exercise, decided to take the fun out of it, telling us all to tone it down a bit, actually tone it down a lot, so that it'd be more "realistic."

240 Creed

"The M240 Bravo is a general-purpose machine gun. It can be used on a pipod, tripod, aircraft, or vehicular mount. The M240 Bravo is a belt-fed, air-cooled, fully automatic machine gun that fires from the open-bolt position. Ammunition is fed into the weapon from a 100-round bandolier. The gas from firing one round provides the energy for firing the next round. It has a maximum effective range of 3,725 meters, weighs 27.6 pounds, and is 49 inches long. The M240 Bravo machine gun supports infantry units in both offensive and defensive operations. It provides the heavy volume of close and continuous fire needed to accomplish the mission. The M240 Bravo is my primary weapon. Without my M240 Bravo machine gun, I am useless. Without me, my M240 Bravo is useless. I must master my weapon, as I must master my life, so together we can Kill and Destroy our Enemies."

I wrote that *Full Metal Jacket*–influenced shit down on a piece of card stock paper with a black Sharpie marker and taped it up on my barracks wall, right next to my headboard. That way, every night right before I'd go to bed, I'd read it to myself several times so I'd have it memorized.

I hoped that if I stuck with it, and learned everything there was to learn about the M240 Bravo, then one day they'd move me up to machine gunner.

Shoot 'Em in the Face!

The M4 fires a 5.56-caliber round, which is a high-velocity bullet, but it doesn't necessarily drop or kill the person the first time. What usually happens is the bullet will just go right through the individual.

When we did CQM training (close quarters marksmanship), I was instructed to double tap the trigger with the barrel pointed center mass at the individual's chest area and then to quickly point the weapon at the target individual's facial area and shoot the guy in the face with a single shot. Bang, bang, then bang to the face.

This is to make sure that the individual is KIA.

The lieutenant told us that he wanted us to yell, "Shoot 'em in the face!" all in unison whenever we were released from a platoon formation at the end of the day.

The Birdcage

The first time I saw one of our Stryker vehicles retrofitted with the "birdcage" parked at the motor pool, I remember thinking to myself, "Damn, we're going into combat riding around in those things?"

The armor added about more than four thousand extra pounds to the Stryker and approximately twelve to fourteen inches to each side. The birdcage, in theory, works the same way as the chicken-wire fence in *The Blues Brothers* did. In case you have no appreciation for fine cinema and have never viewed this classic, or maybe you've just forgotten the scene I'm referring to, it's the part where Jake and Elwood get the band back together, and they have that gig at some Okie redneck bar that plays both kinds of music, country and western, and they open up the set by playing the song "Give Me Some Lovin'," and the stage that they're playing on has a chicken-wire fence in front of it to shield the band from the incoming Budweiser bottles being thrown at them by the local rednecks. The bottles impact and explode on the chicken-wire fence first, rather than on Jake and Ellwood as they try to play.

The birdcage around the Stryker works the same way. The RPG hits the birdcage first and explodes before it hits the Stryker armor. At first I was very skeptical of the birdcage because I thought it was just a quick fix, and more importantly it made the Strykers an eyesore, and it wasn't till we got to Iraq that the birdcage became a beautiful sight to see. As we all found out later, they do indeed work. (Kinda like braces, they're embarrassing to have on and an eyesore to look at, but they work.)

Hurry Up and Wait

The infantry is a pretty cool job, but that's only when you're actually doing something, like blowing shit up, shooting at targets, or out in the field playing "war." When you're not doing job-related stuff, the infantry can be one of the most uneventful jobs in the world.

Typical day in the infantry:

Before you go to bed, you set the alarm clock for 5:45 a.m., and when it wakes you up the next morning, you throw on your PTs (physical training clothes), quickly shave, and then walk down to the company area. Even though PT formation is not till 0630, you're required to be at the company area at 0600.

From 0600 till first formation you stand around and wait, and during this time the squad leader makes sure that everybody is there. If it's 0610 or so, and somebody is missing, the squad leader will send somebody down to the missing person's room to bang on his door, because nine times out of ten if the person's not there at 0600 it's because his alarm clock didn't go off (or he drank too much the night before).

At 0630, the first sergeant comes out and does a "salute report." That's when we find out who is "out of ranks," or missing.

Then the formation is released and each squad conducts PT on their own, which could be anything from running, to lifting weights at the gym, to playing basketball.

PT is from 0630 to 0730, and after that you have an hour and half to either go back to your room and sleep (which is what I usually did), go to the chow hall for breakfast, or both.

Then at 0900, everybody meets up at the company area again, this time wearing BDUs, and if there's nothing to do, you just stand around and wait. Sometimes there will be a class taught, like how to assemble and reassemble an M4 or M240 Bravo, or a land navigation class, but most of the time the squad leader will tell you to go back to your rooms and clean your equipment, which means hang out in your barracks room and if you have a PlayStation play video games, or watch movies. Around 1600 everybody meets up back at the company area and stands around smoking and joking, while a couple privates sweep and clean.

Then everybody gets in formation again and the First Sergeant comes out and tells us what's going to happen the next day, or if there's any news, and then the workday's over.

At the end of the week, we get a "safety brief." That's where the First Sergeant and the CO tell us not to do anything stupid over the weekend, like try to get on post while drunk behind the wheel, or get arrested in a bar brawl, or bang some skank without a rubber. After the safety brief, the workweek is over, and you're released. And the party begins.

Dear Diary

When I was living in San Francisco, prior to Army life, I kept a diary of my so-called life in a journal of sorts, which I showed to absolutely nobody, except to a couple of close friends, but I didn't allow any of them to read it. I just showed it to them, and was like, "Hey, this is what I do when I'm bored, and no, you can't read it."

I wrote in that journal, not because I had any aspirations of ever becoming a writer, but because I didn't have any aspirations to do anything at all whatsoever, and writing about it was just a way to make the days go by a little bit faster.

It was just pages and pages of diary entries, written in tiny microscopic handwriting, of mundane everyday stuff like hanging out on Haight Street, or about the bums that would beg for spare change down on Market Street, run-ins with the SFPD, drunken nights in Mission District bars, hole-in-the-wall used-book stores, people I'd meet on the bus, street corners, the things I'd do, thoughts, observations, etc.

And on some of the pages I did cut-and-paste collages of random things I'd find and collect, such as ticket stubs, bus passes, receipts. Every here and there I'd pretend I was Pablo Picasso going through his cubism phase and I'd draw like a little scribble of something stupid.

One of the turning points that finally made me want to join the military was the day I came home from work, exhausted, and I picked up my journal and started reading it from beginning to end.

It was the most depressing piece of literature I'd ever read.

At the time, like I said earlier, I was going through this mid-twenties thing. It was shortly after my twenty-sixth birthday, I was like "Holy shit, I'm gonna be like fuckin' thirty soon, my life is *soo* over," and reading what I wrote down on paper confirmed that I was doing absolutely nothing with myself, that every day was the same as the day previous, and most importantly, I wasn't doing anything to better my situation. There was no escape. And I then realized that if I didn't do something quick I'd probably spend the rest of my life living like this.

And that was probably the moment when I said fuck it, and got my ass down to that recruiting station.

Writing in that journal helped pass the time, and I found it to be somewhat therapeutic. It was a release, made the days go by a little bit faster, made them somewhat bearable, and it also gave me something to do, since I wasn't really interested in doing anything else and I didn't really have a whole lot of money to do anything else either even if I wanted to.

So when word started circulating that hard times were coming my way, and it was clear I was headed to the Middle East, I instinctively went out and bought a half dozen or so field journals, so I'd have something to do when I got there.

Part Two

Punish the Deserving

18 Oct 2003

We had a battalion run this morning at 0630 from the company area to Carey Theater. Carey Theater is the on-post one-dollar movie theater that's located right next to the bowling alley. It was about a 3.5-mile run. I am so out of shape from all the drinking and partying on the weekends that it's not even funny. Ever since we got finished with JRTC, the whole platoon has been partying and drinking every night like it's our last one on earth.

Once we all made it to Carey Theater, they marched us in and we got seated and our new battalion commander, a lieutenant colonel from Ranger Battalion, came out, shaved head, and with a tomahawk in hand for effect. (We are the Tomahawk Battalion.) He came out with this stern face on and said, "Men, this is not a peacekeeping mission. We will not be handing out bread, we will be handing out lead."

It was like something out of *Patton*, in fact, while he was up there on that stage with that tomahawk in his hand, pacing back and forth, the whole time I was imagining this: an American flag unfolding behind him, as he was saying a bunch of things along the lines of, "Men, all this stuff you've heard about America not wanting to fight the Global War on Terrorism, and wanting to stay out of the war in Iraq, is a lot of horse dung. Americans traditionally love to fight. All *real* Americans love the sting of battle. My God, I actually pity those poor terrorist bastards we're going up against. We're not just going to shoot these non-compliant bastards in the face, we're going to cut out their living guts and use them to grease the gears of our Strykers and the bolts of our weapons. We're going to rip into them. Spill their blood and shoot them in the belly. We're going to hold on to him by the nose, and we're going to kick him in the ass. We're going to kick the hell out of him all the time, and we're going to go through him like crap through a goose. All right now, you sons of bitches, you know how I feel. Oh! . . . I will be proud to lead you wonderful guys into battle anytime, anywhere. That's all."

We were all a little nervous about receiving a new battalion commander just weeks before deployment, but whatever concerns we had about the guy prior to this were pretty much extinguished after this first encounter with him.

And then out of nowhere he explained to all of us why he was carrying around a tomahawk in his hand, which we had all been kinda curious about. Holding it up for all of us to examine, he explained that the tomahawk was the symbol of our battalion, and it is a close-quarters weapon, used to destroy the enemy with swift, decisive blows to the head, and that was exactly what we'd be doing in Iraq.

In a straight-up fashion, he informed all of us that we would be going to Iraq to do offensive operations, stability operations, and to counter mortar ambushes.

For some reason I thought that this upcoming mission to Iraq was going to be over quickly and that we'd be doing more peacekeeping-type stuff. Basically stand around Iraq for a year and be sniper targets, hand out MREs to some starving Iraqi kids, or maybe stand around a

TCP (traffic-control post) and wait for a car bomb to show up.

But instead it sounds like we're going to Iraq for some guerrilla warfare, urban style.

19 Oct 03

I called my parents today to tell them the good news, that their son will be going on his first all-expenses-paid business trip in a couple weeks to a place called the Sunni Triangle in some country called Iraq.

My father's exact words when I told him: "That's not good."

I then called my sister to tell her the good news, and she told me that, "You know Mom is getting really worried about you traveling to the Middle East."

I then called my brother to tell him the news and he told me, "Well, have fun playing cowboys and Indians out there."

I then called my wife and told her the good news, she said, "Congratulations, you got what you wanted!"

For the first time since basic training at Fort Benning, I went to church this morning at Soldier's Chapel. I went because Pfc. Pointz, a Stryker driver in my platoon, asked me to go with him to church the other night, so I figured why not, it probably wouldn't hurt to check it out. I'm not an atheist, but I'm also not a religious person. Not a lot of people at this service, which was kinda sad. Just Pointz and me, and a half dozen other adults (nonsoldiers). That's it.

20 Oct 03

Another brief at Carey Theater. This brief today was about dealing with the media. They told us there will be embedded reporters with us when we get to Iraq. I don't know how I feel about having reporters with us. I watched how the embedded reporters reported the twenty-one days to Baghdad, and it was pretty sickening how they covered it. The media reported the war the same way they would have if it was the fucking Super Bowl of the century. Good vs. evil. America vs. Iraq. Us vs. Them. Right vs. Wrong.

I'd watch the news, and they would show some war footage, and then they would break to a Britney Spears Pepsi commercial, and then when they come back from commercials they have some ex–Special Forces guy give us the point spread for the game, and then they go into some more war footage with some embed, reporting the war all pumped up and excited like he's actually playing in the fucking game, and then they'll even break for a halftime show, like get an old retired general that they probably found walking around some PX, and have him tell all of us what he thinks it's like over there, and what we're going to do next, and how they're going to fight in the second half of the game, and then they'll cut right back to a commercial with some guy on a cell phone saying, "Can you hear me now?"

They also informed us what our mission in Iraq would be, in case reporters ask:

- We are here to help Iraq restore its independence.
- We will work to eliminate the enemy that continues to hinder progress for the Iraqi people.
- Our efforts support the continuing fight in the Global War on Terrorism.
- We will remain in Iraq until our mission is complete.

The second half of the brief was about rules of engagement. A female captain came out and asked us a hypothetical, what-if question. "If your convoy was going under an overpass, and there were women and children on the overpass throwing rocks down at us, what should you do? Do you shoot or not?"

The first answer that came to my head was no, you don't engage, you don't fire unless you see a weapon, so, no, I would not fire. I wondered why she said women and children, like why not say people instead, or was women and children for effect?

One soldier in the auditorium instantly yelled out, "Light 'em up!" Which was followed by some laughter. But there were also people in the auditorium who disagreed with the "Light 'em up!" answer. As soldiers were debating with each other on what should be done in a situation like that, the battalion commander stepped up, and I could tell that he wasn't really digging on what this captain was trying to do here, and he said that he needed to say something to his men, and she handed the brief over to him, and he then asked us a non-hypothetical question.

"How many of you have been to combat?"

Several people raised their hands. The captain I noticed did not.

"How many of you have been shot at?"

Almost all the raised hands stayed raised.

"Then you understand that it doesn't matter if it's a woman or a child, if they have a weapon, they have a weapon. And if you feel threatened, you feel threatened."

He then told all of us not to worry about doing the right thing, that if we wanted to do the right thing to go out and rent a Spike Lee movie. He then stressed to us that if we felt threatened, pull the trigger. It's better to be safe than sorry, better him dead than you.

We were each handed a small piece of paper and were told to fold it up and keep it in our wallets.

Rules of Engagement

1. Enemy paramilitary and designated terrorist forces remain declared hostile and may be attacked subject to the following instructions.

   a. Positive identification (PID) is required prior to engagement. PID is reasonable certainty that the proposed target is a legitimate military target. If no PID, contact your next higher commander for decision.

   b. Do not engage anyone who has surrendered or is out of battle due to sickness or wounds.

   c. Do not target or strike any of the following except in self-defense to protect yourself, your unit, friendly forces, and designated persons or property under your control:

   - Civilians
   - Hospitals, mosques, churches, shrines, schools, museums, national monuments, and any other historical and cultural sites

   d. Do not fire into civilian-populated areas or buildings unless the enemy is using them for military purposes or if necessary for your self-defense. Minimize collateral damage.

   e. Do not target enemy infrastructure (public works, commercial communications facilities, dams), lines of communication (roads, highways, tunnels, bridges, railways), and economic objects (commercial storage facilities, pipelines) unless necessary for self-defense or if ordered by your commander. If you must fire on these objects to engage a hostile force, disable and disrupt but avoid destruction of these objects, if possible.

2. The use of force, including deadly force, is authorized to protect the following:

   - Yourself, your unit, and friendly forces
   - Enemy prisoners of war
   - Civilians from crimes that are likely to cause death or

serious bodily harm such as murder or rape

- Designated critical infrastructure, including public and private financial institutions, government buildings, known or suspected WMD sites/materials, oil fields and related equipment, public utilities including those that generate power, petroleum, or water for civilian use, commercial fuel stations, hospitals, and other public-health facilities.

3. Treat all civilians and their property with respect and dignity. Do not enter a mosque unless required for mission accomplishment and authorized by higher headquarters.
4. Detain civilians if they interfere with mission accomplishment or if required for self-defense.
5. CENTCOM General Order No. 1A remains in effect. Looting and the taking of war trophies are prohibited.

Remember:

- Attack enemy forces and military targets.
- Spare civilians and civilian property, if possible.
- Conduct yourself with dignity and honor.
- Comply with the Law of War. If you see a violation, report it.

These ROE will remain in effect until your commander orders you to transition to post-hostilities ROE.

Civilian Rules of Interaction

Nothing in these rules of interaction limits your obligation to take all necessary and appropriate action to defend yourself and your unit.

1. Be firm, but be courteous. You can afford it—you have the gun.

2. You are the foreigner.
3. Their culture *is not* your culture, their customs *are not* your customs. They do not care about ours—we need a working knowledge of theirs.
4. Do not humiliate or publicly embarrass an Iraqi. Their culture demands that the insult be avenged to regain "face." This could range from verbal protest to RPG attack.
5. Do not put an Iraqi's forehead on the ground. If you do, you will make an enemy of him and his entire family.
6. Do not put your foot on an Iraqi. (See bullet #5.)
7. Do not stare at females. It is a huge insult to their family and causes the entire family to lose face.
8. Do not confuse an inability to speak English with stupidity.
9. When using an interpreter, look at the person you are speaking with, not the interpreter. Use short simple sentences.
10. Shake hands very gently when meeting someone. Expect the handshake to last longer than normal and don't pull away first. If you do, it's a sign that you don't like the person.
11. Expect not to get much done during your first meeting. Getting down to business is considered rude. Sit down, drink tea, smile.

21 Oct 03

Another briefing today at Carey Theater. We had some ex-military guy discuss the threat of terrorism and what to expect from the enemy in Iraq. We watched several terrorist training videos up on the big screen. These guys seemed poorly trained and badly equipped, in fact a lot of us laughed our asses off while we were watching. In one video a terrorist tried to clear a room with an AK, and forgot to turn off the safety to his weapon. They told us that these people fight dirty and love to plant mines and booby traps. They can make a bomb out of an RPG round and just about anything else.

All these pleasant briefs are starting to give people in my platoon crazy dreams. Pvt. Evans told me that he dreamed that I got shot in the back in an ambush. Downham dreamed that I got my eye blown out of its socket.

Ever since this new battalion commander arrived, I've noticed a lot of dramatic changes going on around here. One of the changes I'm glad about is our battalion motto, which is "We Serve," which for some reason always reminded me of the fast-food industry when I heard it. The new BC immediately gave us a new battalion motto and mind-set as soon as he got here: "Punish the Deserving," which is just a politically correct way of saying "Kill the Enemy."

I've noticed that his attitude is rubbing off on a lot of the other officers around here as well, because a lot of them are now carrying around tomahawks with them everywhere they go. And this morning we had a company formation bright and early and they informed us that our company commander (CO) was being replaced, and we will have a new company commander to take his place in a couple days. They didn't give us any details on why this sudden change was made.

This is interesting, all this just three weeks prior to deploying to Iraq.

22 Oct 03

Today we got the Iraqi customs and language brief. I fell asleep during the first half of the brief, but when I woke up, the soft-spoken civilian guy who was giving it, who looked to be of Middle Eastern descent, told us all a bunch of stuff about it being impolite to show the locals the bottom of your boots, and then we all got a quick crash course in Arabic. He would say something in Arabic, and we'd all repeat it. Like do they really expect us to memorize anything that was taught to us today? We're going to Iraq for at least a year, and we all get a one-hour course in Arabic, and they expect us to be able to speak a little of it after this brief?

Today we were all handed our deployment orders, and I was informed that my exact date of deployment would be on the 13th of November.

Thirteen has always been my lucky number.

23 Oct 03

The briefing on unexploded ordnance and land mines was kind of a sobering class. They showed us graphic photographs of what an IED (improvised explosive device) or land mine can do to a human body, and it reminded me a lot of the *Red Asphalt* videos that they would show at drivers' ed class in high school, you know, the movies filled with scenes of reckless and drunk-driving accidents shown just so you'd know what one looks like if you ever get into one. Really informative stuff.

I never got to watch one of those films in its entirety because my drivers' education teacher, Mr. Trunnel, completely lost it and kicked me and a fellow student out of his class and sent us to the principal's office when we started acting like Beavis and Butthead, banging our heads, saying "Hell yeah, dude, that's fucking awesome!!" as we high fived each other during one of the blood-and-guts scenes.

I don't think this UXO brief would be a proper time or place to re-enact that behavior.

The sergeant that was giving us all the class on UXO and land mines informed us that they think there are sixty mines for every square mile in Iraq, and as he was describing to us what a land mine could do to a human leg, I looked over at smiling Frank Blough who was sitting next to me and noticed that he was meticulously scribbling the words "WE'RE ALL GONNA DIE!!" in thick black pen on a blank sheet of paper in his field book.

24 Oct 03

Today we went to the gym on North Fort to see if our paperwork was correct before our deployment to the sandbox. It was kinda like the part in the movie *Pearl Harbor* where Ben Affleck and Josh Hartnett go from station to station getting checked out.

One of the stations we all had to go to was the dreaded vaccine station, where we received more shots than a basketball game into both arms. We lined up like cattle to the slaughter with our medical-record folders, and nurses in civilian clothes injected us. I knew a couple of them—anthrax and smallpox—but had no idea what the hell the other ones were. I don't think I want to know, either.

One of the last stations that I had to clear was a mental-health examination station. I filled out all the forms and the next thing you know I'm pulled over to the side and speaking with some Army captain. He looked over my exam results and said, "You know I can prevent you from going to Iraq with these test results being what they are?"

I then asked him why, and he said that according to my answers, I was an alcoholic. I kinda chuckled, and he said that he was serious, and he explained to me that Iraq is a dry zone, and how does he know I'm not going to wig out or something if I can't drink over there?

I explained to him that I wasn't no alcoholic, that I'd just been drinking a lot lately because we'd all been partying pretty hard because we all know that it's going to be at least a year before we can drink again.

He signed off on my sheet and said I was free to go.

That evening I sat in my room by myself and drank beers while watching *Apocalypse Now.*

I'm Worth a Quarter Million, Dead

Authority
To USC 1475 to 1480 and 2771, 38 USC 1970, 44 USC 3101, and 3397, November 1943 (SSN)

Principal Purposes
"This form is to designate beneficiaries for certain benefits in the event of the service member's death. It is a guide for the disposition of that member's pay and allowances if captured, missing, or interned. It also shows names and addresses of the person(s) the service member desires to be notified in case of emergency or death. The purpose of soliciting the SSN is to provide positive identification."

We were advised in this Army document to sign up for their life-insurance policy, and $250,000 is how much it's going to cost Uncle Sam if I'm killed in combat in Iraq. I filled out the paperwork and took the maximum coverage available and had it all set up so that my wife would get every penny if I got killed over there. I told her to use the money to go to school and do something she really wanted to do, like travel or start her own business, and also to give a chunk of it to my brother and sister.

"I fully understand that if I am captured, missing, or interned, my designation of allotments to dependents from my pay and allowances serves only as a guide to the secretary of my service. The secretary may alter my designated allotment in the best interest of myself, my dependents, or the United States government."

Then I signed my name above the line that said "Signature of Service Member."

Fuck This, I'm Going to Canada

Julia flew over to spend my second-to-last weekend with me before I take off to Iraq. Before she showed up I got drunk up on the third floor of the barracks, and Julia arrived at about 1300, and my roommate was gone for the night so I snuck her into the barracks. She spent the night and in the morning we got up and I took her to the chow hall for breakfast, and after that we started up the rental car and drove all the way to Victoria, Canada, where we spent the weekend. We had a dinner at some nice Irish restaurant, and stayed at some bed and breakfast, in the Oriental suite, which was cool.

The car that we rented had a stereo in it, and I listened to talk radio the entire way back. A lot of things were happening in Iraq. It seemed like these terrorists could give a damn about the Geneva Convention. They are even targeting the Red Cross people, and there are a lot of suicide bombings. In one attack, thirty-five people got hurt.

A lady on the radio was comparing this war to the Vietnam conflict, and saying how the two were similar on the home front, and she even went so far as to say that the liberals here in America could care less about the troops, and how the liberals deep down wish that tons of U.S. soldiers would die in Iraq, and that every time a soldier dies it makes the Republicans look bad.

These people on the radio also said that all these little attacks that are going on over there could just be a prelude to something big, and that things are steadily getting fucking crazy over there, and we have yet to see the worst of it. In ways it's like the wild, wild West over there, gunfights and explosions and death every single day.

I said good-bye to Julia at the airport one last time Sunday night. It was kinda weird. I was thinking to myself that this might be the last time I'd ever see her. Who knows what could happen in one year's time? She told me to be safe and to not do anything stupid over there, which I reassured her that I would. And we kissed and I stood there and watched her walk through the metal detector in her white T-shirt, low-cut blue jeans, and black high heels, and I wondered how much things would change, and if she would still love me a year from now. She blew me a kiss and waved at me as she walked off to catch her flight.

I stood there and watched her until she disappeared.

Hey, Dad

We had a four-day weekend right before we were scheduled to deploy. I flew home to my parents' house to hang out with them one last time before I left. I brought with me a printout of a *Washington Times* article that described the Stryker vehicle as an overrated, underarmored, overpriced piece of shit that had shitty armor that couldn't protect soldiers from RPGs. Not really something a soldier wants to read about when he's about to go to war in that vehicle. I brought it to the dinner table for my dad to read, hoping that it would be a discussion piece, but my dad just flipped through it, unimpressed, and said something along the lines that reporters usually have no idea what the hell they're talking about, and then he asked me what I'd been up to that day, and I told him nothing much.

Slosh Ball

I failed dum-dum math my freshman year in high school, so I had to retake it my sophomore year, and that's where I first met Gabe.

On the first day of class he showed up wearing a Dead Kennedys T-shirt, which kinda shocked me, because nobody at my high school listened to the Dead Kennedys, let alone wore one of their T-shirts. That was, like, unheard of.

I sat next to him in class, said What's up, and I told him all about how I used to read about them in *Thrasher*, and how I used to listen to them a lot when I skated this plywood skateboard ramp over by my parents' house several summers back. The older high school kids that skated the ramp would bring over boom boxes, and we'd all skate while listening to classic Dead Kennedys songs. Songs like "Too Drunk to Fuck," "Nazi Punks Fuck Off," "MTV—Get Off the Air," and "Holiday in Cambodia." I told him how I used to write the DK logo on my skateboard, school binder, everything. But I stopped listening to them once I stopped skating. (The high school kids all graduated and moved away and the city tore down the ramp, so I quit skating.)

I told him it had been a while since I listened to the Dead Kennedys, and I asked him if he could make me a mix tape of all their stuff, and he said sure, and the very next day he came to class with a cassette.

This was 1991 or 1992. There was no such thing as MP3s or CDRs or downloading music. People got their free music from mix tapes. Listening to that tape, I started to get heavily into punk and skateboarding again, and I guess you can say that it all started because of the DK tape that Gabe gave me. We've been close friends ever since.

In high school Gabe wrote for the school newspaper and was

their Gonzo journalist. He wrote a pro-Unabomber article, and when he was assigned to report on the high school football game, instead of writing about the game he wrote about how everybody on the team was on steroids and how everybody in the stands was drunk off their asses. So he was pretty cool, and whenever I'm back home visiting my parents, I always make the effort to stop by and see what's up with him.

The last time I saw Gabe was when I got back from basic training, and when I told him that I'd joined the Army, his jaw dropped and he said, "You dumb motherfucker!"

After we got done catching up, we then debated the politics of the war for several hours over beers. Gabe thought the war was all about money and oil and he didn't believe America would ever catch Saddam. I on the other hand kinda had a pro-war leaning, and believed that Saddam was a threat, and that we would catch him. We disagreed on a lot of things, but at the same time we agreed on a lot of things as well, and since we were friends, it was all okay.

When we finished up all his beers, we decided to go continue this discussion somewhere else. Gabe suggested that we go over to that bar that I fucking hate going to. At first I refused to go, but after a couple minutes of arm-twisting, I finally gave in. When we got there, I (of course) bumped into a guy that I was okay friends with in high school. We played on the football team together. After we exchanged hellos, he asked me what I'd been up to, and I told him that I was in the Army, infantry in fact, and that I was home visiting my parents, because in a couple days I'd be leaving for Iraq.

He just nodded his head and said, "Cool . . . yeah, me and the guys have been playing slosh ball all day and we're just hanging out drinking right now . . . Well it's cool to see you again, man."

We shook hands, and that was it. He then went over and sat down with his slosh-ball buddies, who were all sitting around a table with pitchers of beer getting drunk and watching the football highlights.

After a couple beers, we decided to call it quits and Gabe gave me a ride home. On the way I said to him, "You know what . . . if I die over there, no one would give a fuck."

The next day I was on a plane back home to Fort Lewis.

Meat Tag

A meat tag is basically your dog-tag information (name, Social Security number, blood type, and religion) tattooed on your side, usually under your armpit. Soldiers get the meat-tag tattoo so that when an IED blows them into a million fucking pieces, there's a better chance for the carcass to be identified.

There's probably not a single military post in the States that doesn't have a bar, pawnshop, strip club, and/or tattoo parlor located conveniently within hand-grenade range of its main gate. Fort Lewis is no exception. We have all of those and then some: massage parlor, hooker hotel, crackhouse, meth lab, used-car lot, Taco Bell, etc. All there to suck the money straight out of Joe's pockets.

The Army actually has a list of establishments and businesses off-post that soldiers are not allowed to frequent. This kinda backfired on them because some soldiers used that list as a travel guide.

Anyway, the on-post equivalent of the *Village Voice, The Fort Lewis Ranger*, printed an article saying that soldiers were flooding the local tattoo shops last-minute to get ink done before deployment, and that the meat-tag tattoo was a soldier favorite. They even wrote that several of the local tattoo shops were doing the meat tag for free on soldiers as a "Thank you to our troops serving abroad" type of thing. As soon as they read the words "free" and "tattoo," a bunch of guys in my platoon decided to be all hooah and go out and get them done. There was a lot of the "I'll get one if you get one" type of talk going on. We even had a "meat-tag party" semi-planned out. All of the guys go out after work one day and get them done and then return back to the barracks for a classic all-out drunken party.

The problem was we couldn't find out which tat shop was inking the soldiers for free. We called every single shop in the area code. Once we figured out that there was no such thing as a tat shop that was handing out meat tags for free, and that the going rate was forty to sixty dollars a tag, a lot of the guys wimped out and decided not to get one after all.

There were already a couple of soldiers in my company who had the meat tag, but Sgt. Vance was the first soldier in my platoon to actually go out and get one after reading the article. This was his second enlistment. The first time, he barely missed the whole Bosnia/Kosovo thing, so this trip to Iraq would be his first combat deployment. He told me that he wanted the tag so that when he was chilling on the sandy beaches in San Diego he'd have a cool story to tell people who pointed and said, "What the hell is that?"

I got my meat tag because I was running out of ideas for things to get tattooed on my skin. At the time I already had thirteen or fifteen tattoos on various parts of my body, so I figured a meat tag might be a cool addition.

When I got it done, at a tattoo shop in Olympia, I told the tattooist to leave the religion part blank. The reason why they put your religion on your dog tags is so they know what kind of religious rite to have at your funeral. I had the religion on my dog tags changed right before I left for Iraq from "Christ-No-Denom" to "Rastafarian," which is like the legal religion of Jamaica. I thought it'd be humorous to have some incense burning and a little Marley playing on the boom box during my twenty-one-gun salute, in the event that I got waxed in Iraq.

Conversation with My Recruiter:
Recruiter: Since you're only enlisting for two years you probably won't be deployed anywhere, which is good.

Me: But I want to be deployed.

Recruiter: Oh, well, umm, I meant, umm, Afghanistan, you probably won't go to Afghanistan. You never know, now with this whole Global War on Terrorism thing, we're sending troops all over. In fact, the way the world is now, I can almost guarantee you that in your two years in the Army, you'll be deployed somewhere, probably Iraq or something. In fact I'm sure of it.

He didn't lie.

We're All Gonna Die!!!

A lot of idle time prior to our one-way flight to Iraq was spent watching all the classic war flicks. *Apocalypse Now, Full Metal Jacket, Platoon, Hamburger Hill, Patton, The Dirty Dozen, Black Hawk Down, In the Army Now*, all that. Most of us grew up watching these movies over and over again and can recite word for word countless lines from each, and most of us were probably here in the Army because we watched these movies one too many times. Horrocks and I were in his barracks room one time after work, drinking some beers, watching the HBO movie *Live From Baghdad*, when we got the idea for the "We're All Gonna Die!" theme party.

There is a part in the flick where Desert Storm is about to kick off and all the reporters are inside some Baghdad hotel bar, getting drunk on the eve of the invasion, and they are celebrating with a "We're All Gonna Die" party. As soon as that scene came up in the movie, Horrocks and I just looked at each other, and we just knew that that was what we had to do next, and we said to each other, "Dude, We're All Gonna Die Party!!!!"

We had it all planned out. Horrocks would supply the AO (Area of Operation), which would be his barracks room, and I was to supply the tunes. I had bought an iPod shortly before, so that way I'd have some tunes with me in Iraq. I downloaded a "We're All Gonna Die" mix on my iPod for the party. It was just basically a bunch of songs about war and death and getting killed. (Mostly by Slayer.) The room was decorated with a huge strand of toilet paper with the words "We're All Gonna Die!" written across it in black ink, and I hooked the iPod up to some PX-bought speakers.

The party was a huge success. Almost everybody from our platoon showed up with case upon case of alcohol bought at the Shopette and we all got completely wasted. Barracks parties are pretty much the same as out-of-control frat parties, minus the girls. Toward the end of the evening, at a point when everybody in attendance was completely trashed and well beyond the legal limit to do anything, several soldiers from the platoon decided to drunk-drive their vehicles over to the nearby PX and steal a couple shopping carts from the parking lot and bring them over for a spirited game of Shopping Cart Javelin.

Shopping Cart Javelin: You put a heavily intoxicated soldier in each shopping cart and place an equally intoxicated soldier behind each of the shopping carts, and then each shopping cart is pushed full speed at the other until there's an enormous impact that's reminiscent of a head-on auto collision, which of course receives thunderous applause and cheering each time from the surrounding spectators.

I remember standing there with a beer in my hand watching all this go down, thinking to myself, Damn, so *this* is "America's finest." And a couple days from now, I'll be going to war with these fine young men.

Cheers.

Anti-Hero

Minutes before I stepped onto the bus that would take all of us to the McChord Air Force Base, where we would be put on a civilian plane that would take us all to the Middle East, I called my wife, then my parents to say one last good-bye, since I had no idea when the next time I'd be able to talk to them would be.

My mom picked up the phone, and we talked. My mom refers to Iraq as "scary place," and she didn't like the idea of me going, but she told me to go over there and to try my hardest and do my best, kinda like the same advice she gave me right before my first day of public school. She told me to be safe and if they ever tell me to do something that I don't want to do, then don't do it.

I remember the advice my mom gave me for dealing with schoolyard bullies when I was in elementary school. She told me that I was to *never* start a fight or get into one, and to always walk away, but if some bully pushed me, I was authorized to push him back, but to do it twice as hard to him. My mom then said, If they shoot at you, you make sure you shoot back at them twice as hard, okay? I laughed and reassured her that I would, and then she told me again to be safe, and to call her the first chance I got and to always write home, and then she handed the phone off to my father. I wondered what he would say to me, since he was a decorated Nam vet, and the only advice I can recollect him ever giving to me prior to this was "Many a foolish man has trusted women," something about

"The path to hell is paved with good intention," and, of course, "Go to college."

The conversation was brief. I don't really think my dad knew what to say to me, so he just said, "Don't go over there and try to be a hero and get yourself killed, because ten, twenty, thirty years from now, nobody is going to care anyway." And that was it. He told me to be safe, and for me to write and call home every chance I got. Which I failed to do.

13 Nov 03

I'm writing this entry on a plane from Germany to Kuwait. I slept the whole time from McChord AFB to Rhein AFB in Germany. I'm suffering from a severe hangover and trying to hide it the best I can. We arrived at Rhein at about 3:00 a.m. local time. The AFB was packed with soldiers in desert camouflage, all headed to Kuwait, Iraq, and Afghanistan. The other soldiers were tripping out on our new ACUs (the new army uniform). It felt like everybody was staring at us. I overheard one soldier say, "Damn, those guys look high speed!"

We were only in Germany for a couple hours. I heard that we flew over the North Pole to get here. I bought a German Pepsi at a concession stand in the airport. German Pepsis taste kinda weird. I think a lot of soldiers roll through Rhein on their way to the Middle East, because when I went to the latrine to take a dump, the stall walls were completely covered with soldiers' names and units, and where they were headed. Most of the tags were for soldiers going to Afghanistan. I pulled out my pen and wrote: "CB11B—IRAQ—13NOV03 to ????" I wondered if it would still be up there a year from now.

On the flight to Kuwait, we had to fly in full kit, with our duffel bags and our weapons placed under our seats with the barrels pointing away from the aisle, and with the bolts taken out and kept in our cargo pockets. It's night over Germany, and the German sky has got this cool gloomy-cloud thing going on right now. I would love to come back and visit Germany someday. I don't know what the hell is wrong with me, I'm on a one-way flight to hell on earth, but I am filled with excitement, and I haven't felt this good in a long time. I can't believe this is happening. I'm looking around at everybody on this plane and everybody else is in high spirits as well. Smiling, laughing. You can't help but also think about which of us isn't coming back. I'm trying not to think like that. Right now on the plane they're showing an Arnold Schwarzenegger film. I can't wait to take my first step on that Middle East sand.

Dramatis Personae

Gun Team One calls itself the "Hollywood" gun team because back at Lewis on some training exercise, some Associated Press photographer showed up and they all got their pretty little faces photographed and the photo made it to some local newspaper. The media attention went straight to their heads. The Hollywood gun team: Pfc. Cortinas, Spc. Ramos, and gunner Spc. Horrocks.

Gun Team Two, which we jokingly called the "Vegas" gun team (because we were so damn "money"), consisted of Spc. Evans, gunner and team leader; Spc. Scroggins, ammo bearer; and yours truly, assistant gunner.

Spc. Scroggins is a brother from the streets of Baltimore, Maryland, who just had a little baby girl. He's covered in jailhouse-looking tats, loves basketball, is a hip-hop/rap enthusiast, and is always carrying around a pen and paper so he can write his rap lyrics down. Every now and then, he'll come up to me and do a spoken-word performance of some of his stuff, and ask me what I think of it.

In his old unit, back in Korea, he was also on a gun team, and he's been extremely helpful to me as a mentor ever since I've known him. He's taught me a lot about the machine gun. He'll break it down for me, without all the military jargon and textbook shit, and tell me exactly how it is, on the real. He told me that memorizing the training manuals is all a bunch of useless bullshit and doesn't mean a damn thing when it comes to pulling the trigger and throwing lead down range. He taught me that all I gotta do is just get behind that muthafucka and just fire it.

Sgt. Fisher is our squad leader, and I think he's from Texas. This is his second deployment to the Middle East. The first time was in Desert Storm. I remember back at Lewis he showed me a dog tag that was off some dead Iraqi soldier. I like Sgt. Fisher a lot because he was exactly how I envisioned what a sergeant in the United States Army should be like. He's always swearing and cussing and pissed off about something. And he's a good NCO, he's hard but fair, and always looks out for his Joes. He's also an old-school headbanger from back in the day who is way into metal and thrash. He hates Social Distortion, but that's okay because one of his favorite bands is Slayer. He's married with a couple kids.

Spc. Horrocks is from Blackfoot, Idaho. His prior duty station was up in Alaska, and he takes great pride in letting me and everybody else around him know that he was in the 1-7-duce up in Alaska, and was an M240 Bravo machine gunner in his old unit. He proudly claims to know everything there is to know about the gun, and even refers to himself as an "M240 guru." He loves hunting, the great outdoors, the Army, and telling stories about everything he's ever done. He's kinda boastful, and a little arrogant, but not in a way where he comes off as a jerk or a dick, but in a way where it comes off kinda funny, and it makes him an extremely likable and fun guy to be around. Whenever he talks about himself (which is a lot) he'll close both his fists and start pointing at himself with his thumbs to emphasize that he's the shit. I've hardly ever seen him without a smile on his face, and I don't think he's ever been depressed or gloomy about anything.

Pfc. Cortinas is this eighteen-year-old kid from Texas who comes from a huge family and looks like he should still be in high school. When he showed up to the unit, I could tell that he was kinda lonely, and one time walking back to the barracks from the company area he was telling me how he doesn't know anybody, and he's too young to hang out with anybody because everybody was way older than he was, and he has nobody to hang out with on Friday and Saturday nights because everybody is out getting drunk in bars. So I gave him the door code to my barracks room and told him he could hang out with me whenever he was bored, and if I wasn't in my room he could play around on the Internet on my computer or watch my movies. And we became friends after that. I'd help him out, and he'd help me out, like every now and then he'd shine my boots when they were all fucked up, and sometimes he'd iron my uniform. A good kid.

Doc Gifford, the combat medic for our platoon, was also attached to weapons squad. Spc. Gifford is from a small town in Montana that has a total population that's comparable to the size of my class in high school. Gifford always carries a *Rolling Stone* or *Spin* magazine tucked away in his flak jacket and is into punk and alternative music, and he always has toys on him, like DVD players, MP3 players, digital cameras. And junk food.

Spc. Blough is from Washington state, and is the TC (truck commander) for our vehicle, Bravo Victor 24. He operates the .50-cal on our Stryker and has photos of his wife and kids taped up by his hatch inside the vehicle. Blough is also way big into heavy-metal music, BMX bikes, off-roading, and Harley-Davidson motorcycles.

We call Pfc. Evans "Lil E" because his last name is Evans, and we already have an Evans in our squad. So to avoid confusion, we all call him Lil E.

Lil E is the driver for our vehicle, possibly one of the best drivers in the platoon, and is a hip-hop enthusiast along with his best friend and partner in crime, Spc. Scroggins.

14 Nov 03

Landed in Kuwait at about 1200 local time. There was not a cloud in the sky, just miles and miles of desert. Kuwait looked pretty uninhabited as we flew in. Not a lot of cars driving around, little or no green fields or trees outside of Kuwait City. You could see the Persian Gulf, and right beside the airport several Patriot-missile systems were set up. I was expecting it to be hot and humid here but it's actually pretty nice, California weather, cool and sunny.

As soon as we got off the plane we immediately boarded buses driven by locals and were told to keep the window shades closed as we drove to Camp Wolf, located ten minutes away. On the way there we passed a destroyed aircraft on the side of the road. I wondered if it was from Desert Storm.

Once we got to Camp Wolf, they filed us all into this tent, and after an initial brief they lined us all up and had us swipe our ID cards through this credit-card/ATM-machine kinda thing, which immediately activated our combat pay.

15 Nov 03

It was a three-and-a-half-hour bus ride from Camp Wolf to Camp Udari. I don't remember a damn thing about the bus ride to Camp Udari because I was so exhausted from the jet lag, pretty much passed out. A couple times I did wake up and look around and everybody else was also passed out. We showed up to Camp Udari in the middle of the night, and once we gathered up our duffel bags, we went to our tent. Camp Udari is pretty much a tent city. But that's okay, morale is high and I feel pretty good about this deployment so far.

The chow hall here is a million times better than the ones we have back home. They serve nonalcoholic beer at the DFAC (Dining Facilities Administration Center). I tried one just so that I could say that I did. It tasted like shitty, cheap beer. I took one sip and threw the rest out. I think my body sensed that there was no alcohol in it, and thus wanted nothing to do with it. There's also a mini-PX here that sells CDs, DVDs, foot powder, junk food, and whatnot. Next door is a Subway sandwich store and a Burger King!!! No way!

It's kinda boring here, and I don't know why but I'm kinda antsy and can't wait to get the hell out of Kuwait and up into Iraq. I told Spc. Horrocks that today, he said, "A wise team leader once told me, be careful what you wish for, because you just might get it."

Horrocks reminded me of when we were at JRTC, and we were all just sitting around bored out of our minds and waiting, and all you wanted to do was go into "the box" (the field), and once you were in the box, all you wanted to do was get the fuck outta the box. He told me that's how it's going to be here. Everyone can't wait to get the hell out of Kuwait and into Iraq, but once we're all there, we're all going to be wishing that we outta there. I told him that he was probably right.

16 Nov 03

Since I've been here I've been hanging out a lot with Spc. Horrocks and Sgt. Vance. Both of them are as enthusiastic about being here as I am.

Big news today. At the early morning formation, the First Sergeant came out and told the company that our mission has been changed, and that they have a new mission for us. We'll be doing offensive raids in Iraq, in the worst possible areas in the country. Our first mission will be about two weeks long. We're not supposed to talk about it at all because it's classified.

19 Nov 03

We had a battalion run bright and early this morning. Three and a half miles at a nine-minute-mile pace in the sand. At times I didn't think I was going to make it, but I sucked it up and finished the run without falling out. The last mile felt like the Mogadishu Mile. At the end of the run we had a huge formation in front of a conex (a large shipping container), which our battalion commander climbed on top of and did one of his motivational speeches with tomahawk in hand. He told us that everybody that was planning on ETSing (ETS: estimated time of separation) while in the theater is shit out of luck and that they are stop-lossing all of us.

I remember back at Fort Lewis when he specifically said, "As far as I know, nobody is stop-lossed and if you are ETSing in the theater you will be able to do so."

He also said that a lot of insurgents from Iran are entering Iraq.

20 Nov 03

We're living out of these tents right now that the Kuwaitis gave us. We can't smoke anywhere near the damn things because supposedly they're highly flammable. They also issued us Army cots to sleep on. They told us back at Fort Lewis that we'd be living out of luxurious air-conditioned conexes once we got here, but I haven't seen any of that. The showers suck. They always run out of water and the water is always cold, too.

About thirty feet in front of our tent we have a bunch of unsanitary port-a-shitters set up for us. These are more vile and nauseating than any roadside gas-station shitter I have ever seen. Half of them are overflowing with shit and piss.

I can tell that a lot of the soldiers are pissed off about stop-loss because most of the graffiti on the walls says stuff like "Fuck Stop Loss" or "Stop Loss = The Draft." At night, people use the port-a-shitters as jerk-off booths. People will bring flashlights and glow sticks to give them some light to see their spank mags. All the plastic port-a-crappers look like giant glowing lanterns.

Last night I went to use one of the port-a-johns, and I could hear the guy in the crapper next to me service himself while watching a porno video on a mini portable DVD player. It was pretty difficult trying to take a dump while listening to that.

In exactly a week from today Miss America is coming to Camp Udari to visit the troops, on Thanksgiving Day.

21 Nov 03

Wake-up was at 0300 this morning. Got only a couple hours of sleep and then we all boarded Pfc. Cannon's Stryker because our Stryker had something wrong with it and needed to be fixed. We went to the shooting range that's located way the hell out there in the middle of the Kuwaiti desert to zero our weapons. It was about an hour-and-a-half drive. Pfc. Cannon drives his Stryker like a goddamn fucking psychopath. He purposely aims for every single bump along the way and tries to get the vehicle airborne.

I'm writing this entry from inside the Stryker at the zero range. About twelve hundred meters away are a bunch of camels just walking in the desert. Spc. Horrocks and I pull out an M14 and look at them up-close through the sight. They look pretty fucking huge. Horrocks says, "Damn, I wish I could blow up a camel!" Horrocks isn't the first person I've heard say that when they see a camel, so I ask him, "Why does every single white guy from the sticks say that when they see a camel?" He laughs and says, "I also want to blow my load up in Miss America when she comes here!" Which is another thing I hear people say.

24 Nov 03

Got some good news today. Sgt. Fisher, my squad leader, has now officially made me one of the M240 Bravo machine gunners for the platoon. When I first showed up to the unit back in February they made me an AB (ammo bearer) and my job was just to carry ammo, and then they moved me up to AG (assistant gunner), where my job was to carry ammo and a tripod, and every single day I've been in this unit I have busted my ass to move on up to the gunner position. Today I got my shot.

Yesterday Sgt. Fisher came up to me and asked if I would like to be a gunner, and I told him straight up that there was nothing else in this world that I wanted more than to be an M240 Bravo machine gunner in the infantry. I was dead serious when I told him this. He said that today I would get my shot at the range, and if I hit every target and showed him that I was proficient on the gun, he'd move Spc. Evans from the gun to AG and move me to the gunner slot.

I was extremely nervous at the range, but I hit every single fucking target center mass perfectly. It was one of those rare occasions in life where one can do no wrong. Sgt. Fisher stood next to me and he would point out targets—"three hundred meters, ten o'clock"—and I'd fire and hit it, and then he'd say, "one o'clock, four hundred meters," and I'd fire and hit it, and so on. I've hardly ever heard Sgt. Fisher give anybody a compliment, but after that he congratulated me on a job well done and said that I was now our new M240 machine gunner.

Spc. Horrocks is the other M240 Bravo machine gunner in my platoon. Later on in the evening I was sitting on the cot inside the tent, cleaning the machine gun, when he came up to me and said, "Welcome to the gun." Horrocks was a machine gunner in his last unit up in Alaska, and he has this total romantic image of what a machine gunner should be like. He told me that now that I was issued a machine gun, I had to give it a name. I asked him what he named his M240, and he proudly said, "Maxine," after a sexual conquest that a heavily intoxicated Horrocks had prior to this deployment.

I thought about it for a second, and then I told him that I would name my M240 "Rosebud." He said that was a cool name, and then with a smile asked me, "So who's Rosebud?" I could tell that he was probably suspecting Rosebud to be the name of some lap-dancing stripper or something like that. When I broke the news to him that it was inspired by the movie *Citizen Kane*, he said, "Citizen what?"

I then explained to him that *Citizen Kane* was an old black-and-white Orson Welles movie, and that Rosebud was the name of the main character's sled, which in the movie symbolized Kane's lost childhood, and then I joked that if I got killed while behind the gun I'd probably mutter the word "Rosebud" as my last dying word.

He then called me a weirdo and walked away.

Dear Mom and Dad, I'm Dead

Last night the platoon leader, Lt. Williams, put out that he wants all of us to write a "death letter" addressed to either our parents or our loved one to be delivered in the event that we become KIA.

Almost everybody in my platoon thinks that's morbid and a stupid idea, and a lot of them are simply refusing to write one. I wrote a letter and kept it inside my flak vest. I decided not to write my wife a death letter just because I already told her how much I loved her and everything that I wanted to say to her in case I don't make it, and there was no need for me to repeat myself. So I decided to write my parents one instead. I never told them sorry for all the headaches I caused them when I was younger. They did everything that they possibly could to straighten me out, but I never once listened to them, and I felt bad about that, so I wrote them a letter and put it inside my body-armor vest.

Here is what I wrote:

Dear Mom and Dad,
You're right.
I should have gone to college instead.
Love,
Colby

I took the letter out and threw it away when we got to Mosul, because having a death letter on me kinda creeped me out, and I wrote it more as a joke than anything else, and I didn't think my parents would see the humor in it if they ever did receive it.

All of You are Going, Some of You Will Not Be Coming Back

26 Nov 03

Received good news and bad news today. Sgt. Fisher put out that we'll be doing ambushes in Iraq, and that where we're going, people like to fire RPGs at Americans and quickly disappear. The bad news: The CO also said that where we're going, they expect somebody from Bravo Company will be getting killed, and will not be coming back.

Thanksgiving

The line at the chow hall for lunch was insanely long A) because they were serving a Thanksgiving meal, and B) because Miss America was there to support the troops. The inside of the chow hall was all decorated in festive Thanksgiving decor, and they were serving pie, ham, turkey, and of course stuffing, and nonalcoholic champagne. Miss America was there, serving the chow, dressed in desert cammo, the words "Miss America" written on her name tape. Surrounded by a bunch of photographers as well as salivating soldiers with digital cameras, she served me my Thanksgiving meal, and I later heard that she came out and started singing to the troops, and one of the songs she sang was "God Bless America," and that she cried when she sang it.

The other night somebody broke into the mini-PX and stole $10,000 worth of merchandise, so they had us on lockdown for a majority of the day. They had us dump all our duffel bags out, and they went around and searched all the Stryker vehicles. I was figuring it was probably an inside job, like somebody who worked for the PX, or maybe some contractor. Who knows?

29 Nov 03
Our First Sergeant came into our tent at 0545 and yelled for us to wake the fuck up and get into a single-file line and take our shirts off. We all lined up dog tired, asking each other what the hell was going on. The First Sergeant inspected our bodies front and back for scratches and made us show him our knuckles and our fingernails. After he inspected us all he said that last night between 2400 and 0300 a female soldier was raped right outside our tent in a port-a-shitter. This rape was totally premeditated because right next to the port-a-shitters are these huge gas-powered generators that are loud as hell, you could stand next to one and scream as loud as you can and nobody in the surrounding tents would hear you. A sergeant later told us that if any member of the press asked about the rape, we were supposed to tell them that we knew nothing about it.

Why didn't they ask us if anybody had heard or knew anything about the rape instead?

Our CO later told us that the victim was tied up with some 5/50 cord and gagged with her own panties, and that CI had forensic evidence and that they would probably make an arrest in the next couple weeks. He said the victim will be returning to the United States when she recovers. I hope they catch the sick fuck that raped her and execute him via firing squad.

Rumor has it that the woman faked her rape so that she could get out of this deployment.

No word if that rumor has any truth to it.

Hell Is My Destination

We left Kuwait at the crack of dawn, driving north into Iraq, where we'll be for the next year. They told us there was a 25 percent chance that we'd be ambushed on this initial drive up. We spent last night a mile away from the border. I pulled guard duty with 1st Sgt. Mayo, while everybody slept inside their vehicles or slept on cots outside. We talked as we walked and did laps around the vehicles. I thought it was pretty cool that a First Sergeant was pulling guard duty.

We talked for most of the night, and Sgt. Mayo gave me a lot of advice on what to do if I chose to stay in the Army. He told me to get as much as I could out of the Army because the Army was going to get as much as they could out of me. He told me to take advantage of the education benefits, and if I chose to stay in the Army, to go to as many schools as possible, like Ranger School and Airborne.

First Sgt. Mayo was a pretty cool guy; he told me all about his experience at Ranger School, which was something I'd always wanted to do. We also talked about Iraq. This convoy would go from Camp Udari in Kuwait all the way through Baghdad, north to some small city in the infamous Sunni Triangle. Sgt. Mayo told me not to tell anybody, but he'd heard that they expect us to take 2 to 3 percent casualties in Samarra, which is our destination.

On the border separating Kuwait from Iraq, they had several huge chain-link fences that went as far as the eye could see in either direction. They had dug a moat, too, which was littered with thousands of empty Hajji-brand water bottles used by U.S. forces.

Once we passed the checkpoint at the border, it hit me. I was like, holy shit, this is it, I'm entering a combat zone. Cool! I noticed a sign on the side of the road that said, "Welcome to Iraq." And underneath, in black pen, someone had written, "Good Luck." I had all sorts of emotions going through me—excitement, concern, fear, eagerness, and disbelief all rolled into one. Iraq looks nothing like Kuwait. Entering Iraq was like visiting another planet. In Kuwait, from what I saw, the people looked pretty comfortable as they drove by in Beamers and Benzes, wearing these white man-dresses and those red-checked headdresses they all wear. The streets in Kuwait City were nice, had streetlights and big houses, and looked a lot like the neighborhoods back home.

That all changed the minute we entered Iraq. There was a little beat village right on the other side of the border which made Tijuana look upper middle class. All the houses looked like they were made out of a mixture of mud and garbage. As we started driving through the village, we were immediately flanked by a handful of filthy homeless-looking Iraqi kids begging for handouts. "Mista! Mista! Water?! MRE?! Mista!" I felt bad for those kids. They don't have a chance in hell growing up in an environment like that.

The rest of my squad rode inside armored Strykers in this convoy, but I got tasked to be the M240 Bravo machine gunner for Sgt. Mayo's Humvee. My friend Pfc. Wescott, who went to basic training with me at Benning, drove the Humvee, which was cool. He was in his mid-thirties and had prior service but reenlisted to be a part of this war. And here he was.

I sat down in the back, poking through the roof of the Humvee, behind the M240 Bravo machine gun mounted up top. If we got ambushed or IED'd on this convoy, like they predicted, we'd be totally fucked because this particular Humvee was a light-skinned model, which meant it had no armor whatsoever on it.

Riding on the back of a Humvee allows for a lot of sightseeing. The reason I joined the Army was to experience Iraq, and so I was in high spirits. *On the road in Iraq.* Hell yeah, Kerouac and Cassady don't have shit on this nigga!

Once we drove through the small village, we pulled onto a concrete freeway and started heading north. It was kinda like the freeways back home, but there was absolutely nothing to look at on either side of the road except miles and miles of absolutely nothing for as far as the eye could see. Every several miles would be a small shack made of weathered plywood and sticks. They were like mini-convenience stores that sold cigarettes and junk food. And every one of these would have a couple Iraqi kids hanging out by it. I wondered where the people who worked these shacks lived, because there wasn't anything else around.

Every time we passed one of these shacks, kids outside jumped up and down and waved at us, which was weird because I was under the impression that Iraqis hated Americans. But these people seemed to be happy that we were entering their country and they let us know it, which felt kinda good, kinda like being in a parade. It was like we were here to liberate their country and they were thankful for that. I was also surprised that the street signs were in English, with Arabic written underneath. Of course several of the signs that we passed had bullet holes in them.

As a machine gunner, my job was to keep my eyes open for any possible threats, like for example, freeway overpasses. I'd make sure nobody was up there with an IED, a hand grenade, livestock, rock, or God knows what to throw down at us. Every time we approached one of these overpasses I'd have the M240 fixed on it, and right when we drove underneath it, I'd swing the gun around, keeping a bead on it as we passed. They said these guys would crouch down when we approached and throw stuff down at us from the other side of the overpass when we crossed under. Every time we'd approach an overpass, my heart raced a little, and every time we'd drive away from one, I'd feel a little relieved. What's cool is that we had several Army Kiowa helicopters shadowing the convoy, hovering not too high overhead. It was interesting watching them work, flying up and down the freeway like wasps. Those guys have a pretty cool job.

All along the way we passed a lot of evidence of war. There were burned-out tanks and military trucks and vehicles of all kinds abandoned along the side of the freeway. Some of the overpasses were peppered with bullet holes, and sometimes you'd see a streak of bullet holes across the freeway itself, probably from a plane or a helicopter. The only nonmilitary vehicles that shared the roads with us were raggedy civilian convoys and trashed Third World–looking buses packed with Iraqis. The women wore the traditional black dresses with the head veils. They would stare at us but as soon as you made eye contact, they would look away. The Iraqi men were a little different. They stare, too, but don't look away, and if you wave, which is something they never initiate, they wave back, nervously.

We drove all day, stopping only to refuel. Then at about the time the sun was dropping to the horizon, clouds appeared out of nowhere and it started to rain, hard. The concrete road was now a semi-paved mud track. The ride was getting bumpy and the temp dropped dramatically. I was wearing my military-issue neoprene ninja mask thing to keep my face warm, and underneath my BDU top I wore snivel gear, but I was still freezing my ass off.

Once it started raining I was in a world of discomfort. My clothes were soaking wet with freezing water and I had honestly never been that cold before in my entire life. My whole body shook, and my fingers and toes went numb. At one point it got so bad that I swear to God I was actually hoping that we would get ambushed or IED'd so I'd be put out of my misery. It was that cold.

I thought we'd never stop, but finally, really late that night, we pulled into a little fuel point in the middle of butt-fuck to get a couple hours of sleep. It was raining hard and we pulled into this muddy fuel point and parked the vehicles. As soon as we parked, the first thing I did was light up a cigarette, since I hadn't had a chance to smoke all day. First Sgt. Mayo came by and chewed me out for smoking, because I happened to be standing next to a huge fuel tanker that had the words "Highly Flammable" in giant red letters on the side. My bad.

I grabbed my sleeping bag and a cot and tried to sleep underneath a huge truck that was parked next to us. It was perfect. I had the cot set up nice and was all cozy inside my sleeping bag when 1st Sgt. Mayo came up and told me that sleeping underneath a truck that was in heavy mud was probably the dumbest fucking thing in the world to do. The truck might sink in the mud while I was sleeping and kill me, which at the time would have been okay with me. He told me to find somewhere else to sleep, so I set the cot right next to the Humvee and grabbed a poncho.

I tried to sleep through the rain and the cold but it was impossible, even though I was extremely tired. So I smoked a couple cigarettes underneath my poncho, which seemed to warm me up a bit. I slept a little bit but it was like half-sleep. Then we woke up at dawn and drove to Baghdad.

Back on the road, we followed these huge traffic signs along the freeway that directed us to Baghdad. We got caught up in a traffic jam while driving through Baghdad, and the whole time I was thinking "ambush." That was really the first time that we actually drove through a densely populated area. I hate to say this, because it's extremely racist, but every single fucking person there looked like a goddamn terrorist to me. Every single one of them. And dude, they were all over the place.

I saw a couple people with AK-47s on a bridge hanging out. They had no uniforms on, and they kinda freaked me out when I saw them, but they were probably Iraqi police, because nobody in my platoon shot them when we drove past, and they didn't seem too scared when they saw us.

We pulled into a fuel point that was located in a bombed-out airstrip that used to belong to Saddam's military. There were a couple of bombed-out hangars, and while the vehicles were getting fuel I got out and walked over and had a look. Inside the hangars there were painted murals of Saddam, one of Saddam on a horse walking over an Israeli flag and the other of Saddam doing a *Siegheil* hand gesture with a Scud missile in the background headed toward Israel.

On the way out of the fuel point, 1st Sgt. Mayo handed me a tent stake and told me to whack any little kid who tried to fuck with our Humvee. We were told not to throw candy, food, or water bottles at any of the kids begging for handouts that we passed on this convoy. As soon as we left the airfield, there was a mob of bratty Iraqi kids screaming for money and MREs. Once they knew we weren't giving them shit, they flipped us off and yelled, *"Fuck you!"* in perfect English.

07 Dec 03

We made it. None of us got ambushed on the convoy here, which is good. We drove past the New York City of Iraq, Baghdad, which was kinda cool. We passed several huge mosques, and like most holy places of worship, regardless of faith, they looked beautiful.

Right now we're at some shithole FOB (forward operating base) called Pacesetter, located somewhere in butt-fuck Sunni Triangle. Just when you think the living conditions couldn't possibly get any worse, they do. The accommodations here at FOB Pacesetter make the place where we stayed in Kuwait look like the Four Seasons.

There is absolutely nothing here at Pacesetter for us.

Nothing. No phone center, no Internet, no PX, no gym, no running water, no basketball hoop, no Burger King, no MWR (morale, welfare, and recreation) center, nothing. There's not even a shower here. Supposedly they're working on them and we'll have some showers in a couple days. We'll see if that happens.

All this place is is a bunch of circus tents with Army-issued cots inside of them. There's not even a port-a-shitter here. The shitters are just sheets of plywood nailed together to form makeshift outhouses, they're communal, which means you can take a shit and thumb-wrestle with the person next to you if you want to. The shit drops into a barrel. And when the shit barrel is full, a two-man detail is required to remove the shit and burn it.

There's no pissing allowed in the poop barrels, you can only shit in them, so right next to every one of these outhouses are two black PVC pipes that go straight into the ground. Those are the urinals. There's no wall for privacy, and a hundred meters in front of these piss pipes is a line of Strykers belonging to another company of soldiers, and every now and then some pervert will watch you whip it out and piss in the tubes.

08 Dec 03

Last night a Humvee got IED'd on the convoy route called Ambush Alley, and they had us run down to the motor pool and get all locked and loaded and ready to storm out and kick ass. Then, for whatever reason, they canceled the mission, which totally pissed me off and bummed me out. We rolled out at 1600 for our first combat mission—a TCP (traffic-control point) at some nearby village. Morale is at an all-time high. Everybody is amped. Everybody had their cameras out and was taking squad photos before the mission. In the Stryker we have a stereo hooked up and we were blasting "Seek & Destroy" by Metallica. Finally we all loaded into the Strykers and we left the main gate and drove for a while when all of the sudden the vehicles stopped. We stayed stationary for a while, then we were informed that our mission had been canceled, and we were told to return to the FOB. On the way back, we heard over the radio that a Stryker in 3rd Platoon, which came along with us on this mission, had had a serious rollover accident into a ditch. There were two urgent medical evacs, and the driver was submerged in water underneath the vehicle. He was stuck there for forty-five minutes. I hope he's still alive. Back here at the tent, the mood is extremely somber.

09 Dec 03

I'm finding out all the details of the Stryker rollover and it's making me literally sick to my stomach. We were supposed to be leading that convoy out there last night, but somehow things got all switched around at the last minute and 3rd Platoon somehow ended up in the lead. Somehow on the way to the TCP they fell into a deep ditch that had water in it. The back door was combat-locked, so nobody could get out of the Stryker, and it was on its back submerged. As of right now, my friends Spc. Blickenstaff, Sgt. Bridges, and Spc. Wesley are dead. Sgt. Mata was dead, but they revived him. We haven't even done our first combat mission yet and we already have three dead.

1ST BATTALION, 23RD INFANTRY REGIMENT
FOB PACESETTER

1030 HOURS. . . . . 12 DECEMBER 2003

Prelude
*Invocation ....CH (CPT) Gutting
Comander's Tribute ....CPT Robinson
Scripture Reading .... CPT Tiffner
Remarks by Fellow Soldiers
Memorial Tribute ....CH (CPT) Gutting
*Benediction .... CH (CPT) Gutting
*Last Roll Call ....1SG Swift
*Firing of Volleys ....1/23 INF BN
*Sounding of Taps
Postlude

*Please stand

In Memoriam
SSG Steven H. Bridges
Bravo Company, 1-23 INF BN
Born: 22 August 1970
Died: 8 December 2003

SPC Christopher J. Wesley
Bravo Company, 1-23 INF BN
Born: 7 August 1977
Died: 8 December 2003

SPC Joseph M. Blickenstaff
Bravo Company, 1-23 INF BN
Born: 26 September 1980
Died: 8 December 2003

11 Dec 03

We had our first combat mission today. It was to secure an area of Ambush Alley so that the convoys can drive through without getting hit. We dismounted the Strykers at a three-way intersection and I had the machine gun locked and loaded and directed down the road facing traffic. A couple combat helicopters hovered overhead. Some guys in the platoon had bayonets fixed on their weapons. Strykers all over the place with .50-cals scanning, dismounts here and there. The whole thing was an awesome sight—lots of local foot traffic in the area, the town we were in is called Ad Duluiyah (pronounced *Dee-lu-lee-ah*). It's located somewhere in the northern part of the Sunni Triangle. This place looks like an issue of *National Geographic.* People commuting by donkey, people walking with dead chickens, all the cars looking totally destroyed, and it's a miracle any of them still run. This one guy ten feet away from my gun position was killing baby lambs and gutting them right there and then. Located right behind my gun position was an elementary school, which was completely covered in bullet holes. When school was out, all the schoolkids came over to me and they all just stared at me in amazement. Every now and then one of them would point at my 9mm, or my bayonet, or my machine gun, and they'd whisper softly to each other curiously. An Iraqi lady in full traditional veil and everything walked past me and said "Good morning" in English. (It was 3:00 p.m.) I'm shocked that a lot of these people speak English.

The kids here are definitely more well behaved than the ones in Baghdad. One little schoolgirl offered me a candy bar. I motioned with my hands that she should eat it. She opened up the candy bar and broke it in half and offered me a half. Talking with my hand, I gave her back the half she offered me and told her I was full and she should eat it. She smiled and then she started blowing me kisses. Her older sister, who was on the other side of the street watching all this going on, ran over and grabbed her by the arm to take her away. They both giggled and laughed hysterically as they walked away, the little girl blowing kisses the entire time.

12 Dec 03

We did an area-presence mission yesterday in a small village near Ambush Alley. We had a couple of counterintel agents with us and three linguists, two of them female, both of whom were extremely cool and friendly. I noticed that the Iraqis, especially the female Iraqis, were completely tripping out at the sight of a female in uniform, like they would point and act all shocked when they saw them. I asked one of the linguists what this was all about, and she told me that some of the women thought that they were total sluts for wearing pants and working with men, and some thought that they were totally awesome and wished they could do that, too, and so they looked up to them.

The area presence was just a meet-and-greet with the locals to gather up intel and to find out if the locals were anti-American, etc. We pulled security while the intel agent and linguists took their helmets off and joked and played around. I was handed a bunch of gifts, and my cargo pockets were filled with oranges, pomegranates, candy, a Pepsi, etc. Slowly, more and more people showed up, and soon each and every one of us had a couple little kids hanging out next to him. I was surrounded by a bunch of little kids and they all started giving me lessons in the Arabic language. They would teach me a word, and I would write the pronunciation of the word in pen on my hand and practice on them.

After the four-and-a-half-hour meet-and-greet, we searched a nearby orchard for weapons caches.

Didn't find shit.

Can We Go Home Now?

When word started circulating among the guys that Saddam had been captured, at first I thought that it was another "Joe rumor," and I didn't think that it was true. A Joe rumor is a rumor that Joe spreads that's highly untrue and at times very comical. Like the Joe rumor that circulated right when we got to Kuwait that we might go back home because the Army didn't know what to do with us.

But then when the First Sergeant came out and told us all that in fact the rumor was true, that in fact today we had caught Saddam up in Tikrit, I believed it. The First Sergeant also told us that this meant absolutely nothing to us, and that our mission had not changed, and that we still had a job to do. I and the other guys were kinda bummed out that it wasn't us that caught Saddam. Even though the First Sergeant said that nothing had changed, I wondered if this meant that the war in Iraq would be over soon.

The Battle of Samarra

When I found out that I wouldn't be going into the city with the rest of the platoon when they rolled into Samarra, a suspected terrorist hot spot supposedly filled with non-compliant forces armed to the teeth with IEDs, RPGs, and AK-47s, I bitched about it like a little schoolgirl to the rest of my squad.

Sgt. Fisher caught wind of me complaining to the rest of the guys in the squad, and he came up to me in the tent and sternly told me to stop crying like a little girl about it, and not to worry, this was only one of our first missions, we'd be here for an entire year, and that "You'll get your chance."

While the rest of the platoon would be kicking down doors and kicking ass street by street, block by block, Spc. Evans, my team leader, and I would be tasked out to the guys in mortars, who would be on the outskirts of town, far away from anything. Our job would be to pull security on their position, and if there were detainees that had to be taken to the command post, we'd be there to escort them in for questioning.

We had a midnight to 6:00 a.m. curfew placed on the city, and at first we had pretty liberal ROEs (rules of engagement), which were to shoot *anybody* out past curfew. Shortly before the start of this mission they changed that to *detain* anybody out past midnight.

We rolled into Samarra in the middle of the night and parked our vehicle on the outskirts of the city, where the guys in mortars were set up. We just sat there for hours and stared into the city, and somewhere out there our platoon was conducting raids on houses that belonged to suspected terrorists. Every now and then I'd hear single gunshots. Later in the night, we got a call about a couple detainees that had to be brought in for questioning. Our job was to take them over to the command post.

Two of them—a mentally retarded Iraqi guy who was walking around like a Jerry's kid past curfew, and an Iraqi police officer who was drunk off his ass. We loaded them onto the backs of our Strykers, and as we were driving away from the city all hell broke loose in the neighborhood that I knew my platoon was conducting operations in. The whole neighborhood lit up and I could hear hundreds and hundreds of rounds being fired and ricocheting bullets and tracers streaking up toward the night sky. It looked like a bottle-rocket factory had just caught on fire.

Spc. Evans and I looked at each other and commented that it looked like our guys were in one hell of a firefight. Then we heard over the radio, *"Stop shooting!! You're shooting at us!"* and then I heard another person over the radio yell, *"No,* you *stop shooting at us!"* and then *"Cease fire! Cease fire! You're killing him!"* Confused, I looked over to Spc. Evans and said, "Dude, I wonder what the hell is going on."

Evans just shrugged and said, "I don't know."

Whatever it was, it didn't sound or look good.

Light Him Up!

Once the sun came up over Samarra the next morning, we parked the Strykers around this abandoned slaughterhouse right outside the city, and Spc. Evans and I met up with the other guys from the squad.

Sgt. Fisher claimed that what happened last night was divine intervention, and he kept on saying over and over again that he was going to start going to church from now on. Even though I could never imagine Sgt. Fisher ever going to church, I don't think he was kidding around.

We placed the M240s up along this berm, and the guys on gun one—Spc. Horrocks, Pfc. Cortinas, and Spc. Ramos—told me all about what happened.

Spc. Horrocks started off by telling me that he almost got killed and that he better not ever hear me crying about not going out on any missions. He said that it was shortly after curfew had been lifted in the city, and this guy, who was probably on his way to work or something, pulled out of his driveway, turned on his hazard lights, and started to drive away. Horrocks said that the guy was in between their blocking positions—2nd Platoon on one blocking position, 3rd Platoon on another—and the guy pulled out of the driveway and Spc. Horrocks pointed him out to the platoon leader and to

Sgt. Fisher and they both told him to keep his eyes on him. And as soon as they said that somebody yelled, *"Light him up!"* So everybody pointed their weapons at the vehicle and started lighting him up, and Horrocks was right in the middle of it along with Sgt. Fisher and the platoon leader. Sgt. Fisher then started to shoot over Horrocks's head with his M4, at which time Horrocks, who was the closest guy to the vehicle, then pointed his M240 Bravo machine gun at the guy in the car and pulled the trigger, but he was only able to fire off a three-round burst before his gun jammed.

I interrupted his story and asked why he shot at him, since he was closest and didn't see a weapon on him. He said that he fired because everybody else was shooting, and he didn't know if they saw something he didn't.

His gun had jammed because when we got to Kuwait, both 240s were issued a "nut sack," which is this thick nylon sack that holds a belt of M240 ammo. When the Army issues you something, they usually issue it for a reason, but I took my nut sack off right before we rolled into Samarra, because when we had tested them out at the range in Kuwait, they totally sucked and would malfunction and jam the gun every now and then. I figured I'd rather take a good ass-chewing for not having it on my weapon than have it on and have the fucker jam on me at the moment of truth when I needed my gun to work. Horrocks left his on. He was there, I was not. If Horrocks had taken that stupid sack off his gun, that gun would not have jammed, and who knows what would have happened.

But back to the story. While everybody was shooting at this vehicle, dropping mags and reloading and shooting, people finally started yelling, "Cease fire!" and the shooting stopped, and the Iraqi in the vehicle started saying, in sheer terror, "No, mista! No, mista! Don't shoot!" while at the same time doing the universal sign language for "I surrender and I'm unarmed," which was that he had both his hands up in the air as he slowly started to get out of the vehicle. Horrocks described the look in the guy's eyes as one of just pure fear, and he said that he would never forget that look. And then they started to shoot at him again.

"What?!" I asked Horrocks. "Why did you guys start shooting at him again?" Horrocks said that it was because somebody yelled out that the guy had a weapon, and thus everybody went back to lighting him up.

"Who the fuck yelled, 'Light him up' again?" Horrocks didn't know who had said it, but it came from 3rd Platoon.

Again people were yelling, "Cease fire!" and the shooting stopped again, so they called over the combat medic, Doc Gifford, to see if the guy was dead or alive, and miraculously the fucker was still alive. Doc Gifford only found a couple bullet holes in him, all in nonlethal parts of his body.

Horrocks told me how the guy was smart because once the shooting started up again, he fell to the ground and pretended like he was dead. Since the guy was still alive but obviously in a lot of pain, Doc Gifford decided to shoot him. Not with a bullet, but with morphine. But even he missed. This was his first combat casualty, and probably out of nervousness he accidentally shot himself up in the thumb with morphine and was now all drugged up and no longer "in service," as they say.

Two United States Army infantry platoons were shooting at this guy, almost all of them awarded expert marksmanship badges, armed with semiauto and fully automatic weapons, with some of the best sights on their weapons that money could buy. Thousands and thousands of rounds were expended, some shooting at near-point-blank range, and only a couple rounds hit this individual, and in nonlethal areas.

If I had witnessed something like that, I'd probably start going to church.

Months later:

> "In Samarra, Iraqis have taken to calling the Stryker Brigades the 'Ghost Riders,' because they arrive in near total silence, strike the enemy without warning. The terrorists in Iraq have plenty to fear from the 'Ghost Riders' of Fort Lewis, Washington." *[Applause.]*
>
> —President George W. Bush
> Fort Lewis, Washington, 18 June 04

Samarra Slaughterhouse

What they had us doing after the first night in Samarra was stage over at that abandoned slaughterhouse outside of town, and whenever there was a mission for us to do inside of Samarra, like a patrol or a TCP, we'd leave and go into the city, do our mission, and then return to the slaughterhouse.

Samarra was only supposed to be a two- to three-day mission so we had packed accordingly, but somehow it ended up lasting almost two full weeks. Thus Samarra turned into one long suckfest that felt like it would never end. At night we slept on the ground right outside our vehicles, with only our ponchos and poncho liners to keep us warm. Since it was winter in Iraq, it was always pretty cold, but once nightfall came, the temperature would dramatically drop to the point where it was hard to sleep from shivering so much, and your feet would go numb, and then to make matters worse it would start to rain. We had our ponchos set up as tents to keep us dry, but it rained so hard that the water was coming up from the ground, so a lot of us decided to sleep inside the slaughterhouse, which completely smelled of death, stale blood, and animal feces. And after a couple days, the slaughterhouse started to smell of human feces.

We Need Smokes, Dammit!

After day three or four, everybody started running out of cigarettes, and we were slowly turning into crack addicts, to the point where soldiers were almost on the verge of offering oral sex for a cigarette. Horrocks told us all not to worry about being out of smokes because he said that he told his sister to send him a care package with a carton of Marlboro Lights, and as soon as that got here, we'd all have nicotine. But the thing was, we were out in the field, and it was highly unlikely that we would have a mail call in the field. Thus, we were all in a world of shit, so we improvised—we began acquiring our smokes when we did TCPs.

TCPs are kinda exactly like those damned alcohol-sobriety checkpoints they have back home, but instead of looking for drunks or stoners with a nickel bag of weed stashed in their glove compartments, we're looking for terrorists and weapons of mass destruction, and praying to God that the car that pulls up to our TCP ain't no goddamn car bomb.

Basically how a TCP works is we'll set up on a street, park the Strykers, dismount the guys, pull over every car, sometimes every other car, depending on what type of mood we're in at the moment, and search the vehicle for terrorists and weapons. If the line gets long, we'll search just cars that fit the profile of what we're looking out for at that time, like, let's say, a white Opel. (Opels are, like, the official car of Iraq. It seems like every other car here is an Opel.) When the vehicle pulls up to the TCP, we kindly tell the driver to step out and we'll check the glove box, trunk, and under the seats, tell the driver to lift up the hood, and then we say, "*Shookran*" (thank you) and let them go.

Sometimes the Iraqis who would pull up to our TCP would be smoking a cigarette. Since we were all nic-ing like crazy, TCPs became a great way to acquire smokes. You'd ask them for a cigarette, and these nice Iraqi people would hand you their entire pack. Spc. Evans even found one car that had an entire carton of Miamis (the Iraqi generic fifty-cents-a-pack version of Marlboro Reds) just lying down in the backseat, and he paid the guy an American twenty-dollar bill for it, which the guy happily accepted. A pack of Iraqi smokes usually sells for fifty American cents, so paying twenty bucks for a carton is like somebody paying several hundred dollars for a carton in America. The platoon leader, being a nonsmoker, caught wind of this and saw that we were buying and bumming smokes off the Iraqis out on TCPs and said that he didn't want any of us doing it again.

A couple days went by, and we got a mail call. Almost all of us received Christmas care packages. Horrocks received a box from his sister, and we all circled around him as he opened it, acting like we were all his best friends. He opened the package, quickly tossed all the contents onto the ground without paying any attention to what they were, looking all over for the carton of smokes. He couldn't find it anywhere. He then picked up the letter his sister had written him that was inside the package, and it said something about how she forgot to get him that carton like he requested, but that it would be in the next care package.

Merry Christmas

We started Christmas morning with "Operation Grinch," which was just another TCP somewhere in a residential part of Samarra. In one of the houses, a little Iraqi girl came out and said, "Merry Christmas" to us in perfect English. After the TCP, we drove to the command post and had a Christmas dinner. And that was that.

To Be Continued . . .

When we finally returned to Pacesetter, they had showers set up for us, and we all took showers. Then we packed up our stuff and got ready to go up north, to a place called Mosul. A lot of time was spent hanging out in the tents.

The only other soldiers in my platoon that I knew were also writing in journals were Sgt. Vance, Spc. Horrocks, and Spc. Wenger. Sometimes when I'd be sitting on my cot writing an entry in my journal, I'd look over and see Sgt. Vance sitting on his cot writing away in his journal, too. Which was cool, because if Sgt. Vance, who I would consider to be a pretty masculine guy, was also writing in a journal, then I didn't feel so weird about writing in mine.

I knew that Spc. Wenger kept a journal because I vividly remember him coming up to my cot once when I was writing away, asking me if I was keeping a journal so that I could write a book someday, which made me laugh, and I told him no, I had no plans to write a book, and I was just keeping a journal to pass the time, and to have something to help me remember what it was like here in Iraq when I'm older. He then told me that he was keeping a journal as well, but he planned to turn his into a book someday. I said, "That's cool, man."

I wrote in my journal for the same reasons that Sgt. Vance and Spc. Horrocks were writing in theirs, and that was so in twenty or thirty years I could pick it up and remember what it had been like to be a soldier in Iraq.

The next day, out of boredom, I made the mistake of reading all my journal entries, from beginning to end, and I didn't like a single thing that I had written down.

What bothered me was that the experience of "combat" so far was nothing like I had expected it to be. War, thus far, for me, was quite possibly the dullest, most anti-climactic experience I'd ever been through in my entire life, and the only thing I was really combating in Iraq was boredom. The only shooting that my platoon had done so far to date was at a poor Iraqi who had probably been on his way to work, in a car that had probably had a "God Bless America" bumper sticker on it. That's it.

What kind of war journal is that?

And it was all repetitive, and every day was pretty much the same as the day before, and I realized that I was writing about the same shit over and over again. I cringed at some of the stuff I was putting down on paper. It just wasn't coming out right, and I was like, if I don't want to read this now, what makes me think I'll want to read it later, when I'm older? So I stopped.

I closed the journal, tucked it away in my rucksack, and it wasn't till about month eight of my deployment that I started writing again.

Part Three

BLOGGING FROM A COMBAT ZONE

> War is not only a practical necessity, it is also a theoretical necessity, an exigency of logic . . . That war should ever be banished from the world is a hope not only absurd, but profoundly immoral.
>
> —Heinrich von Treitschke

I found out about this blog website stuff in an article in *Time* magazine. It sounded like a good way to kill some time out here in Iraq, post a little diary stuff, maybe some rants, links to some cool shit, thoughts, experiences, garbage, crap, whatever. I have no set formula on how I'm going to do this, I'm just going to do it and see what happens. You think the Sex Pistols knew what the fuck they were doing when they first started jamming? They just fuckin' did it.

About me: I am an 11B infantry soldier in the United States Army, currently in Mosul Iraq. Our mission: to locate, capture and kill all noncompliant forces here in Iraq. So far we've done pretty damn good. I've been here for about eight months now, and I have no idea how much longer I'm going to be here. My whole outlook on everything has changed since being here, and I've probably aged a great deal over here. So far, this has been one hell of an experience. Lots of lows, and very little highs. Every day is the same, a patrol, an OP, a TCP, same food at the chow hall, see the same faces, same streets, etc. Nothing really ever changes here. Time goes by extremely slow out here as well. A little about me, I am from the San Francisco Bay Area, I've also lived in Cleveland Ohio, Los Angeles, and New York Fuckin City.

FYI: In case you're wondering how and why I got the name "MY WAR" as a title to this website, it's a Black Flag song, here are the lyrics to that song:

MY WAR
My war you're one of them
You say that you're my friend
But you're one of them
You don't want to see me live
You don't want me to give
Cuz you're one of them
My war you're one of them
You say that you're my friend
But you're one of them
I might not know what a friend is
All I know is what you're not
Cuz you're one of them
My war you're one of them
You say that you're my friend
But you're one of them
I have a prediction, it lives in my brain
It's with me every day, it drives me insane
I feel it in my heart, that if I had a gun
I feel it in my heart, I'd wanna kill some

I feel it in my heart, the end will come
Come on!!
My war you're one of them
You say that you're my friend
But you're one of them
Tell me that I'm wrong
Try to sing me your ego song
You're one of them
My war you're one of them
You say that you're my friend
But you're one of them
My war.

Posted by CBFTW on Tuesday, June 22, 2004

I posted my first real weblog entry on the Internet without telling a single soul about it, except Doc Haibi, our combat medic, and the only reason I told him was because I read an article called "Meet Joe Blog" in *Time* magazine, and I went up to him right after, showed him the article, and asked him if he'd ever heard of such a thing as "blogs." He told me that he had no idea what the hell they were and that he'd never heard of them before.

Shortly after I asked Haibi what a blog was, I went to the Internet cafe, checked them out, and came back and explained to him what they were, and that I had started one up myself, and that if he told anybody in the platoon about it, I would (figuratively speaking, of course) kick his ass.

I didn't tell my wife, my parents, my siblings, my friends back home, my roommate, or anybody else in my platoon about it. The fewer people that knew about it the better, so that way I wouldn't get into any trouble in case the Army did have a problem with these blogs. And I'd also feel weird if people I knew read my personal writing.

To me, showing somebody else your writing is kinda like showing somebody a naked photo of yourself, and quite honestly, I didn't want anybody to laugh at me. With the Internet and the blog format, it looked like I could write whatever I wanted to, post it, and people I didn't know at all would be able to read what I wrote without me even knowing that they were, and I would remain totally invisible and nameless. If they liked it, cool, if not, whatever.

Attention to *Details*

Every day after dinner chow, usually at around 1900, came what was called a "poop meeting." A poop meeting was when we all got the poop on what was going on the following workday, found out about upcoming events and missions planned for us, and whatever information and news there was for us to know about.

At 1845 the entire squad would meet over at the squad leader's conex front door, and once everybody from the squad was physically there, our squad leader would come out, sit down on his little plywood porch, we'd all light up a smoke, and he would open up his little field notebook thing, his "poop book," where he had all the information written down, and then he'd give us the poop.

Usually he'd start off the poop meeting with something like, "The commander is noticing that a lot of soldiers are not wearing their eye pro (protection) out on missions, and he wants to remind everybody that it is mandatory to wear eye pro once you leave the wire. The CO also doesn't want to see anybody talking to and hitting on any of the females at the gym and/or chow hall, and the First Sergeant doesn't want to catch anybody out of uniform and going to the Internet cafes still dressed in their PT uniform. You got that, Buzzell?" (First Sergeant flipped out one time when he saw me at the Internet cafe in my PT uniform.)

And then if there was a mission for us the next day he'd tell us, "At 1300, we have a mounted patrol, and then from 1400 to 1700 we have an OP up on OP Abrams, so at 1130 tomorrow, everybody meet up at the motor pool, because we're all going to go to chow together as a platoon, and then after that do our patrol and OP." And then he'd tell us that we'd need to bring a couple cases of water with us, as well as a case or two of MREs, and for us to make sure that those items got onto our vehicle before we rolled out. Or if there was a raid or some joint patrol with the INGs (Iraqi National Guard) or Iraqi police, we'd be notified of it, and/or given an OP Order (operation order) for it.

At the tail end of every poop meeting, we'd be notified of any casualties or attacks that had taken place the previous day in Mosul, our new home, an ancient city 150 miles north of Samarra. It seemed like every single day there was at least one casualty or attack somewhere in Mosul.

This would be told to us the same way that the media reports war casualties to the people back home, like for example he'd say, "Today there was an IED that went off over by the traffic circle, none dead, but several are missing limbs. The airfield got mortared twice last night, two Global Security contractors got killed, and ummm . . . Oh, yeah! Laundry turn-in! That's tomorrow at zero nine, make sure you guys all turn in your dirty laundry and that your laundry slips are completely filled out."

And that would be the end of the poop meeting, we'd be released to go back to our rooms, and if there was no mission planned for us that evening, some soldiers would go to the Internet cafes, MWR center, gym, or just hang out in our rooms and watch bootlegged Hajji movies or play video games.

But if the mail truck showed up that day, mail would be handed out to the squad right after all the poop had been given to us. To make sure I'd never run out of reading material while out in the shit, I subscribed to as many magazines as possible before I left the States. I went to the mag rack at the PX and grabbed as many of those annoying subscription slips that fall out whenever you open 'em up as I could, filled them out, and mailed them in.

I find that infantrymen are into the macho testosterone literature when it comes to the monthly periodicals, mags like *4X4 Monthly, Soldier of Fortune* (which I subscribe to, just for the articles), *Guns & Ammo, Men's Health, Bodybuilding Monthly, Outdoor World,* and of course the soft-core bubblegum skin mags like *Maxim, FHM, Stuff,* and so forth. Pornography and magazines like *Playboy* and *Penthouse* are of course not allowed in Iraq, for reasons that have to do with not offending anyone and being sensitive to the Islamic culture or some shit like that. (Even though they sold porno in downtown Mosul, and all the rooms that our Iraqi interpreters lived in had walls completely covered in *Maxim* pin-up girls.)

So I subscribed to magazines that I liked but knew that not a lot of other soldiers read, like *Thrasher, Mad, National Geographic, Time,* and *Details,* which I caught a lot of hell for and which brought up a bunch of questions about my sexuality among fellow squad members. To this day I seriously have no idea why the fuck I subscribed to *Details,* I just did. At every mail call I would dread when the new issue would arrive, because my squad leader would read off the name of whoever the letter or package was addressed to and then toss it aimlessly at that person.

I knew exactly when the new *Details* arrived because he'd always freeze right before he read the name of the addressee (me) and with this confused look, he'd say, "What the fuck is this?" and he'd flip it over and show the rest of the squad the cover, which would always be some sexy cover shot of, like, Vin Diesel or Justin Timberlake. He'd then throw the mag at me and say something like, "Don't ask, don't tell."

Of course everybody in the squad would get a laugh out of this, and say things like, "Dude, you're a *homo*!" and I of course would feel the need to explain myself. "Look, dude, *Details* is *not* a mag for gay people! Check it out, there's tons of hot chicks in here." And I would open it up and flip through the pages to try to prove to the guys in my squad that *Details* was a totally hetero mag, which backfired on me because when I did every single page I opened up to had a full-page photo of some girlie man doing his best *Zoolander*.

Subscribing to *Details* resulted in people laughing at me and cracking San Francisco jokes, which I was totally immune to by then. What I'd end up doing with my *Details* was whenever my roommate Horrocks wasn't around, as a joke I'd rip out all the boy pictures and tape them up on his walls.

A Joe Blog

For a while they were working us to death, multiple missions per day, but at this current stage of my deployment, month eight (June 2004), we had more downtime than we knew what to do with. A lot of hours of the day were spent doing two things: jack and shit. I had just got done reading *The Rise and Fall of the Third Reich* in its entirety, and was running low on new books to read and things to do and was getting bored with hanging out at the gym every day, when at this one particular mail call, the new *Time* magazine came in, and I brought it back to my room and read an article called "Meet Joe Blog."

The article grabbed my attention. I was like, What the fuck is a "blog"? It sounded totally nerd to me. The article said that a lot of these so-called "bloggers" were just people talking about their everyday pathetic lives via rants and stories, and some were wannabe amateur journalists who took it upon themselves to become the media, and a lot of them were becoming extremely popular.

This whole blog thing reminded me a lot of the fanzines I used to read back in the nineties. Fanzines (or "zines") were just amateur publications, each with a certain theme or interest, that were self-published, usually at a Kinko's, and distributed independently, either through a mail-order DIY (do it yourself) distro, or at small hole-in-the-wall independent bookstores and record shops. Hardly any were done to turn a profit or with any commercial interests, and most people that published zines paid to have them published themselves and never made a dime from them, which made them more personal and real. And they also became an alternative to bigger magazines, kinda like how this article in *Time* was saying that these self-published blogs were becoming an alternative to the media.

The thing that caught my eye in the article was a brief paragraph that said that there were Joes doing them in Iraq and they even had a name for them: "mil-bloggers." I did a double take when I read that part. I was like, No fucking way! That's impossible! There's no way in hell that the military would allow such a thing to happen.

Out of curiosity I walked down to the Internet cafe, which was about twenty-five meters away from my living conex, and went online to find out for myself what the hype was all about. More importantly, I wanted to check out the mil-blogs that were coming out of Iraq. But I didn't end up spending too much time reading these soldier-written blogs, because some of them had been shut down and most of the ones that weren't shut down were just saying a bunch of brainwashed rhetoric, like "Oh, the Iraqi people love us, we're doing the right thing, I love the Army, I love my job, I love my country, I love our president." That gets old after a while, and if I wanted to read stuff like that I'd go to the official U.S. Army recruiting website.

I looked around and I couldn't find a single blog out there that was written by somebody who locked and loaded their weapon every day, went out on missions, and saw for themselves up close and personal what it was really like out here. Most of these mil-blogs seemed to be written by soldiers who were REMF (Rear Echelon Mutha Fuckers) and had jobs that hardly ever required them to leave the FOB. And for some of them a combat deployment in Iraq was pretty much like a YMCA summer camp (with of course an occasional mortar attack). I looked around but I couldn't find any that were written by a Joe who was in the combat arms, or a Joe who was in the infantry—somebody who saw and experienced the kinds of things that I was seeing and experiencing. I'd been in Iraq for a while now, and we were doing multiple combat missions per day, countless raids, countless missions, and being in an infantry platoon, we were spending most of our time outside the wire, thus I probably had a different perspective than someone who never left the base.

Fuck it.

Without even thinking twice about it, I decided right there and then to start up a blog. Why not? If these soldiers and even officers were doing them and saying all sorts of moronic shit, and the military was allowing it to go on, I might as well do one, too. And who knows? This could be kinda fun, a great way to kill some time out here.

So I went on the blogger homepage and set it all up. It was about as easy as setting up an e-mail account, they had it all prepackaged and ready to go for you, and most importantly, unlike fanzines, it was free to publish, so it didn't cost me a dime.

I wanted to stay anonymous, so I went with the blog URL and screen name of CBFTW, which is just my first and last initials and the FTW tattoo I have on my arm (Fuck the World).

I didn't want my peers reading my stuff and thinking I was some kind of fairy for geeking out with an online Web journal, writing my feelings and experiences down, and, most importantly, I was kinda cloudy on what the Army's policies were about these sorts of things. Even though there were other soldiers doing them, there had to be a catch-22 somewhere. So to stay out of trouble, I decided to stay anonymous and keep my blog under the radar for as long as possible.

Months later, in the motor pool.

Squad leader: "Buzzell, get over here!"

Me, standing at the position of parade rest: "Yes, sergeant?"

Squad leader: "What the hell does that CBFTW shit stand for on your website?"

Me: "Sergeant, it stands for Colby Buzzell Fights the War."

Squad leader, analyzing my answer while nodding his head with this look that says, "Good answer even though that's the biggest load of bullshit I've ever heard."

Sgt. Vance, who just happened to be walking by: "What does FTW stand for if somebody lower-ranking than you asks?"

Me: "Fuck the War."

Being a lifelong Oakland Raider fan, the art fag inside me chose the gray-and-black color scheme as a template for the blog.

The multicolored templates looked kinda fruity, and I wanted to present a darker reality of what was going on in Iraq. Black and gray set the mood perfectly.

Now I had to come up with a name for my website. Hunter S. Thompson, somebody who I was reading a lot of at the time and one of my all-time favorite writers, immediately came to mind. Even though *Fear and Loathing* was not my number-one book by the man (*Hell's Angels* was), I thought about naming the site "Fear and Loathing in Iraq" as a nod of respect to HST, but I decided to use that as my subtitle instead. I didn't want to jock his shit too hard. And after fifteen minutes of racking my brain for a good main title, I decided to go with a Black Flag song, "My War," just because Black Flag is one of my favorite punk bands, and "My War" sounded kinda tough: MY WAR—FEAR AND LOATHING IN IRAQ.

I then put a jpeg image of *Guernica* at the top of the website. In case you're from Blackfoot, Idaho, and you have no idea what the hell *Guernica* is, it is a painting by Pablo Picasso, a man who once said that a "painting is not made to decorate apartments, it's an offensive and defensive weapon against the enemy."

Quick history lesson: *Guernica* is about the aerial bombing of that town during the Spanish Civil War that left sixteen hundred civilians killed or wounded and is considered one of the greatest antiwar paintings of our time. It's also one of my favorite paintings, it has that Slayer-album-cover feel to it, which I like. I also had my barracks room back at Fort Lewis decorated with a *Guernica* print.

Now when I looked at it, it kinda reminded me of Iraq, in a way. The dark colors, the grays, and the women with outstretched arms with that look on their faces that says "Why?" reminded me of the house raids we were doing, the scared crying Iraqi women in the corner, holding their babies, who were also crying, while we searched the house. The animals reminded me of all the animals that roamed freely in the streets there, at times they seemed just as scared of us as the people. And the fallen soldier with a broken sword stirred up a bunch of emotion as well. Of course if you look by the fallen soldier's hand, in the bottom middle of the painting, you see a little flower growing, which means hope comes out of destruction. Which hopefully is the case with Iraq.

I then put a Smiths album up on my profile that depicts a soldier with the words "Meat Is Murder" written on his helmet, just because I've always been a Morrissey fan and I always thought that album cover looked kinda cool (you know, the whole duality-of-man thing). I then put this disclaimer up, which I cut and pasted without permission from some female officer's blog, hoping that it would cover my six in case the Army ever decided to come down on me for anything that I would post:

> **This website is privately operated and is designed to provide personal information, views and commentary about the author's experiences in Iraq and elsewhere. The images depicted and opinions expressed on this website are solely those of the author and contributors and not those of any agency of the United States Government, expressly including, but not limited to, the Department of Defense, the United States Army, or the United States Army Reserve. The site is not designed, authorized, sanctioned, or affiliated by or with any agency of the United States Government, expressly including, but not limited to, the Department of Defense, the United States Army, or the United States Army Reserve. Users accept and agree to this disclaimer in the use of any information accessed in this website.**

Then to test the blog out and to see if it worked I Google-searched "The Infantryman's Creed," which was this song we had to memorize back at basic training that was part of the whole brainwashing process from civilian to cold-blooded infantry killer. We had to sound off with it every time we entered the chow hall. I copied the creed, and then posted it up on the blog as a first entry.

THE INFANTRYMAN'S CREED
I am the Infantry.
I am my country's strength in war.
Her deterrent in peace.
I am the heart of the fight—
wherever, whenever.
I carry America's faith and honor
against her enemies.
Never will I fail my country's trust.
Always I fight on—
through the foe
to the objective,
to triumph over all.
If necessary, I fight to my death.
By my steadfast courage,
I have won two hundred years of freedom.
I yield not—
to weakness,
to hunger,
to cowardice,
to fatigue,
to superior odds,
for I am mentally tough, physically strong,
and morally straight.
I forsake not—

my country,
my mission,
my comrades,
my sacred duty.
I am relentless.
I am always there,
now and forever.
I AM THE INFANTRY!
FOLLOW ME!

Volleyball Iraq

Our Forward Operating Base (FOB) is named after our honorary 1st Sgt. Marez, who died of old age as soon as we arrived in Kuwait. FOB Marez was located in Mosul, which is the second- or third-largest city in Iraq. Mosul is conveniently located south of heaven and 350 kilometers north of Baghdad. If Baghdad is to Iraq what New York City is to the United States, then Mosul is probably the Detroit of the shit-hole. With its high crime and murder rate, it was an ideal location for any soldier who wanted to spend his combat deployment living in hell.

A haven for noncompliant forces of every genre—insurgents from Syria and Iran, who came for the excitement of fighting in a guerrilla war against the American infidels, former regime members who planned and financed attacks against "coalition forces," bomb makers, Islamic fundamentalist psychopaths, jihadists, mercenaries, mad mortarmen, common thugs and criminals, bored teenagers—you name it, we got it all in Mosul.

When we first got to Mosul to replace the 101st Airborne Division up in the northern theater of Iraq, we were all issued living quarters called "conexes." Two soldiers per room. Each room equipped with two beds, two wall lockers, two mini trash cans, and two ugly blue-and-yellow rollout carpets. Spc. Horrocks and I shared a room. Him on one side and me on the other. Each living conex was also equipped with a little porch light right above the front door.

They told us all immediately that we were not authorized to turn on or use the porch lights at any time whatsoever, because at night the enemy might key in on the lights from outside our FOB and drop mortars on us while we were sleeping or some shit like that.

When I first got there, I was walking to the chow hall for some lunch and I heard a mortar hit somewhere on the other side of our FOB, and like a total combat cherry who doesn't know shit, I completely hit the dirt, like how you see them do in the movies. On the other side of the street from me, a sergeant with a 101st Screaming Eagles combat patch sewn on one of his shoulders didn't even flinch or break stride when the explosion went off. He just looked over at me and shook his head and kinda laughed. After he told me to get the fuck up, he said, "Welcome to Mosul, kid."

On another one of my first nights at FOB Marez, I was sleeping when Spc. Horrocks grabbed me and said, "Wake up! We're being mortared!" Horrocks and I always kidded around with each other, and I thought this was one of his dumb jokes or something, because I figured if we were being mortared I'd hear it and it would wake me up. So I said, "Horrocks, man, stop fuckin' with me, dude, I'm trying to sleep, man." And right after I said that and was about to go back to sleep, I heard the whistling of two incoming mortars and then I heard them impacting our FOB. Alarmed, I got my ass outta bed, physically pushed Horrocks aside, ran out the door to the concrete mortar bunker that was five feet in front of our conex door, pushed the guys that were already inside outta my way, and got my ass in there in a heartbeat.

At FOB Marez, people got used to mortar attacks, and over time thought nothing of them. It seemed like every day a mortar landed somewhere on the FOB, and every now and then to mix things up a bit some fuckin' nut on a one-way trip to Allah would drive his or her VBIED (vehicle-borne IED, a.k.a. car bomb) to one of our gates and set it off.

Some days at Marez we'd only get one mortar, some days a couple mortars, sometimes the mortar would explode, sometimes it was a dud. Sometimes it was a mortar, sometimes a rocket. Sometimes at night, in the morning, during the day. Sometimes a couple weeks would go by without one. And whenever there was a gap between attacks, bewildered soldiers would take notice and say things to each other like, "Hey, notice how we haven't been mortared recently? I wonder what the hell's going on?"

As far as I knew, and I asked around, we didn't catch a single one of those mortarmen in the act of mortaring our FOB the entire time we were there.

Not one.

We had the technology to pinpoint precisely where the mortars were being fired from almost instantly and could have had the guys in artillery return the favor and fire a huge shell right back at them, right down their mortar tubes, and blow those motherfucking Ali Babas to bits, but we didn't do that. Probably because the guys who fired the mortars at us did it from "friendly" civilian neighborhoods, and we didn't want to blow up any Iraqi civilians who might be in the wrong place at the wrong time.

So instead we had hundreds of concrete mortar bunkers set up throughout the FOB to seek cover in during an attack. They also made for great shade when you wanted to sit down and enjoy a cigarette.

Over at the airfield, there was a sign that reminded us what to do in case a mortar attack happened. The sign had a drawing of a stick-figure guy dropping a mortar in a mortar tube with these words underneath: "In case of mortar attack, stay calm, get low."

Remember: Stay calm, get low.

Several months after we first arrived at FOB Marez, somebody came up with the bright idea to build a volleyball court right next to our conex to help boost the morale of the soldiers and give the troops something positive to do in between missions and whenever there was downtime. Overnight, the volleyball court became very popular. I would walk past the volleyball court and there would always be a game going on with a bunch of shirtless soldiers and a handful of cheering soldiers sitting around the perimeter of the court watching and waiting to get in on the next game. I think half the reason the volleyball court became such a success was it gave the soldiers an excuse to take their shirts off and get a tan in the treacherously hot Iraqi sun while showing off their beach muscles and their tattoos. A lot of the soldiers that played were of course decorated with various Army-themed tattoos—unit crests, crossed rifles, dog tags, etc.

Since the volleyball court was such a hit, they decided to place these huge, heavy-duty industrial bright-as-fuck night-lights around the court so that the soldiers could enjoy some night volleyball. I swear to God they must have gotten these lights shipped to us from Yankee Stadium or some shit like that because as I just said these lights were *bright as fuck*.

One night, I was sitting down on my desert-camo lawn chair that I had bought at the PX for seven bucks right outside my conex front door with my porch light off, of course, enjoying a Miami-brand cigarette, staring up at the stars over Mosul, when the Hajjis decided to get in on the game, and they keyed in on those lights and volleyed a bunch of mortars to the area around the volleyball court, which was a little more than fifty meters or so away from where I was sitting enjoying my smoke. About a half dozen soldiers from my company received Purple Hearts while playing volleyball that night. (Q: How'd you get your Purple Heart? A: Playing volleyball in Iraq!)

Nobody was severely wounded or anything like that, thank God. Just minor shrapnel wounds to various parts of the body. No meat tags were used to identify any of the volleyball players.

Needless to say, night volleyball was canceled until further notice after that.

Mad Mortarmen Gone Wild Home Video

I always wondered who the Iraqi mortarmen were that insisted on hitting our FOB almost on a daily basis. I always pictured these mortarmen doing this illegal deed in a hurry and scared to death the entire time, yelling at each other in Arabic to "hurry the fuck up!" because every time we got called out to try to catch these sons of bitches and turn them into martyrs minutes after they mortared us, they were always gone like the wind.

Then one day one of our interpreters brought with him to work a training/propaganda video that he had somehow acquired in downtown Mosul that showed exactly how these rat bastards mortar our FOB. It showed three Iraqi men, all wearing black ski masks, laying out the mortars all nice and neat and all in a row in broad daylight. It showed these masked mortarmen taking their time prepping the mortar tube and getting the mortars ready with no feeling of being rushed or any fear whatsoever of being caught or blown to bits by nearby U.S. forces out on a countermortar mission.

Then the camera pans onto our forward operating base, where you can see the water tower, chow hall, and guard towers, and then the camera goes back to the three individuals, who are now dropping mortars into the tube, and after each mortar is fired they'd all yell, *"Allah akhbar!"* which in English means, "God is great."

We'd yell, "Get some!" when we'd fire at the enemy. They'd yell, *"Allah akhbar!"*

They patiently fired seven or eight mortars, and then they stopped and slowly packed up their equipment, and then they all drove away in an old beat car. Probably to go get some burgers and congratulate each other on a job well done.

Task Force 121

I was outside my room smoking a cigarette when Sgt. Laufo came by with a huge smile on his face and told me that on tonight's raid, which our platoon would lead, we would be working jointly with Task Force 121. (Sgt. Laufo was a guy we called Sgt. L because we couldn't say his name properly, but he was also one of the biggest Samoans I'd ever met and a natural leader, the type of guy you want to follow into combat.)

Hell, yeah. Doing a joint mission with Task Force 121 in Iraq was every infantryman's wet fucking dream. The only problem with working with them was that none of your friends were going to believe you when you told them that you did when you got back home.

Task Force 121, from the scarce information I gathered about them off the Internet, is pretty much a team created by

Donald Rumsfeld comprised of a bunch of Navy SEAL and Delta Force All Stars, mixed with a bunch of CIA spooks. In fact, the intel that was gathered for this raid was given to us from CIA intel. But we were told very few details about Task Force 121.

Before every mission, an operation order is put out to all the squad leaders and platoon leaders and platoon sergeants in the war room, where they go over the OP order, discuss the whole mission in detail, bring out the maps, go over whatever questions people have about the mission, and times of movement, order of movement, and ROEs are fully explained, all that stuff. Once the OP order is given out to all the squad leaders, the squad leaders then relay the OP order to their squads.

At around 1630, my squad leader put out our squad's OP order for the mission, which was that we were to be the inner cordon for this raid, and we would just basically hang out outside of the house, pulling security for the rest of the platoon while they stormed in, and if they needed us for whatever reason, we'd be there to rush in and help out.

The impression that I got about us being on this mission with Task Force 121 was that we were just along for the ride to get credit for detaining this guy, and credit for conducting this mission, since Task Force 121 is on the hush and hush.

While in my room, doing pre-mission PCIs (pre-combat inspections) on my equipment, making sure that everything was functioning correctly on my weapon, oiling the bolt with CLP, and double-checking to make sure that I had fresh batteries in my NODs (night observation device), me and Horrocks talked about how cool it was that we were doing a joint operation with Delta Force, and then we started getting carried away with the quoting of lines from the movie *Black Hawk Down.*

Horrocks was like, "Dare me to go up to them and say, When you D-Boys are on the five-yard line, you gonna need my Strykers!"

He then walked up to me, showed me his trigger finger, and started squeezing it and said, "You see this? That's my safety."

As overdramatic as I possibly could, I then said, "You know what, Horrocks, once that first bullet goes past your head, politics and all that shit just goes right out the window." And then I said, "People ask me all the time, why do you do it, Buzzell? They don't understand, it's about the man next to you. That's all it is."

> TARGET INDIVIDUAL: Major general in the fedayeen, suspected of arms dealing and organizing attacks on coalition forces
> CODE NAME: "Bonnie"

Every time we did a raid we'd give the target individual a code name, usually a female name, and then there was a code word for when the target individual was captured, and that code word was called over all the radios so that everybody knew that we had caught our guy. That code word tonight would be "Budweiser." The king of beers.

We marshaled out of the motor pool at around 0015 and drove to meet up with Task Force 121. We stopped the vehicles on the side of the road and dropped the back ramp to talk to them, to make sure that everything was still a go.

Horrocks, Ramos, and I were sitting in the back of the vehicle with our combat medic, Doc Gifford, and our new guy, Pfc. Warren. This would be Pfc. Warren's first combat mission. Lucky bastard, his first mission in theater was with Delta Force.

The Task Force 121 guys rolled up in a Third World–looking minivan that looked like every other minivan in the country, dirty and kinda beat up. I remember looking down at the license plate on the front of their vehicle and noticing the Arabic plates, and for some reason I thought that was weird. One of the Delta guys exited the minivan and walked up to us and spoke with our platoon sergeant and asked if everything was still a go, and it was, so he walked back to his vehicle, and we raised the back ramp.

As soon as the ramp lifted, like a bunch of geeks we all looked at each other and said, "Wow! Did you see the NODs that guy was wearing?" And we talked about the vehicle they cruised up in, the uniforms they were wearing, the completely different equipment they had. And of course we all wished that we were them.

At around 0200 we showed up to the area where the target individual's house was located, and we parked the Strykers in some shitty-ass field that was all muddy and covered in garbage. As soon as we dismounted from the vehicles the stray dogs that hung out in the neighborhood immediately started barking at us, like they always do.

We all gathered up, and from there we made our way to the target individual's house, where Task Force 121 would meet us at. We crept to the house at a semi-rushed pace. The neighborhood we were in looked to me like it was an upper-middle-class neighborhood by Iraqi standards, most of the houses were two stories and all looked pretty well kept. The street we were creeping on even had streetlights, and was fairly well lit because of that. We were all fully locked and loaded, and all of us were trying our hardest to act and look as professional as possible for Task Force 121, when all of the sudden a camera flash went off.

Holy fucking shit.

One of our guys had pulled out his disposable camera because he wanted to take a photo of us on our way to working with Task Force 121, and he didn't realize that the flash was on. Sgt. Castro flipped out and chewed the soldier out. We all felt extremely embarrassed about what happened, and then continued anyway.

We set up our gun teams right there in front of the house, which was semi-close to a street corner, and pulled security down the streets while the line squads from our platoon and Task Force 121 blew the fuckin' door up with a huge breaching charge and stormed into the house side by side to detain the target individual, code name "Bonnie."

After the charge went off, a couple of people in the neighborhood woke up, and you could see a few of the lights in nearby houses being turned on. While I was outside, in the prone position behind the M240, the Kiowas immediately showed up and they hovered above us, and at the same time I could hear explosions from the door breaches going on inside the house, and lots of thrashing around and yelling while they were inside clearing the building. Then the minivan that the Task Force 121 guys were using drove up and parked right outside the house and a couple guys stepped out of the vehicle and went inside.

My squad leader yelled at Horrocks to pay attention and scan his sector, which infuriated Horrocks. "Sergeant! I'm *fucking* scanning!!"

Shortly after, we got the Budweiser message over our Icom radios.

The raid itself lasted a little under an hour. The less time you spend on a raid the better. Basically, all you want to do is storm into the house, grab your guy, search the house, grab whatever stuff you need for evidence, and leave. And that's pretty much what we did. The line-squad guys who were inside the house and searched it told me that the Task Force guys told them to look for anything that was post–Gulf War era—documents, photos, manuals, terrorist-camp graduation photos, etc.

After we got the Budweiser message, we pulled the Strykers up and started loading back onto the vehicles. The Task Force 121 guys went their own separate way, taking with them everything that was gathered up inside the house. Bonnie was catching a ride in our vehicle back to the FOB, and three other detainees, Bonnie's sons, rode in the back of the other vehicles.

Bonnie had a gray man-dress on and a green plastic sandbag over his head. He also looked like he had a weight problem. We put him in the back of our vehicle, I sat across from him, and Sgt. Horrocks sat next to him, telling him to "Scoot over, you fat fuck!" and then Horrocks said something about payback for September 11 to Bonnie. I wanted to say something to Horrocks about how the guy was probably just as surprised as us when September 11 happened, but whatever. Budweiser scooted his fat ass over, and he just sat there. We returned to the FOB at around 0330, our First Sergeant then briefed us about operational security, and said that he better not catch any of us talking about this raid at any of the phone centers or at the Internet cafes.

I returned to my room feeling pretty good. How many people can say that they've been on a successful joint mission with Delta Force in Iraq? Probably not many.

Dramatis Personae Mosul

Shortly after we arrived at FOB Marez, they completely recast the entire weapons squad with new characters.

They decided to move our squad leader, Sgt. Fisher, over to headquarters, and move our old NBC (nuclear, biological, chemical) NCO over to our squad and make him our new squad leader. He looks a lot like Private Cowboy in the movie

Full Metal Jacket. He's an ex-marine. (Oops, my bad, there's no such thing as an ex-marine, that's right, once a marine, always a marine, sorry.) Once he came over to weapons everything completely changed. They moved my team leader, Spc. Evans, over to 2nd Squad, and Spc. Ramos got moved to headquarters, and Pfc. Cortinas and Spc. Scroggins both got moved to 1st Squad, and our combat medic, Doc Gifford, got moved to an entirely different FOB. The only remaining guys in weapons squad were the driver and TC to our vehicle, Spc. Blough and Lil E, and both the machine gunners, Horrocks, who had by this point been promoted to sergeant (but would later move on to 3rd Squad), and myself.

Spc. Warren was a new guy who came to Iraq shortly after basic and was only in weapons squad briefly, and then they moved him over to 3rd Squad, where he became a driver for their vehicle. They moved Pfc. Pointz from 3rd Squad over to weapons squad. Pointz was originally a driver for 3rd Squad's vehicle, but they kicked him out because the guys in 3rd Squad were way more scared of getting killed due to his bad driving than they were of any daisy-chain IEDs planted on Route Tampa. Pfc. Pointz was from Michigan, liked sci-fi novels, Dungeons & Dragons, and trench coats. Nuff said.

Spc. Benitez, a thirty-something old man, got sent over to us from an entirely different platoon. All I knew about him was that they sent him over to weapons squad, and he was prior service, like was in the Navy or some shit like that.

Pvt. Malcolm, who'd been kicked out of countless squads, got sent over to us because they had nowhere else to put him and they didn't know what else to do with him. So we took him. There was also Pfc. Fritsche who joined our squad about this time. And then we also got a couple replacements, Spc. Cummings and Spc. Haibi. Spc. Cummings came to our unit straight from Korea. He grew up in Port Angeles, Washington.

Very mellow, laid-back kinda guy. At times almost too laid back, but a cool kat.

Doc Haibi, who I would consider to be intellectual and a man filled with infinite wisdom, was our new combat medic. Haibi was prior service, ex–11 Bravo infantryman, who switched over to become a medic because he thought he was too old to be an infantryman. (He's like late thirties.) He served in the Army National Guard down in Florida (where he's from) for a bunch of years, and then got out, and then got back in, but this time he got back in as active-duty so that he could come over here to Iraq and see the shit with his own two eyes. He's married with a couple kids.

Goof Troop

I don't know what it's like in the Marines, and I wondered if this was like a "Marine" thing, but on one of my squad leader's first days, he lined us all up in a squad formation out in front of our conexes and said a little something about how he wanted us all to bond as a squad, and that he wanted us to come up with a "squad motto."

Nobody has a squad motto. That's, like, completely fucking lame.

At first we all thought that he was just kidding around and we all just sorta stood there and looked at each other like, is he for real? Spc. Cummings was the first to laugh out loud, and he asked him, "Are you serious, sergeant? You *really* want us to come up with a squad motto?" Our squad leader of course replied that he was totally serious. I then immediately got a flashback from high school and I remembered one of my friends calling the kids that drooled on themselves and went to special class "goof troopers." So jokingly I brought up the idea of "Goof Troop" as a squad motto. Surprisingly, he liked that name a lot and decided to use that as our squad motto, which made me wish I had just kept my fucking mouth shut because he actually used "Goof Troop" to address us all from there on out, and it completely embarrassed the hell out of us.

Sgt. Horrocks, who was now a team leader, even asked him one time to stop calling us Goof Troop because the other squads were kinda laughing at us. He didn't seem to mind though. Weapons squad used to be a shit hot squad, but now that it was almost completely dismantled, and almost overnight had become a squad full of misfits and discards, I then took it upon myself to appropriately name the Stryker that we rolled in the "short bus," and if they would have let us, I probably would have painted that on the side of our Stryker as well.

Our squad leader wasn't a bad one, but he had an entirely different leadership style than Sgt. Fisher, and I never did fully adjust myself to it. He was more about Army regs and policies, and he liked to let everybody know that he was the man in charge, the figure of authority, and the dominant male in the relationship. For as long as I could possibly remember, I've always had problems with authority figures, and even though, thank God, I've never worked in the fast-food industry, he reminded me of the managers you'd see at like a Burger World who would take their jobs way too seriously and yell at their employees if they fried the fries a different way than they did.

In the real world, if I ever had a boss like him, I'd probably quit.

In fact, after that whole "Goof Troop" thing, I know I would have thrown my apron down and quit.

But in the Army, there is no quitting. If you don't get along with somebody, or your personality clashes with anybody in your chain of command, like a team leader or a squad leader, you just bend over and take it in the ass. After a while though, it doesn't hurt as much, and sooner or later you don't even feel it anymore.

And that, my friend, is when you truly know that you're in the Army. When you no longer feel it.

FUCK YOU, MOSQUE

Three Loud Explosions

I can hear small arms fire right now coming from outside the wire as I write this entry. On my way to the Internet cafe that they have set up for us on this FOB I heard three loud explosions, about 5 minutes apart, followed by some brief small arms fire. We have cement mortar bunkers set up all over this FOB for us to seek cover in during an attack. From a cement shelter I observed three very large dust mushroom clouds from right outside the wire from where the explosions took place. No word yet what just happened. The craziness begins . . .

Posted by CBFTW at 9:54 A.M., June 24, 2004

Right after I posted that entry up on the weblog, I ran to my room to find out what the hell was going on. When I got to my room, Spc. Cummings came up to me and told me that the whole platoon was rolling out and for me to grab my shit and get my ass to the motor pool ASAP. So I ran into my room, threw on my gear, grabbed the M240, and ran as fast as I could to the motor pool. As I was mounting the M240 on the gun mount on the back of the vehicle, I was informed that those three loud explosions that I had heard earlier coming from outside the FOB were actually car bombs, not IEDs, as I had suspected.

Spc. Cummings and I were the gunners in the back air-guard mounts on the Stryker, me behind the locked and loaded M240, and Cummings at my side as my AG. Pfc. Pointz was filling in as TC and behind the .50 on our vehicle, next to him was our platoon sergeant, Sgt. Hoerner. Pfc. Evans was our driver, and we had Spc. Benitez, a young Iraqi interpreter, and our combat medic, Doc Haibi, with us in the back of the vehicle. Sgt. Horrocks and our squad leader were away on leave, so Spc. Cummings covered down as our squad leader.

As we sped as fast as we could outta the FOB, all I could hear over and over again over the radio was: "Warning! Enemy in area!" I always got pumped up with adrenaline whenever I heard her calmly say, "Warning! Enemy in area!"

The way the computers work inside the Stryker is that behind the TC hatch you have what you call an FBCB2 screen, which is like this computer screen that has a graphic map of the area that you're operating in, and whenever there is contact somewhere, somebody reports it on the FBCB2 and a red triangle will pop up in the area where the enemy is located, so that every single Stryker and everybody in the battle space knows exactly where the contact is and exactly what the threat is. And when that red triangle pops up on the FBCB2 screen, automatically a recorded female's voice will come over the radio saying: "Warning! Enemy in area!" to let everybody know that, well, duh, there's enemy in the area.

I heard the reason why they have a female voice say the message is because somebody did some study way back when and found out that infantry soldiers (men), when extremely tired, fatigued, and/or confused, will be more alert and pay attention to a female voice than to a man's voice. (If they really wanted to grab infantrymen's attention, they should make her say the "Enemy in area" thing all orgasmic and sexy, with heavy breathing like a phone-sex operator.)

We drove down Route Tampa, which is the main route in Mosul, as fast as we could to get to the Sheikh Fatih police station, which was currently under siege, and from what we heard on the radio, completely taken over.

As we raced as fast as we could to where the attacks were taking place, I observed several burning remains of cars on the side of the road. I also saw some completely abandoned Iraqi National Guard trucks in the middle of the streets. Route Tampa was usually a pretty busy main road, with lots of storefronts and apartment-looking houses and local traffic, but now it looked like a ghost town. All the storefronts were locked up and there were no cars driving anywhere. On the radio on the way to the police station I was hearing the bitch say, "Warning! Enemy in area!" over and over again on the radio.

As soon as we got to the Sheikh Fatih police station (call sign: Three Whisky), we parked our vehicle on the main street to the left of the police station several hundred meters away. To the right of our vehicle was 1st Platoon, and to the right of them 3rd Platoon, and to their right was MGS (missile guidance set) and mortars. They were all engaging the police station and the huge mosque that was located right next door to it with .50-cals and small-arms fire as soon as we got there.

Our TC, Pfc. Pointz, started rocking the .50-cal and Spc. Cummings and I were pulling rear security, which means we were facing away from the action. Our job was to scan our sector and make sure nobody tried to shoot at us from behind. I couldn't help but turn around every couple seconds and take a look at the shooting. Our combat medic was inside the Stryker eagerly poking his head out every now and then from Cummings's air-guard hatch to take a peek at all the action. The shooting came in waves, there would be a barrage, and then it would die off, and then it would start up again, and then die off.

I pulled out my digital camera and started taking a couple photos of all this going on. As I put the camera away and went back to scanning my sector, I looked over to the mosque and saw a white flash leave a TOW-mounted Stryker, and that white flash then went straight into the front of the Sheikh Fatih police station, making a thunderous explosion. Me and Spc. Cummings both saw the TOW leave the Stryker and engage the police station, and after the explosion, we just looked at each other and yelled at the same time in unison, "*Whhhoooooaaa! Holy shit!*" Then all of a sudden the shooting stopped and all you could hear were all the soldiers cheering from all the Strykers parked around the mosque and the police station like it was a goddamn eighty-yard touchdown pass at a Raider home game.

Nothing motivates men to slay their enemy like a TOW missile impacting its target. Nothing.

Then once everybody stopped cheering, everybody started engaging the mosque and the police station again with small-arms fire. The Iraqi interpreter inside our vehicle was covering his ears. I looked over to my side and I saw a hand holding a digital camera poking out of Spc. Cummings's air-guard hatch like it was a submarine periscope.

It was Doc Haibi taking photos from inside the vehicle. Then over the radio I heard somebody broadcast that we were now taking fire from the mosque tower. Fuck that shit, so I grabbed an M4 rifle from inside the Stryker and started engaging the mosque tower. By now every single fucking barrel was pointed at the tower of the mosque and engaging it. In fact, for a second there was a dust cloud around the tower from the thousands of bullets impacting it. Even our combat medic, whose job was to treat casualties, not create them or become one, couldn't resist getting in on this and he literally stuck himself up out of the air-guard hatch next to me where Spc. Cummings was and both of them together were engaging the tower.

Then a TOW missile was launched from a Stryker and impacted the top part of the tower where the balcony railing was located, making a huge explosion, but amazingly it didn't take down the tower like it does in the movies.

Once again, everybody stopped shooting to cheer like it was another touchdown for the home team.

I expended a whole thirty-round magazine of 5.56, and as I was putting another full magazine into my weapon I looked over at a nearby Stryker and there was a soldier in the back air-guard hatch hysterically throwing up the heavy-metal devil-horn hand signal like it was an Ozzy Osborne concert, yelling, "*Who hoo! Fuck you, mosque! Fuck you!*" Again everybody started engaging the mosque with everything they had. While this was going on I was in total disbelief that we were actually engaging a mosque. Like isn't this against some kind of Geneva Convention thing?

When the shooting slowed down, 1st Sgt. Swift, who was riding in Bravo Victor 22, made the call over the radio for us to move in and secure the perimeter of the mosque and the area around the police station, which kind of made me nervous because all I was thinking about was, Fuck, I hope there's nobody up in that tower with a fucking RPG, because if there is we're totally fucked.

There was still light sporadic gunfire as we pulled up and parked on a side street that went parallel to the mosque. Bravo Victor 21 had its guys dismounted on the ground, and their vehicle needed two people to pull air guard, so Doc Haibi and Spc. Benitez dismounted from our vehicle and moved on over to Bravo Victor 21. Spc. Benitez brought along the other M240 machine gun with him. First Sgt. Swift was already on the ground with 2nd Squad, and he caught a glimpse of the guy in the tower and started engaging him with his M4, at which time

I heard over the radio, "We're taking fire from the mosque! Up in the tower!"

Fuck that shit, so I then directed my M240 Bravo machine gun toward the tower and pulled the trigger completely back and didn't let go until I was completely out of rounds. Links and brass shells spitting out of the right side of my weapon, making a huge mess all over. It was fucking beautiful. (Almost burned the barrel.) I sprayed all up and down that tower, which had four or five slim windows, until I expended my ammunition. As I reloaded the 240 with another belt of 7.62, I was thinking to myself, "Jesus Christ, I can't believe I'm actually shooting at a holy place of worship." I thought we weren't allowed to do this kind of thing.

Fuck it.

"Get some! Get some! Get some!"

At this point in time everybody was unloading on the thing. The whole time I was shooting the machine gun, I would fire a good three-to-four-second burst into a window, and then I would go to the next window and fire a burst, then the next window. I went up and down that tower three or four times, yelling, *"Get some!"* every time I fired a burst (like they do in the movies).

Then everybody started yelling, "Cease fire! Cease fire!" and everybody reluctantly did. Our platoon sergeant then screamed over the radio, "If I see one of our guys drop down in the hatch and not shoot back, I will pull him out of there myself and smoke his ass in the middle of the street!"

We pulled up through a back street alongside the mosque and parked right next to the back side gate. Everybody in the Stryker dismounted the vehicle to go secure the area, and our medic went to go treat any casualties, and I stayed on the vehicle and pulled security with the M240. We were close enough to the mosque that I could inspect the damage. I was amazed that the tower was still standing after the ass-kicking we'd just given it. The mosque and everything around it were completely covered in bullet impacts.

Finally the INGs showed up in their pickup trucks. (This was the first time I'd seen any INGs or ICPs that day.) A couple of the ING soldiers had Special Forces tabs sewn on their shirt sleeves; rumor had it that these ING soldiers got their SF tabs from the American SF soldiers who trained them. We secured the outer perimeter of the mosque while the SF-tabbed ING soldiers, as well as regular ING soldiers, entered the mosque. It was pretty interesting watching them operate. You could tell that the ING soldiers with the SF tabs were the leaders because they gave out the orders and directed the men, they seemed extremely confident and had that same cocky leader aura, a lot like our own SF guys have.

Our job then was to secure the area while the INGs went inside the mosque to clear the building and kill whoever was inside. They told us all to cease fire on the mosque and not shoot because INGs would be on the roofs and whatnot. Shortly after they entered the mosque, a couple ING soldiers dragged out a dead body and placed him up against a wall on the side of the road about ten to fifteen feet from my gun position. I couldn't see what he looked like because he was covered with a blanket of sorts. The ING soldiers laid his body on the ground, then walked away. A couple minutes later, a curious ING soldier walked up to the body and lifted the blanket. He was a young guy, his mouth and eyes were wide open, and he had the stereotypical Al Qaeda terrorist beard.

Then this older overweight Iraqi lady, dressed in traditional black Arab attire, holding several plastic bags filled with groceries in one hand and a little boy's hand in the other, came out of nowhere from this street corner right next to where the body was. She didn't speak English, but with her hands she explained to me that she lived on the street, and that she wanted to go home.

For the last, I don't know, couple of hours, there'd been a huge-ass fucking firefight here, the kind that you could probably hear a couple miles away because my ears were still ringing. TOW missiles, .50-cals, small-arms fire, thousands and thousands of rounds and all sorts of crazy explosions, and this lady and this kid had to have heard all of this, and you would think that they'd probably want to stay the fuck away from any area where U.S. forces were engaging enemy forces, but yet that didn't bother her, she just wanted to go to her house with her groceries and continue her day like nothing was going on. I nodded yes to her, and allowed her to walk to her house with her kid. I felt really bad doing this, because there was the dead body lying on the street now, and if I allowed them to walk to their house they'd both have to walk right past the body and observe it.

I was expecting them to completely trip out on it. But they both looked down at the body, saw that it was a dead body, said absolutely nothing, looked up, totally expressionless, no shock whatsoever, and continued to walk to their house. I'll never forget that.

The INGs were now on the roof of the mosque, and I felt kind of nervous for them because I seriously was expecting a trigger-happy soldier to accidentally shoot one of them. Thank God nobody did. In situations like that I was more nervous of our own guys than I was of any terrorist.

Once the INGs were inside, we moved our vehicle over to the front of the mosque, and from there I got to see the damage that was around us. Thousands and thousands of brass shell casings all over the place, TOW-missile wires in the street, chunks of concrete, cars completely blown to bits and overturned, I mean the whole AO looked like a war zone, which of course is what it was. You could even see the huge craters in the ground from where the car bombs had gone off. I was amazed at how much damage they could do.

I then looked over to my platoon sergeant, Sgt. Hoerner, who was sticking out of his hatch, as he was looking around the mosque and the surrounding area assessing the damage, and then he looked over at me and with a huge smile said, "Man, this is collateral damage like a muthafucker!" We both laughed, because one of our key mission tasks was to keep collateral damage to a bare minimum, but I guess that all goes out the door once you take fire from a mosque.

One of the TOW missiles that was fired didn't go off, so we had to sit around and wait while somebody placed an explosive charge on it and blew it up. Lots of soldiers had their digital cameras out taking footage of that. I stayed in the vehicle the whole time the INGs were securing the AO. Our combat medic walked the area, and when he came back to our vehicle he told us all about what he'd seen and what was going on on the ground level, and that there were chunks and pieces of human body parts all over the place.

Once all the dirty work was done and the INGs had finally secured the police station and the mosque, we handed the body of the dead insurgent over to them and drove back to FOB Marez.

My ears were ringing all the way back to the FOB. In fact, they rang for most of the day.

Right when I got to my room and took my gear off, we got the call that we were rolling back out, and that we had to go to FOB Freedom to hand over the radio equipment that we had found inside the mosque that the insurgents were using for whatever reason.

When we arrived there, our platoon leader chose a couple soldiers from my platoon (Spc. Wenger, Pfc. Palmer, and Spc.

Evans) to talk to the media, who wanted to find out what went down that day in Mosul. The ones that didn't get selected had to wait around over by our vehicles for a couple hours while they talked to the media. I wonder why my platoon leader didn't ask for volunteers or pick me. I would have loved to talk to the media and tell them, and everybody else back home, that today, me and Rosebud put a buncha holes in a mosque, and you know what (as I take a drag from my cigarette), I feel pretty damn fucking good about it. But then again, maybe that's why my platoon leader didn't pick me because I probably would have said something moronic like that.

Before Wenger, Palmer, and Evans spoke with the media, a high-ranking Army public-affairs officer (lieutenant colonel) pulled them to the side and briefed them on what they could and could not say. All three told me that the lieutenant colonel stressed to them to tell the media that the insurgents fired first, and we were just there to return the fire, which is true, but he also told them to:

—*Not* say that TOW missiles were used in the attack, but to instead say "internal weapons systems" were used.

Whatever, that's no big deal, that's like saying, instead of telling the media that you returned fire with your M4, tell them that you returned fire with your "self-defense mechanism."

But then he told them to flat-out lie when he said:

—Do *not* mention the fact that the Iraqi police fled from the mosque and the police station, how they didn't even put up a fight, but instead tell the media that they fought well and did an excellent job.

Before we came to Iraq, the Army went totally out of its way to make sure that we had everything that we needed. They issued us brand-new Camelbaks, brand-new desert-camouflage uniforms, gloves, pads, sappy plates (body armor), brand-new Wiley X sunglasses, and they even provided us with answers to the questions that the media might ask us once we get here.

It was issued to us on this small green card-stock piece of paper that we were told to fold up and place in our wallets. It explained to us how to talk to the media, what to say to the media, and it came with answers to the media's questions:

3rd Bde/2nd ID
Public Affairs Guidance

Information you *CANNOT* discuss with the media or public

- **Specific numbers of troops**
- **Specific numerical information on troop strength, equipment or critical supplies (e.g. artillery, vehicles, water, trucks, etc.)**
- **Information regarding future operations, current operations or strikes, including postponed or canceled operations**
- **Information regarding security precautions at installations or encampments**
- **Names of military bases or specific geographic locations of units in the CENTCOM AOR**
- **Details on Rules of Engagement or Force Protection**
- **Any WIA/KIA questions must be referred to PAO**

Info: Accidental release of sensitive information can be remedied by asking reporter not to include in coverage for OPSEC reasons. Report incident to PAO.

Stryker information you *CAN* discuss with the media or public

- **Smooth ride!**
- **Quiet . . .**
- **Fast . . . 60 mph**

- Independent suspension
- Run-flat capability
- Central tire inflation system
- Holds 11: 2-man crew, 9-man squad
- 350 h.p. Caterpillar diesel engine
- Automatic transmission
- Remote weapons station .50-cal or MK19
- FBCB2: See first, understand first, act first, finish decisively!
- Reporter access to Stryker vehicles is limited.

MEDIA GROUND RULES

- All interviews with service-members are on-the-record.
- Media embedded with U.S. Forces are not permitted to carry personal firearms.
- Light discipline restrictions will be followed when operating with forces at night unless specifically approved in advance by the on-scene commander.
- Embargoes may be imposed to protect operational security. Embargoes will only be used for OPSEC and will be lifted as soon as the OPSEC issue has passed.
- Battlefield casualties may be covered by embedded media—Soldier identity must be protected.

OTHER INFORMATION

- If it is believed classified information has been compromised and the media representative refuses to remove the information, notify Bde PAO or IO ASAP. Soldiers MAY NOT confiscate any tape, film or other media equipment.

MESSAGES

Operational

- We are here to help Iraq restore its independence.
- We will work to eliminate the enemy that continues to hinder progress for the Iraqi people.
- Our efforts support the continuing fight in the Global War on Terrorism.
- We will remain in Iraq until told our mission is complete.

Brigade

- We are trained, equipped and ready to perform any mission we are given.
- 3Bde, 2ID soldiers are some of the best trained in the U.S. Army.
- 3Bde, 2ID is an infantry-centric brigade equipped with organic reconnaissance, engineer and artillery assets; augmented with aviation and civil affairs.
- 3Bde, 2ID is soldier-centric; the individual soldier, not the Stryker or equipment, gets the job done.
- 3Bde, 2ID soldiers are confident in the Strykers and the unit's equipment.

I CORPS PUBLIC AFFAIRS GUIDANCE

- Be polite. Remember, it's your choice whether to talk to the media, or to identify yourself and provide your name.
- Be sure you understand the question. Take time to think and don't talk about subjects you are not responsible for.
- Never lie. If you don't know the answer, refer the media to the PAO.
- Don't make off-the-record statements to reporters;

everything is on-the-record.

- **Be brief, use simple language. Don't use acronyms or military jargon.**
- **Don't answer "What if?" questions or give opinions.**
- **Don't say anything you wouldn't want to see in print or on TV.**
- **Don't editorialize your opinions about military or political leaders.**
- **Be in proper uniform.**

This is the official press release that Task Force Tomahawk released about what took place at the Sheikh Fatih police station:

PRESS RELEASE

Release # 06-60
FOR IMMEDIATE RELEASE

Anti-Iraqi Forces Fire on Iraqi Security Forces and Coalition Soldiers from Mohammed Al Noory Mosque
MOSUL, IRAQ (June 24, 2004)—At 11:20 a.m., in response to reports of terrorists taking over the Sheikh Fatih police station in southwestern Mosul, Iraqi Security Forces moved to secure the site and were fired upon by anti-Iraqi forces who were shooting from the Mohammed Al Noory Mosque across the street from the police station. Coalition forces moved to the site to support the Iraqi Security Forces and were fired upon from the Mohammed Al Noory Mosque as well.

Iraqi Security and Coalition forces returned fire on the terrorists in the mosque.

At 1 p.m., Coalition forces reported that Iraqi Security

Forces and soldiers from 1st Battalion, 23rd Infantry Regiment have taken back the Sheikh Fatih police station from the anti-Iraqi terrorists. Iraqi National Guard soldiers have secured the Mohammed Al Noory Mosque as well. There is no word on casualties.

Anyone with information about criminal or terrorist activities should inform the Iraqi Police, Coalition forces, or call the Tips Hotline 813-343 or 780-013. To turn in weapons or munitions, contact any Coalition soldier or call the Hotline (813-343) to arrange turn-in.

The Day After

What happened in Mosul must have been big news back home, because my dad sent me an e-mail saying Mosul was all over the news and he wanted to know if I was okay, my mom is a total worrywart and all she does is watch the news all day to see if anything happens in Iraq. Every time she heard about a death of an American soldier on the tube she flipped out. I sent my dad a reply telling him me and everybody in my platoon was okay, doing well, morale was high, that kinda crap. Left out the details.

Transfer of Power

> We may occupy a country completely, but hostilities can be renewed again in the interior, or perhaps with allied help. This course can also happen after the peace treaty, but this only shows that not every war necessarily leads to a final decision and settlement.
>
> —Carl von Clausewitz

> The June 30 deadline is a fiction . . . You don't set an arbitrary date for the transfer of power to a nonentity.
>
> —Senator John Kerry

UNCLASSIFIED
TRANSITION OF IRAQI SOVEREIGNTY
31 May 2004
(U) Purpose: The intent of this document is to provide leaders and soldiers with talking points for use in conversation with the local populace and community leaders. Talking Points are unclassified. They are intended to provide the basic information and direction for conversations that are appropriately tailored for a given audience. *Know your audience.*
(U) You should not read these talking points verbatim. Not all talking points should be provided to every audience. Present only those talking points appropriate to the situation. Background paragraphs are provided solely for the use of the person delivering the talking points and should not be read or presented to the populace.

Background: The transition to sovereignty will occur on 30 June. Nonetheless, polling data and anecdotal information indicates that Iraqis remain confused and/or ill informed regarding what post 30 June will mean to the average citizen. These talking points are prepared in order to provide information for routine engagements.

SOVEREIGNTY TALKING POINTS—
WHAT WILL HAPPEN:

- On June 30, the occupation will end, the Coalition Provisional Authority will dissolve, and a new Iraqi Interim Government (IIG) will assume stewardship of Iraq.

- On June 30 Iraqis will be in charge of and responsible for Iraq.
- As the Coalition hands over power to the people of Iraq, Iraqis will be responsible for their future.
- All of the ministries will be under control of the Iraqi prime minister.
- Iraqi ministries will be directly responsible for their ministry's policies, strategies, and budget.
- The Coalition senior advisor's role shifts to that of a technical assistance provider. The need for technical assistance is determined by the minister.
- The independent electoral commission of Iraq, a UN-sanctioned commission composed of Iraqis, not the Coalition, will publish the rules for elections in January 2005.
- The multi-national forces—Iraq will remain under the authority of UNSCR (UN Security Council Resolution) 1511.
- Coalition forces will continue to work closely in partnership with the ISF to protect and defend the Iraqi people and their vital national interests.
- The Iraqi armed forces will be a principal partner in the multi-national force operating in Iraq under a unified command pursuant to the provisions of UNSCR 1511.

SOVEREIGNTY TALKING POINTS—
WHAT WON'T HAPPEN?

- Daily life for Iraqis will not improve dramatically overnight but will continue to improve as rebuilding continues on a determined pace.
- Coalition nations will not cease their work in assisting Iraq rebuild its infrastructure.
- Coalition nations will not cease providing an experienced

corps of advisors to the Iraqi government and ministries if requested to do so.
- **Coalition Forces retaining the right to self-defense.**
- **Coalition nations will not stop conducting combat operations to kill or capture anti-Iraqi forces until the ISF is prepared to assume this important security task.**

They told us that the "battle tempo" would be slowing down dramatically for us after the country was handed over to the people of Iraq. In theory, we would just hang out at the FOB and be like Iraq's older brother, and if younger brother was out there getting picked on or getting his ass kicked, we'd pause our PlayStation games, grab our gear, head down to the motor pool, put on our cowboy hats, start up the Strykers, and big brother (U.S.) would show up, start punishing the deserving, throw some lead and maybe a couple TOW missiles around, and then return back to the FOB and pick up where we left off. We'll see if it actually works out that way.

The Bad Hands

Another day of waiting for hostilities to erupt again. Spent a majority of the day conducting weapons maintenance. One of our interpreters went by the mosque that got shot the fuck up the other day and he told me that they placed a huge banner out in front of it that reads: "This mosque will be closed for two to three weeks. The Bad Hands did this."

I could have told you right then it was going to take longer than two to three weeks to get that bad boy serviceable again.

My War Soundtrack

I spent a lot of good money on goodies before I left to go to Iraq, things like digital cameras, waterproof field journals, and a 30-gig iPod, which I downloaded more than 932 hours of music onto. Occasionally I carried the iPod with me out on missions. I'd keep it inside an empty ammo pouch on my flak vest, and even though we were not allowed to do so, I would always bring it up to the guard towers whenever we did force protection. Sometimes I would listen to it while on patrols, sitting in the back of the Stryker, and sometimes, out of boredom, if I was sticking out of one of the back air-guard hatches, I would sneak a solo earpiece into one ear and listen to music while we drove around looking for anti-Iraqi forces.

The iPod comes with a "playlist" feature, on which you can organize and create different themed playlists, and it even has a feature that allows you to name the playlists.

Here are some of the songs that I put on and labeled as my "Stryker Soundtrack" playlist:

"Kill the Poor" / Dead Kennedys
"Anything and Everything" / Slayer
"Stuck in the Middle with You" / Stealer's Wheel
"What a Wonderful World" / Louis Armstrong
"Speak English or Die!" / S.O.D.
"Bombs over Baghdad" / OutKast
Theme song from *The Good, the Bad, and the Ugly*
"Imperial March" from *Star Wars*
"Kill 'Em All" / Metallica
"Let's Start a War," "Army Life," and "Blown to Bits" / The Exploited
"Stars and Stripes Forever"
"Welcome to the Jungle" / Guns N' Roses

"Ride of the Valkyries" / Richard Wagner
"Paint It Black" / Rolling Stones
"Die, Die, My Darling" / Misfits
"Give Peace a Chance" / John Lennon
"You're Nobody Till Somebody Loves You" / Dean Martin
"Shiny Happy People" / R.E.M.
"Show You No Mercy" / Cro-Mags
"Bullet in the Head" / Rage Against the Machine
"We Care a Lot" / Faith No More
"Danger Zone" / Kenny Loggins (*Top Gun* song)
"Romper Stomper" / Transplants
"It's Clobberin' Time" / Sick of It All
"Iron Man" / Black Sabbath
"Sunday Bloody Sunday" / U2
"Orange Crush" / R.E.M.
"Killing an Arab" / The Cure
"I Don't Care About You" / Fear
"Seek & Destroy" / Metallica
"Attack of the Peacekeepers" / Jello Biafra with D.O.A.
"Highway to Hell" / AC/DC

FOB Marez

Here is a list of fun and exciting things to do at FOB Marez if you ever (God help you) end up there:

The Phone Centers
We had several of them at FOB Marez. We had an AT&T phone center by the chow hall, which was open 24/7 and always had a huge line of sullen soldiers trying to call home. And in between the chow hall and our living conexes we had an Akcell phone

center that was open till 0200 that was run by some Turks. Ten bucks got you a thirty-minute phone card. There's a ten-hour time difference between Mosul and the West Coast, a seven-hour time difference with the East Coast. So the best time to call home was usually late at night or really early in the morning.

One time I was at the Akcell phone center calling my wife, and I noticed that somebody had written on the wall, "If you're looking for a good time, and you want to be fucked, call: 1-800-USA-ARMY."

Whenever the phone center was closed, that meant that somebody had just gotten killed in Mosul, which pissed everybody off because then you had to wait a day or two before you could call home or check your e-mail.

They would close all the phone centers and Internet centers down until the family of the deceased soldier had been contacted, then open them up again.

Internet Cafes

We had several of these located on our FOB. The line for the MWR free Internet by the chow hall was usually pretty long to get on a computer, and once you were on, there was a thirty-minute time limit, which only gave you enough time to quickly check your e-mail and respond to a couple of them.

The Hajjis had several Internet cafes available for soldiers, but they charged two dollars an hour and the connection sucked, it always cut out, and most of the computers were totally contaminated with viruses (from Joe looking at Internet porn), and it was always packed with bored soldiers spending hours and hours surfing hotornot.com.

Several of the computers were equipped with webcams, which was a good thing for the married soldiers who wanted to see their wives (as well as for the single soldiers who tried to get girls in chat rooms to "support the troops" privately via webcam).

Previous to my blog, I'd usually go to the Internet cafe, like, two to three times a week just to e-mail friends and family and to buy stuff online. But since I started the blog, I found myself going to the Internet cafe every opportunity that I could. Not to post new entries but to read the comments that people would leave on the blog, as well as to read the handful of e-mails that I was now getting from readers.

Chow Hall

The chow hall was also probably one of the most dangerous places to be on our FOB, and there was a pretty good chance you'd get a Purple Heart if you ate there, if not at chow hall, then on your way walking to and from chow hall. I would even bet that more soldiers received Purple Hearts on the way to and from chow hall from mortar shrapnel than on actual combat operations.

There was only one chow hall located on this FOB and it was exactly a quarter-mile walk from where my room was and it was run and operated by KBR (Kellogg, Brown & Root) people, mostly Filipinos.

The food was pretty good, in fact it was a million times better than the chow halls back at Fort Lewis, and it was pretty much all you can eat, like they didn't scold you if you felt like going back for seconds.

Sunday was the night to go. That's when they served the good stuff, like lobster tail, steaks, you know, the gourmet shit. They had about a half dozen TVs inside, all tuned to AFN (Armed Forces Network) Television.

A couple days before Mother's Day, a female soldier was

killed outside of chow hall by a mortar, so higher put out that full kit (helmet, body armor, weapon, etc.) was required to eat at chow hall. So you had to throw on full kit, which weighs a ton, and road-march your ass down there in the 110- to 120-degree temp, walking uphill, both ways.

I'm not kidding, it was an uphill walk both ways to chow hall, because on the way there, you had to walk down the hill and then up, and on the way back, it was down the hill and then up.

For a while there, in the summer, I'd eat there every other day because I didn't feel like going through all that just to get a meal. When I was hungry, I'd just grab an MRE. Needless to say, I lost a couple pounds.

Gym

We had a huge gym set up there for us by the MWR people, fully air-conditioned and everything. State-of-the-art cardio machines, weights, an indoor basketball court and aerobics room. They had a big-screen TV inside connected to a satellite dish, but it went out every couple hours, and when it did work it was usually on Armed Forces Network TV.

The only thing that sucked about the gym is that whenever we received a mortar attack, the gym people would freak out and close the gym down, and always right in the middle of your workout.

They had a boom box inside the gym that played music while you worked out, and it seemed like the only CD that those people owned was Metallica's *Black Album*, because they played it nonstop.

Hajji Shops

These were located throughout the FOB. All of them owned and operated by an Iraqi citizen and all of them reminded me of those ninety-nine-cent stores back home. Most of the stuff they sell is pure crap.

This one guy who opened up his shop over by the chow hall briefly sold Honda scooters to soldiers for $400 to $500 each. The fuel point on FOB Maraz only provided diesel fuel, so he also sold the fuel to go along with the scooters, and since he was the only guy at the FOB who sold fuel, he could charge whatever he wanted. Chain of command finally told him that he was not authorized to sell scooters to soldiers. I can't figure out if they shut down his scooter business because they didn't like the idea of soldiers on scooters, or if it was because they didn't like the idea of an Iraqi charging whatever the hell he wanted to for gas. Hmmm . . .

Cool things you could find at Hajji shops: Saddam Hussein memorabilia, "Welcome to Iraq" postcards, Cuban cigars, "tourist maps" of Iraq, fake Rolexes, brass pots and pans made from melted-down shells, washing machines, rugs, candy, bootlegged CDs and DVDs, sodas (or "pop" as you guys from Michigan call it), mountain bikes, and other miscellaneous crap like that.

The most popular items that the Hajji shops sold were definitely the bootlegged DVDs. Some of the movies were extremely poor quality, like it's some guy with a handheld recorder filming from inside a movie theater, and you can hear people talking to each other, and every now and then see a silhouette of a guy in the audience get up from his seat to go take a piss or buy some popcorn.

AAFES PX

What was cool about this place was you could shop with your ATM card or Star card. Buy all your soap, shaving, foot-powder stuff. They also sold pretty much everything you needed, like DVD players, big-screen TVs, protein powders, magazines, non-bootlegged CDs and DVDs, laptops, digital cameras and camcorders, PlayStations, Xboxes, video games, whatever you can think of.

The PX also sold Operation Iraqi Freedom memorabilia and souvenirs of every kind, like OIF shot glasses, coffee mugs, beer glasses, mouse pads, key chains, hats, magnets, buttons, jackets, wallets, sweaters, etc.

You could also purchase at the PX the T-shirt that says you've been in Iraq. They had a wide assortment of decorative OIF shirts to choose from. The lamest shirt that they sold was probably this one that had Arabic writing on the front of it, and on the back it said, Who's Your Bagh-Daddy? Almost every PX in Iraq sold the Bagh-daddy T-shirt.

And when you purchased something in cash at the PX, they didn't hand you change back in dimes and quarters, instead they handed you OIF POGS, which act as currency at any PX.

They also sold condoms at the PX (Trojan non-lube). People bought them, too, which makes you kinda wonder.

The Fruit-Juice Stand

Owned and operated by an Iraqi lady and her husband. For two bucks you got a big cup of banana strawberry smoothie or whatever fruity combo you wanted. Which were great on the extremely hot days when you just wanted to chill out with a cold drink. I'd usually buy like two of them when I went there.

Tailor Shop

Just an Iraqi with a sewing machine, you pay him a couple bucks and he'd sew on whatever patch you wanted on your uniform, like your CIB (combat infantryman badge) and combat patch.

The tailor shop over by the airfield could embroider Arabic writing on your uniform, so that way you could get your last name, or "Bad Mutha Fucker," written in Arabic on the back of your hat or somewhere on your uniform.

When we first got to Kuwait, a couple soldiers in my platoon got their last names sewn on the backs of their hats in Arabic, and they were immediately told to take that shit off. My unit wasn't allowed to have any Arabic writing sewn anywhere on our uniforms. It had something to do with being infantry, so we hold ourselves to a higher standard than the rest of the Army.

I always saw noninfantry and reservists getting Arabic writing on their uniforms, and it drove me nuts because it was unauthorized to deface the Army uniform like that, but it didn't seem like that policy was really enforced except for us. One time on Armed Forces Network television, I even saw a general with Arabic writing sewn on his uniform.

Public Shitters

In case you gotta take a dump, for your convenience there were port-a-shitters available all over the FOB. They had contracted guys that went around to the shitters all day in their sewage trucks and hosed down the insides of them, and sucked all the shit and piss out of them. I have no idea where they disposed of the waste. Probably in the Tigris. You could find out a lot about soldier morale by reading the writings on the port-a-shitter walls.

The MWR (Morale, Welfare, Recreation) Center
Open 24/7, they had a little movie theater set up there, and every night at 2000 hours they showed a free flick. They had it set up like a real movie theater, with rows and rows of cushioned seats and a digital movie projector, they even provided free popcorn and Gatorade. They showed movies like *Lord of the Rings, Barbershop,* you know, the big Hollywood-blockbuster stuff. Believe it or not, they actually showed *Fahrenheit 9/11* there once.

They also had free Internet and about twenty Dell computers. You could stay on them as long as you liked, as long as there was nobody waiting, but if there were people waiting, which nine times out of ten there were, then you had a thirty-minute limit. The connections were really bad there, and the server was always down. The computers behind the main counter to the MWR center all had Halliburton screensavers.

They had a big-screen TV set up to play movies over by the Ping-Pong and foosball tables, too. Right behind the TV were a bunch of holes in the wall from mortar shrapnel.

They had a room set up with Xboxes and PlayStations for people that wanted to sit around and play video games all day, and they also had a small library where you could steal, I mean check out, books on the honor system. But most of the books they had available weren't even worth stealing, unless you like reading trashy romance novels and sci-fi books, which there seemed to be an overabundance of there.

Public Transportation
Available at FOB Marez, but very unreliable. They ran whenever they felt like it, and they didn't drive on Fridays, which was like a religious holiday or day off for them.

We had Iraqis driving these Third World–looking buses

around the FOB that were un-air-conditioned most of the time, but they did play authentic Middle Eastern music. Sometimes they wouldn't even pick you up, they'd just drive right past or refuse to give you a lift because they claimed to be running low on fuel. (I always felt like cocking my weapon at them whenever they did that to me.) Your best bet was to hitchhike a ride from a civilian contractor.

Ballistic Shades

The Army issued us all new three-hundred-dollar Oakley sunglasses one day. Expensive, sporty sunglasses that are supposedly "ballistic."

I felt like a goddamn snowboarder or some "extreme" guy with them on, but since the Army spent a shitload of money on these "ballistic" sunglasses, we were all forced to wear them, which was bullshit because I was perfectly fine rocking my five-dollar Dirty Harry sunglasses that I bought at a liquor store back home.

One day I was at the airfield, getting a new ID card, because the ETS (estimated time of separation) date on my card was now incorrect thanks to something called stop-loss (a.k.a. the backdoor draft), and while I was in the lobby, waiting for my ID card, I saw a photocopied flyer up on the wall that reminded soldiers to always wear eye pro, and it had a photograph of a poor melancholy soldier who got his face tore up pretty fucking bad from an IED, but his eyes were okay, thanks to the "ballistic" sunglasses he was wearing. I still liked my sunglasses better.

Abu Ghraib

The TV set in the gym is where I found out what was going on in the news back home and saw for myself how the major news networks like Fox, MSNBC, CNN, all reported what was going on in Iraq to the American people. I am entirely convinced that the major news networks were totally unaware and oblivious to the fact that there were cities in Iraq other than Fallujah and Baghdad, because that's all you heard from them, Fallujah and Baghdad. That's it.

It was also interesting to watch the press conferences the president and the generals in Iraq gave. Sometimes I wondered if they were talking about a different Iraq than the one I was in. Especially when they used the words "coalition forces." They must have been talking about Fallujah or Baghdad when they said this, because in Mosul, I didn't see *any* of this so-called "coalition" that they kept talking about. None whatsoever.

The only other people that I worked with on missions were the Iraqi police and the Iraqi National Guard. That's it. And I would hardly consider that a coalition since we pretty much did all the dirty work, and they took all the credit for it.

The TV set in the gym was where I first saw those images of Iraqi prisoners being tortured, and I couldn't believe my eyes. I had just entered the gym and had just started working out when I looked over at the television set and noticed that some of the other soldiers in the gym had stopped working out and were slowly migrating to the TV. I wondered what was on the television that made them do this, and from where I was, it looked like a game of Twister. So I stopped working out and made my way to the TV for a closer look, and I couldn't believe what I was seeing. All that hard work that we did in Iraq, immediately down the tubes. Some of the other soldiers reacted in the same way, shaking their heads in disgust (and of course there were a couple degenerates that chuckled at the images). I was no longer in the mood to work out, so I left the gym and went straight to my room to tell Horrocks about it. I remembered how he flipped out when I told him that San Francisco was now allowing gay marriages, and I couldn't wait to see his reaction to this.

Horrocks was still sleeping, and I woke him up, and I told him all about it, and he agreed with me this would totally fuck us up, because our job was to basically "win the hearts and minds" of the Iraqi people. Now we had to start all over again.

We stepped outside of our conex to smoke a cigarette together and talk about it some more. One of our Iraqi interpreters came by, and I asked him if he had heard about it yet, and he said that he had, and that it was all over Al Jazeera. Great. All three of us came to the same conclusion, and it was that those so-called soldiers at the Abu Ghraib prison were a bunch of idiots, and if it was up to us, as fair punishment, we would let those Iraqis that they tortured torture them. Or, as they say in the Christian Bible, an eye for an eye.

The Dead Don't Talk

Sometimes when we went on missions, and especially raids, our Iraqi interpreters would conceal their identities by wearing sunglasses or covering their faces with scarves or baseball hats. Being an interpreter for us was probably the most dangerous job that an Iraqi citizen could possibly have. There was a high turnover rate, and a lot of them were here today, gone tomorrow. Some of them got killed and some of them quit after they or their families received a death threat.

Some were very well educated and were English teachers at the universities in Iraq, and some were not, like our one guy who, when I asked him how he learned English, excitedly told me that he learned it from "watching American movies!" and went off on naming American actors for me. "Leonardo DiCaprio! Julia Roberts! Tom Hanks!" etc, etc.

Some did the job because it was a job, since there were not too many of those in the country, so that they could feed and take care of their families, and others did it because they had a personal beef with the insurgents and former regime members that were fucking up their country.

This one Iraqi lady who was an interpreter for us, an extremely nice lady, always wore the traditional dress, always had a nice warm smile on her face, and always had some sort of American novel in her hands. Like Dean Koontz or some shit like that. She told me that she taught English at some university before the war and she also told me once that when she heard rumors that the Americans were going to invade Iraq, she prayed and prayed that we would. She told me that she knew Iraq would be a better country without Saddam ruling and that we'd do a lot of good here.

She even jokingly said to me that if the Americans weren't going to come over here, that she was going to physically fly herself over to the White House and beg George W. Bush to "please invade Iraq."

Her prayers were answered and she told me that she wanted to help, so she immediately quit her job teaching English and became an interpreter for us. I learned a lot from her. I'd always see her sitting down on a cot over by my conex area, happily talking with the other interpreters, and when she wasn't socializing with them, she'd be sitting by herself reading. I'd always hit her up for free Arabic lessons, which she'd always happily help me out with, and then we'd talk for a while about politics, Iraqi culture, books, and Iraqi customs.

And then one day, I stopped seeing her around the FOB. So

I went up and asked the other interpreters what happened to her, and they told me that "they" found out that she was working with the Americans, so they murdered her sister.

And I never saw that lady around the FOB again.

Dirty Laundry

Every Tuesday at 0900 was laundry turn-in. That was when we turned in our green dirty-laundry bags to headquarters with a piece of paper that itemized everything in the bag. Twenty-item limit per bag. We also had to sign a waiver that said they're not responsible for lost items, and then we'd throw them all in the back of an LMTV deuce-and-a-half truck, and a day or so later we'd get them back, all nice and clean.

In the end we had the KBR guys doing our laundry, and they did a pretty good job. It came back the very next day, all folded up and smelling clean, kinda like how Mom used to do it.

When we first got to Mosul, we had some Iraqi contracted to do our laundry, which was a total nightmare. In fact, I wouldn't even bother turning in my laundry to them, because it would take several days, and items would be missing, stuff half washed, and a lot of stuff not even washed at all. And when our laundry was returned, all our clothes smelled like fucking gasoline. What the fuck was that all about? It was pretty bad, some soldiers even went as far as to actually buy washing machines from the Hajji shops to do their laundry. But most washed their clothes the old-school way, by hand.

One of our Iraqi interpreters had a moneymaking scam of charging soldiers five to ten bucks for him to do a full bag of laundry. His name was Hussein, and he had a thick mustache and was always wearing a corduroy sport coat and these really sleazy 1970s sunglasses. Every now and then he'd wear a New

York Yankees baseball cap. A real good guy, but he had that used-car-salesman thing going on about him. He was always walking around with a plastic grocery bag filled with absolute crap trying to sell it to Joe to make a buck or two.

Anyway, he had a laundry scam going for a while, and every day he would bang on my door asking my roommate and I if we had any bags of laundry for him. He didn't have a set price for this service that he was providing, and the first time I went through him I handed him a ten-dollar bill to do one half-full bag of laundry and he told me that was way too much. The going rate was around five bucks a bag. I gave him the ten anyways and told him to keep the change.

I went through him for a while, as did a lot of other guys from the platoon. The guy had a wife and some kids, so I had no problem giving him my hard-earned money to do my laundry. Every day he would go home with bags and bags of dirty laundry and a fat stack of cash. And he was making a fat profit for a while doing this.

But then we got the KBR guys to do our laundry for free, which pretty much put Hussein out of business. Because you don't have to be an officer with a business degree from Stanford to know that you just can't compete against free. Hussein then went into arms dealing and had a scam of selling toy BB guns to soldiers. Which of course a lot of soldiers bought and used to shoot the poor innocent pigeons that would hang out on the trees over by our conexes.

One time after returning from chow, I was opening the door to my conex, and I heard a ricochet ping from a stray BB hit the door inches from my head, and the only reason I didn't beat the living shit out of the guy that accidentally fired at me was because I was friends with him, it was an accident, and he could bench a hundred pounds more than I could. So I let it slide.

Chain of command then caught wind of the BB guns and shut that shit down ASAP. So that put Hussein out of another job.

At a different compound in Mosul, COP (command observation post) Blick, they also had an Iraqi that was in the business of doing Joe's dirty laundry. "They" found out that he was working with Coalition Forces (because, I heard, he'd walk home with bags and bags of laundry and his credentials and ID card still around his neck). And one day after work as he was walking home, they shot and killed him point-blank on a busy street in Mosul. About a dozen or so soldiers lost their laundry that day.

It seemed like every month something like that happened to one of our interpreters, either in my company or in another. They either quit because they or their family received a death threat, or they got murdered or mysteriously disappeared.

Arabic 101

We had a day set up for us, right when we first got to Mosul, where we had all the interpreters come out and try to teach us all some Arabic, to get the basics down and learn a couple key phrases, like "Stop, put the weapon down!" that kinda stuff, but of course all Joe wanted to know was how to say pick-up lines and cuss words in Arabic. The only Arabic schooling that we received was a couple of hour-long briefs at an auditorium where some Middle Eastern man came up behind a podium and taught us a couple key phrases, which we all immediately forgot as soon as the brief was over.

The Army's quick-fix solution to us knowing some Arabic was they issued all of us this cool little "Iraqi Visual Language Survival Guide," which enabled us to communicate somewhat with the non-English-speaking natives. It's on this laminated piece of paper that's all folded up and opens like a map, full of little drawings depicting various things on one side, like an angry suicide bomber, an IED blowing up a tank, and a camel, and on the other side are a bunch of survival phrases, like "Where is the latrine?" and next to that is "Where is the latrine?" written in Arabic script.

So if you wanted to ask an Iraqi where the latrine was, all you had to do was open up the survival guide and point at the Arabic text that says, "Where is the latrine?" and it even shows you how to say, "Where is the latrine?" in Arabic: *Wayn Al-khala / Al-mu-ra-fiq.* And you do the same thing on the other side of the visual guide, for example if you're looking for a suicide bomber or a VBIED, you just point at the cartoon drawing that depicts it.

But what usually happened when you would show an Iraqi your visual guide and point at what you wanted him to look at, his eyes would wander and he'd look at the other stuff on the visual survival guide and start laughing, because some of the pictures are kind of humorous, like the cartoon of a soldier getting stabbed and the one where he's being burned to death.

For a while there I was getting pretty fluent in Arabic, and I'd always practice on the Iraqis whenever we did TCPs. I was able to say hello (*Salaam aleikum*), ask them to please step out of the car (*Sayarra*) as we search (*Deft-Tesh*) the vehicle, can you please open your glove compartment (*Check-me-check*), trunk, and hood for us, and then I'd tell them thank you (*Shookran*). Sometimes they'd be shocked at my Arabic and even ask me if I was an Arab.

Another good example of when knowing some Arabic was helpful is when we were doing a dismounted foot patrol through a low-rent part of town or something and everybody was just staring at us uncomfortably, you'd just bust out the smile and the wave and say, "*Salaam aleikum.*"

It would totally ease up a tense situation, make us not seem as threatening to them, and they'd smile back and say, "*Aleikum salaam*" (the return greeting). And that barrier between you and them would kinda go away. Then you got one of your interpreters to politely ask them where the fuck are those goddamn weapons caches that I know you fuckers are hiding?

> Let us first consider the question: Who are the combatants in guerrilla warfare? On one side we have a group composed of the oppressor and his agents, the professional army, well armed and disciplined, in many cases receiving foreign help as well as the help of the bureaucracy in the employ of the oppressor. On the other side are the people of the nation or region involved. It is important to emphasize that guerrilla warfare is a war of the masses, a war of the people. The guerrilla band is an armed nucleus, the fighting vanguard of the people. It draws its great force from the mass of the people themselves. The guerrilla band is not to be considered inferior to the army against which it fights simply because it is inferior in firepower. Guerrilla warfare is used by the side which is supported by a majority but which possesses a much smaller number of arms for use in defense against oppression. We must come to the inevitable conclusion that the guerrilla fighter is a social reformer, that he takes up arms responding to the angry protest of the people against their oppressors, and that he fights in order to change the social system that keeps all his unarmed brothers in ignominy and misery.
>
> —Che Guevara, *Guerrilla Warfare*

Only the Dead Have Seen the End of War

Our platoon got tasked out to do escort missions for a couple officers over at FOB Freedom, which was the other major FOB in Mosul. Basically our job was to act as an armored cab service for these guys (officers) and drive them to wherever they needed to go for a couple days, like back and forth from the Mosul airfield, the ING compound, and FOB Freedom. Fun stuff.

For this escort mission, we had to drive these officers over to the Mosul airfield so that they could check out and inspect these brand-new trucks that we bought for the INGs that cost $17,000 each. One of the officers was a captain who was a pretty cool guy. In fact, he offered to pull air guard on the way to the airfield.

Me and him somehow later got into a discussion about the Global Security civilian contractors, and he told me that the locals downtown were scared to death of them and that they actually refer to them as "Black Death."

He then told me a story that he'd heard from somebody else, that when the Global Security guys would drive around downtown to do their escort mission or whatever the hell they do, if they got ambushed by an RPG or small-arms fire, they'd been known to just unload on everybody and everything around them. Story goes that they once killed forty-six people in a situation like that.

Don't know if there's any truth to that, it's just a story that he heard from somebody who heard it from somebody else.

I know very little about the Global Security guys, we never worked with them, they did their thing and we did ours. The only time I ever saw them was when they were dead or when they got ambushed and my platoon would get called up to go out and secure the area around one of their burning SUVs, or when I was on gate guard and they would drive past us through the gate in their unarmored white SUVs, which was completely mind-boggling to me, because it was psycho enough to drive around town in an armored vehicle with a .50-cal mounted on top.

Either those guys have balls of steel or they're completely missing a couple screws upstairs. Or both.

Who the hell in their right mind would want to volunteer to come to Iraq?

Wait a minute . . . didn't I . . . ?

My friend, who's a lawyer who recently graduated from San Francisco State, once e-mailed me:

"Those global-security guys—I saw you mention them [on your blog] and I don't know if you talk about this, but I think they answer to no legal authority—a-la since they aren't technically soldiers no international law applies. So I think they can do whatever the hell they want and the U.S. can't prosecute them but maybe the Iraqis could—but I don't know how together their legal system is."

Who knows what their deal is and what their purpose in Iraq is. All I know about them is that they made a hell of a lot more money than I did, like six-digit salaries, and I was only making a small fraction of that.

Since me and this captain were discussing Global Security civilian contractors here in Mosul, I told him the story about how we had just got done eating lunch at the chow hall at FOB Freedom and were leaving the main gate of Freedom to return back home to FOB Marez, and I was manning the machine gun out of the back air-guard hatch to our vehicle, and Doc Haibi was up out of the second air-guard hatch with his M4, when a red SUV came out of nowhere and started honking its horn as it tried to enter FOB Freedom as we were trying to exit through the gate, and I looked over and there were bullet holes all over the SUV, the windshield, the sides, everywhere. I remember thinking to myself: Holy shit, how can anybody survive an attack like that? The driver had this wide-eyed look of panic on his face as he was yelling "GET THE FUCK OUTTA THE WAY!" as they drove past us.

When they passed us and I looked at the back of their vehicle, I saw that the back window was completely blown to bits, and there in the back was an individual lying on his back, completely covered in blood.

He looked alive, but barely. After they drove into FOB Freedom, we drove off to go back to FOB Marez, and I was thinking, What the fuck happened to them? And whatever happened to them, it must have just happened a couple minutes ago, and I don't want to drive through what those guys just drove through.

"Holy shit, did you just fucking see that?!" I yelled over to Doc Haibi.

He told me that he had and to expect to take contact and to keep my guard up on the ride back to Marez.

I yelled down a sit rep (situation report) to the guys in the back of our vehicle on what me and Doc Haibi had just seen driving past, and to be alert and expect to receive contact.

Shortly after we exited the main gate of FOB Freedom and were driving down Route Tampa toward the traffic circle, we saw a white SUV parked all crooked up on the middle divide. When we got closer I observed a lifeless body sitting there in the driver's seat, head leaned forward and on the steering wheel, wearing his body-armor vest, with the seatbelt still strapped on him, and the individual still had his black sunglasses on.

It was a Global Security guy.

The vehicle, to me, did not look as shot up as the red SUV, but it was still covered in bullet holes, windows all blown out, and there was fresh red blood splattered all over the white paint of the vehicle.

Fuck.

We stopped the vehicle and dismounted to pull local 360 security around the SUV and to stop traffic. I looked around and realized that we were almost in the same location where we'd been attacked with an RPG several weeks before. Our combat medic slapped on his latex gloves and started the process of putting the man in a body bag and separating his shit.

The guy looked to be in his late twenties, maybe early thirties, to me. Clean cut, athletic build. There was still fresh blood dripping from his face. Doc Haibi pulled out his digital camera and took a quick crime-scene photo.

Directly across the street was a major gas station, with lots of cars lined up to get gas. Sgt. Horrocks ran around frantically with an interpreter to see if anybody saw anything or knew anything about what had just happened. Of course, nobody fucking talked.

Whenever we got attacked or something happened, we'd always run around and ask the people if they saw or knew anything, and they'd hardly ever talk. An interpreter once told me that it was because they were scared to death that they'd get killed if they were seen talking or giving information to the Americans.

The Kiowas showed up and were hovering overhead. Air support is always a great feeling in situations like this. As our medic was putting his body into a body bag and separating this guy's personal belongings, he discovered that he had a letter of resignation on him and a one-way airplane ticket back to London, where I'm guessing he was from.

When we returned to the FOB and pulled into our motor pool, we noticed that they had dragged the blood-splattered

SUV here and parked it for some odd reason right inside our motor pool, a couple parking spots from where we usually park our Strykers.

That white SUV, with the blood all over it, stayed in our motor pool for about a week. Every time I went to the motor pool to get ready to go out on another mission, I had to look at that thing and be reminded of that guy, slumped over, sunglasses still on, fresh blood dripping down his face, and think about his letter of resignation being physically on him when we discovered his lifeless body, and sit there and wonder what were his reasons for wanting to quit. Did he miss his family? Wife? Kids? Was his job too dangerous? Or was he just sick of this war and everything about it and he wanted it all to end?

A couple days later, I was sitting down on the back ramp of our Stryker, enjoying my pre-mission ritual cigarette, when a couple soldiers I didn't recognize because they were in a different company were taking photos of the white SUV, which still had blood splattered all over it, and I overheard one of the guys say to his friend that he couldn't wait to show all his friends back home these photos and tell them that this was some car that he shot up with his weapon on some TCP.

I wanted to say something but I just kept my mouth shut and looked the other way. I figured, What's the point?

July 4

Independence Day. The only fireworks that went off were the ones that we provided. We had a platoon barbecue in the late afternoon. I didn't want to go to it, because it was well over 110 degrees, and I wanted to hang out and read in my air-conditioned living conex instead, but the barbecue was "mandatory fun," as we liked to call these sorts of things in the Army, thus it was mandatory for my ass to be there.

A couple Turks opened up this barbecue stand right by the gym called Mujat's. They sell beef and chicken kabobs as well as cheese bread. I figured I'd live dangerously and order the barbecued lamb kabob, which was chunks of lamb meat wrapped up in a pita-bread thingie. Three bucks. It was pretty spicy, and pretty good. We all sat around these plastic tables outside of Mujat's kabob stand.

The sun was totally out, not a cloud to be seen, and it was extremely hot. On a cooler outside the barbecue stand was a beer advertisement for some European beer that I'd never heard of. It depicted an ice-cold beer, in an icy glass. I stared at it for a while through my sunglasses, silently salivating, when I started getting flashbacks of previous July Fourths.

I wondered about all the friends I'd celebrated with who I'd lost touch with and hadn't seen in years, and what they were doing back home on this day. I wondered if any of them were wondering what I was doing today, or even knew that I was in Iraq. Probably not. I probably wasn't missing much, they were probably doing the same old shit. Buy a bunch of good old all-American beer, like Miller, Budweiser, and Coors, get drunk, go to the park, and watch the fireworks show.

After the platoon barbecue, we all went back to our conexes and got our stuff ready to go back out on another counter-mortar mission up on OP Abrams, where we always go for countermortar missions.

When we left the FOB and got to OP Abrams, like we always did we parked our vehicles, and like we always did we dismounted the guys and sat around with our thumbs up our asses, and like we always did we watched the sun set over Mosul, which is a very peaceful thing to witness. When the sun finally disappeared and it started getting dark we all mounted back up and moved our location to an area nearby, which was an up-and-coming Iraqi suburban neighborhood that was still under construction. A bunch of houses being constructed from cement and cinder blocks. We found a nice two-story house, pulled up along side of it, and our squad dismounted, and we all walked up onto the roof and pulled the rest of the countermortar mission up there.

Then at about 2200, we decided to have our own Fourth of July fireworks, I have no idea what possessed us to do this, or how it started, or whose idea it was, but we all started launching star clusters and illumination rounds up in the air. Our squad leader came around to each one of us and handed us an illumination round. He asked me if I'd ever fired a lum round before, and I told him that I never had. Spc. Cummings, Doc Haibi, and I all stood around him as he gave us a brief class on how.

The illumination round comes in a silver tube. You twist the cap off and place it on the opposite end of the tube, and that acts like a firing pin when you slam it on the ground. Once it ignites, it fires a lum round straight up in the air a couple hundred meters, and the glowing round slowly hovers back to the ground on this little parachute.

Easy enough. Volunteering to go first and show us how it's done was our squad leader. He slammed the lum round as hard as he could onto the concrete roof we were on, but it didn't go off. He slammed it again as hard as he could, and again it didn't go off. Perplexed, he looked at the bottom of the lum round to find out what was wrong with it, at which time he had the damn thing pointed at the class.

"*Whoa!* You got that shit pointed at us!" Doc Haibi yelled as he grabbed the lum round out of his hand. Doc slammed the thing onto the roof himself, and it ignited and sent a lum round into the air. I then sent one flying, too, and watched it slowly glide back to earth.

It was kinda cool; everybody was firing off dozens of them

into the sky, and the Mosul night was now fully illuminated. We had all kinds of illumination rounds in the air coming down on us. Green ones, red ones, white ones. The stray dogs in the neighborhood were going ballistic, barking and howling up a storm. I'm sure all the Iraqis in the surrounding neighborhoods who were watching this go on were reacting the same way, and wondering what the fuck those crazy Americans were doing now.

With the scorching summer heat, barbecue, and the fireworks show (compliments of the hardworking U.S. taxpayer), it kinda felt like the Fourth, but at the same time it felt nothing like the Fourth.

There's a great line in the movie *Apocalypse Now*: "The more they tried to make it just like home, the more they made everybody miss it."

Well, that's exactly how I felt today.

Movement to Contact

One day we did a mounted patrol through one of the major arteries of the city, Route Tampa. Mounted patrols are also known as "movement to contact" missions. The Army used to call them "search and destroy" missions, but since we're a kinder, gentler Army, we now refer to them as "movement to contact."

"Pussification" of the Army is what I call all that garbage. Just like we can't call the enemy the enemy anymore. Instead we call them "anti-Iraqi forces." We used to call them "non-compliant forces." What kind of shit is that? What's next? Are we going to start calling wars "operations" instead?

"Movement to contact" is kinda like fishing, except you're not out there fishing for rainbow trout in the Sacramento

River, you're in Iraq fishing for noncompliant forces armed with RPGs and AK-47s. And guess what you use as bait? That's right, you're the bait.

Movement to contact is when we would go trolling around the streets of Mosul in our Stryker vehicles to see if we could lure some terrorists or insurgents to take the bait and attack us. Then we'd reel them in hook, line, and sinker, and gut them like the bottom-feeders they are, with our razor-sharp tomahawks.

But it hardly ever worked out that way. What usually happened is we'd throw our lure out there, and then when we reeled it in, we'd notice that we'd only gotten a nibble, maybe an RPG or an IED. And then they'd drop the bait and take off. Thus, fishing for insurgents in Mosul can become an extremely frustrating ordeal, because you know they are out there, but you just can't see them. (A much more effective tactic would be dynamite fishing, where you just start throwing sticks of dynamite in the water and just scoop up everything that floats to the top.)

Anyway, on this late-afternoon movement-to-contact mission, there was a mob of protesters, a couple dozen, right there in the middle of Route Tampa, all carrying huge banners with Arabic writing on it, and a lot of the protesters were carrying large framed photos of a smiling Saddam Hussein, and they were all clapping and chanting something in Arabic.

I have no idea what the hell it was all about, so I waved at them with my nonfiring hand as we drove by and several of them nervously waved back. As I was waving I of course had my other hand firmly gripped on the firing handle of my fully automatic M240 Bravo machine gun with the barrel pointed straight at them. Then one raggedy-looking teenage kid decided to be brave and he picked up a rock and threw it at me.

He missed.

The week before an Iraqi kid did the same thing, he angrily threw a rock at me, and when I pointed the machine gun at him and pretended like I was going to blow his ass away, with no fear whatsoever he just angrily motioned with his hands, "Go ahead, shoot me! *I dare you!*"

As we drove away, I thought, "Gee, I wonder what that kid is gonna be when he grows up?"

At one point during our mounted patrol we drove through a large cemetery, which every neighborhood in Mosul seems to have, and we accidentally ran over a couple of the graves. They kinda felt like a subtle speed bump as we ran over them. Oops. Our bad.

The Iraqis are pretty good at multitasking stuff in their environment, like not only can they convert a pair of walkie-talkies into an IED detonator, they have also converted their graveyards into community recreational parks. Like you'll see Iraqi families picnicking at a graveyard like it was Central Park, and almost every single graveyard in Mosul for some reason has a soccer field smack-dab in the middle of it that you'll always see a couple kids playing in, kicking around a soccer ball to each other. Which is always a strange sight, seeing a bunch of little kids kick around a soccer ball on a makeshift soccer field in the middle of some graveyard, surrounded by hundreds and hundreds of tombstones.

Lots of stray dogs, chickens, and cows like to hang out in the cemeteries as well. I've also noticed that the Iraqi people bury their dead differently than we do in America. We dig a deep hole, then we throw the body, which is usually in a casket, into the hole, and then fill the hole up with dirt.

In Iraq, they don't do the dig-the-hole part, they just place the body on the ground, then pile dirt on top of the body until a nice dirt mound forms. There were thousands of little dirt-mound graves at this cemetery. As we were driving through, I saw one cool-looking grave that had an engraving of an AK-47 on the tombstone. In fact I saw a couple of them with AK-47s.

I told my wife that if I ever got killed in Iraq and they brought my dead body back to the States, I'd want the words "I'd Rather Be Here Than in Iraq" written on my tombstone.

She didn't think that was funny.

The Writing on the Wall

FUCK YOU AMERICANS!—Mohammed

—A thirty-foot string of spray-painted graffiti
in English on a freeway overpass in Mosul

Don't Shoot

Whenever we had a patrol at say 1400, what that meant was that we all had to be physically at the motor pool at exactly 1330. For accountability, to make sure everybody was there, that kinda crap. And then once everybody was there, we all lined up as a squad and our squad leader would do what is called a "hands-on inspection," which means he'd make sure with his hands that you had all your equipment on you and that it was up to standard. He'd make sure you had a Camelbak full of water, both knee pads on, gloves on, fresh batteries in your NODs, that you had all your magazines and that they were full of ammo, and he'd also check your weapon to make sure that it was clean and that the bolt was oiled. And then after he made sure that every single one of us had everything that we were supposed to have on us and we passed his inspection, we all jumped in the back of the Stryker, raised the back ramp, and we were good to go.

Off on another movement-to-contact mission, as well as an OP. As we were driving around Mosul, a little Iraqi kid came out of nowhere on this busy street we were driving down and he pointed his toy pistol at me and simulated shooting at me like I was some kind of U.S. soldier occupying his country. What kind of shit is that? The toy guns that the kids in Iraq play with are replica models and look exactly like the real thing. I guess it's to train them on weapons familiarity at an early age or something.

Every now and then we had to drop off stacks of this coalition propaganda newspaper at the Mosul police station, and I flipped through one of the issues once, and there was a little advertisement or public-service announcement that had a photo of a little Iraqi kid holding a replica 9mm and a bunch of Arabic writing around it, something like "Do not point your toy guns at coalition forces."

It wasn't the first time I had a little kid point a toy gun at me. It had happened to me several times actually, and every time, I just figured, and hoped, that it was just a toy and he didn't pull the trigger. But every time it happened on a mounted patrol it immediately jacked my heart rate up, and I wanted to yell at the little kid and give him a good spanking on the ass and explain to him how close he just came to death and to not do that again, but you can't. You just drive on and hope that the next U.S. soldier that he points that replica toy gun at doesn't light his ass up.

We drove around Mosul for a bit, and then we parked our vehicles and pulled an OP up over by OP Abrams. Pfc. Pointz and I pulled the OP from inside a house that was half-built, and the other gun team went up on the roof. Fuck that standing around in the sun bullshit. We went inside and pulled it from one of the rooms with a window overlooking the sector we were supposed to watch. We had some overhead cover, so we had some shade (thank God).

Since our squad leader was with the other gun team, we took turns pulling shifts. One of us would take our K-pod helmet off and sleep for a little bit, while the other guy would stand guard and keep an eye out for our squad leader and make sure he didn't catch us shamming.

A white Honda then pulled up to the house that we were occupying, and four guys in traditional white outfits and headgear, all holding prayer beads, came out. I put my K-pod back on my head and got up to see what was going on. The driver started talking to me in Arabic. I didn't understand a word he was saying, but from how he was saying it, it sounded to me like he was telling me that he was the owner of the house and that he wanted to show the house to the other guys, because they were interested in buying it. It was his house, not mine, so I said sure and let them inside. I watched the owner walk around the house with the three other men, showing them each room and trying to sell them the house. One of the prospective buyers then came up to me and gave me a cigarette. I said, "*Shookran.*"

After that, they all got back into their Honda, waved goodbye to us, and drove off. Shortly after that, we also left. We drove off and drove around Mosul for a while. Driving down the same streets, looking at the same buildings, waving at the same people, over and over and over and over again. It never fucking ends.

When I first got to the unit, I was handed a *Ranger Handbook* and was told to study it. One of the things that the handbook teaches you is "Don't ever march home the same way. Take a different route so you won't be ambushed" (Standing Orders Rogers' Rangers #11). We seemed to go out on missions every day at the exact same times, did the exact same things, drove down the exact same routes, every single fucking day. And then wonder why we got ambushed.

After we drove around for a bit, seeing if anybody was brave enough to try to shoot at us, we returned to the FOB and went straight to the fuel point, and right when we were refilling the vehicle we heard a mortar impact the FOB. Kinda close to us, too.

That's always a great feeling, being at the fuel point when the mortars start coming down.

> The world is a dangerous place, not because of those who do evil, but because of those who look on and do nothing.
>
> —Albert Einstein

Break from Reality

Before my roommate bought himself a PlayStation, he would just sit on his side of his room and watch bootlegged DVDs that he bought at the Hajji shops on the television set that he had purchased off a departing 101st soldier for, like, sixty bucks. Until Sgt. Horrocks got himself a PlayStation, it was kinda hard to get any good reading done, because he'd be bored from watching all his movies over and over again, and he'd constantly hang out on my side of the room and try to talk to me while I was trying to read, which would drive me absolutely nuts. Horrocks is from Idaho, and I don't know if that had anything to do with this, but he loved to talk, in fact at times I had to wait till he went to sleep to read so that I wouldn't be interrupted, and since he's a light sleeper and doesn't like the light on while he sleeps, I had to lie there on my bed and use my Army-issued flashlight as a reading lamp.

After he bought his PlayStation, he hardly ever talked to me. I wish I would have known about this at the beginning of the deployment, I would have gone out and bought him a PlayStation and every single video game I could find myself.

We had just got done with a joint Special Forces mission, clearing a huge section of Mosul with the INGs, and as soon as we got back from the mission, he went straight to his side of the room, took all his gear off, and immediately started up the PlayStation and began playing SO-COM, which is this so-called realistic Special Forces action war game.

I thought that was kinda odd, so I asked him, like, isn't this war in Iraq enough war for you as it is? Like, why would you want to play a stupid video game about combat when you're actually out doing it? Like, isn't that overkill? He then pointed out to me some of the military books that I had on my bookshelf, and pretty much asked me the same thing, why do I read books about war and Iraq, when I'm in a war in Iraq?

I kinda understood what he was saying.

Sgt. Horrocks had his side of the room decorated with what I call the "September 12" look. He had a huge American flag hanging up on his wall, his folding lawn chair was red, white, and blue, and he had a miniature American flag hanging up by his window.

In the middle of our room, we had a *Sports Illustrated* swimsuit calendar hanging on the wall. Every day that would pass we crossed out with a big X. Some months went by faster than others. The months that had a really hot model went by faster than the months that had okay-looking models. Those months seemed to take forever to end. June lasted for two months because we liked the model too much to let her go.

We also shared a coffeemaker, which we kept on my side of the room. By this time we'd been through three coffee machines because we bought them at the Hajji shops, and they kept breaking. We always had a fresh pot of coffee going in the mornings and at night, especially when we had a night operation.

I had a flag hanging up on the wall on my side of the room, but it was the California state flag. I had it hung up more to irritate Horrocks than for any West Coast pride thing. Horrocks had a very low opinion of Californians. He thought they were all a bunch of "fruits" and "nuts," but his main beef with Californians was that they'd all move up to Idaho, with all their California money, buy up all the land, and post No Trespassing signs around it. Somehow that screwed with his hunting, which he loved.

I had an autographed photo of the Governator (Arnold Schwarzenegger) taped up on the wall as well. I had written him a letter, telling him that he was doing one hell of a great job with California, and I asked him for an autographed photo, and he sent me one. I also had a big plywood bookshelf on my side of the room where I kept all the books that I ordered online and read.

I found that at times I had more free time than I knew what to do with, so instead of wasting all that free time watching low-grade Hajji flicks or jerking around on a PlayStation video-game system, I decided to go ahead and read every single book that I'd always wanted to read but for whatever reason never had.

When I first got to Iraq, I wanted to learn as much as possible about the place, since I hardly knew anything about it. So I went online and ordered as many books as I possibly could on the subject, and studied them the same way as I studied my TMs and FMs when I first showed up to the unit.

The PX at the time didn't have any highlighters, so I had to get one from one of the guys who worked in supply, and I'd always highlight a sentence, part, or section of whatever stood out, for whatever reason, and then when I finished the book, I'd go back and read what I had highlighted, and then move on to the next book, and then when I finished that book, I'd go back to the book I read before, and reread only the highlighted parts again. It helped me retain some of the stuff I was reading. I'd also use some of the stuff as quotes on my weblog, which I always peppered with literary quotes. Like that von Treitschke quote that I posted that was a highlighted section in *The Rise and Fall of the Third Reich.*

Here is a list of *some* of the books that I read in Iraq:

Books on Iraq

Saddam Hussein: A Political Biography / Efraim Karsh and Inari Rautsi
The Modern History of Iraq / Phebe Marr
Saddam: King of Terror / Con Coughlin
Islam / Karen Armstrong
Taliban / Ahmed Rashid
A History of Iraq / Charles Tripp

What's sad is, even though I spent a shitload of money buying all those books, and I read every single one of them, some of them twice, I didn't retain much from those books. Like, I vaguely knew what the difference was between a Shiite and a Sunni.

Books on War

The Art of War / Sun Tzu
On War / Carl von Clausewitz

Guerrilla Warfare / Che Guevara
The Iraq War: Strategy, Tactics, and Military Lessons / Anthony H.Cordesman

I thought it'd be appropriate to give these books a once-over. Even though I'm pretty sure that *The Art of War* and *On War* (possibly the most overquoted books in the military) are both required reading at the war colleges and at West Point, I think that some of our generals in Iraq should have reread those books once or twice before they got there.

Books I Always Wanted to Read

Fear and Loathing in America
The Rum Diary
The Proud Highway
Better Than Sex: Confessions of a Political Junkie
Kingdom of Fear
All by Hunter S. Thompson

I had never really gotten to read anything else by Hunter S. Thompson other than *Hell's Angels* and *Fear and Loathing in Las Vegas.* So since I really liked those two, I decided to go ahead and read some of his other books. I loved his writing, his style, but most importantly, I loved his attitude.

The Rise and Fall of the Third Reich / William L. Shirer
Slaughterhouse-Five / Kurt Vonnegut

Books I Read Just for the Hell of It

Notes of a Dirty Old Man / Charles Bukowski

I didn't start reading till after high school and it was Charles Bukowski that got me to read. I was hanging out on Haight Street in San Francisco, shopping for obscure punk records, and out of boredom I walked into this used-book store, just to look around, and the Bohemian-looking guy behind the counter asked me if I needed help with anything and was there anything in particular I was looking for? I told him no, and that I was just browsing. And when I said that, I was standing in front of this huge section that had a ton of books by some guy called Bukowski, and I was like, "Who's this Bukowski guy?" and the guy behind the counter instantly lit up and said, "He's the shit, man!" I told him that I'd never heard of the guy, and instead of him explaining to me what he was all about, he told me to just pick up one of his books and read any one of his short stories or poems, and that I would see for myself that he was the shit. Which I did, and was instantly hooked. I spent the next thirty minutes or so in that bookstore reading his stuff. And before I left the bookshop, I bought *Hot Water Music*, and ever since then I've read, and reread, countless times, every single one of his books.

I bought *Notes of a Dirty Old Man* because I wanted to read something to lift my spirits in Iraq, and I also wanted my roommate Horrocks to be introduced to Bukowski. I remember I loaned it out to him, and sometimes I'd be on my side of the room reading, and he'd be on his side of the room reading Bukowski, and every now and then, I'd hear him bust up laughing and say, "Dude, no way! This guy's crazy!" When he finished reading the book, I asked him what he thought of the guy, and he smiled and said that he was "all right."

Dispatches / Michael Herr
How to Talk Dirty and Influence People / Lenny Bruce
The Red Pony / John Steinbeck

Do I Come Here Often? / Henry Rollins
The Savage Nation and *The Enemy Within* / Michael Savage
Baghdad by the Bay and *One Man's San Francisco* / Herb Caen
Howl / Allen Ginsberg

Books for a Soldier

I bitched on my blog about the MWR library and the fact that most of what they had were trashy romance novels, so people started e-mailing me and offering to send me books. I received boxes and boxes, so many that I ended up donating them to the MWR library. These are just some of the books that people sent me that I read while I was in Iraq.

Soldier / Anthony B. Herbert
Berkeley at War: The 1960s / W. J. Rorabaugh
The Sun Also Rises / Ernest Hemingway
The Town and the City / Jack Kerouac
Nine Stories / J. D. Salinger
Catch-22 / Joseph Heller
Less Than Zero / Bret Easton Ellis
The Thin Red Line / James Jones

Unexploded Mortar Round

I was walking to the Internet cafe at the MWR center with Doc Haibi, and we were talking and I was looking down on the ground, like I usually do when I walk, when I almost stepped on an unexploded mortar round. I stopped, looked at it, looked at Doc, and said, "Is that what I think it is?" He said, "Yeah, that's a mortar all right."

Doc Haibi walked over to a nearby pile of sandbags and

grabbed a couple of them to mark off the area. As he was busy doing that, I walked over to this nearby building and told the NCO there that there was an unexploded mortar about thirty meters away from their door, maybe they should call EOD (explosive ordnance disposal) so that they could come over and blow it. He said thanks, and me and Doc Haibi continued our mission to the Internet cafe, picking up our discussion where we had left off.

Doc Haibi at this time was still the only person that knew that I had a weblog going. He'd ask me about it every now and then, and I'd tell him about the handful of comments and e-mails that I received from people, but other than that, I hardly talked much about it with him. My blog was steadily becoming more and more popular. Not at an alarming rate but slowly. Instead of getting a couple comments and e-mail per day like I was at first, I was now getting a couple dozen. All the comments and e-mails that I was getting from people were extremely positive. Which kinda surprised me, because I wasn't really expecting that. And I guess what that did was made me a lot more confident about writing and posting stuff. So I figured, What's art if nobody sees it? And I went to a couple message boards and websites and posted little ads telling people that I was a soldier in Iraq blogging about it, along with the URL for my website. I also decided to put a hit counter on my website (so I'd be able to see how cool I was). The first day I put a hit counter on my blog, I only received like a couple dozen hits, but the next day I went and checked, and it was doubled, and then the next day that number was doubled, and it seemed like every day the number of visitors to my blog doubled, sometimes tripled.

But Doc Haibi was still the only person that knew about it.

For now.

Dear Mom, Having a Blast in Iraq

One night I went to the free Internet cafe at the MWR center to check my e-mails and shit. Sat down at a computer and noticed the Internet was down. I asked the Pfc. sitting at the computer next to me how long it had been down for, and he told me (thick southern accent): "It's been down for over an hour now. It's starting to piss me off, too. I was chatting with my mom, I haven't talked to her for two weeks now, and it just went out. Whenever it does that it freaks my mom out [laughs]. She thinks I got hit by a mortar or something [laughs]."

This guy was a nice fellow, kind of chatty, like that was way more information than I needed, but he was a nice guy, you could tell that right away. But there was something odd about him. I couldn't exactly tell what it was. The whole time he was talking I was thinking that if there was ever an audition for *Of Mice and Men,* and they needed somebody to play Lenny, this would be your go-to man.

While we waited for the Internet to come back up, we engaged in some Army small talk: What unit are you with? Where you from? What's your MOS (military occupational skill)? And then he said: "Oh, I'm a combat engineer! I've been blown up, like, eight times, so far out here in Iraq! [Laughs]. Yeah [laughs]. That's just what we do. We go out and find them eye-E-deez [laughs]. In fact we got one guy in my platoon that has five Purple Hearts! Can you believe that? And that ain't no shit, either. I've been here in Iraq for like two or three months now. They sent me straight here from basic and AIT [advanced individual training]. Can you believe that!? I've been pretty lucky so far [laughs]. It's been one hell of a ride boy, let me tell you. It seems like every time we go out we get blown up! [Laughs.] My mom doesn't like it when I tell her about that [sad face], but I just tell her that I'm eighteen and she's gotta have faith in me, and faith in my unit."

Everybody Gets Hit

A platoon mate of mine was explaining to me one day that you had a better chance of getting killed driving on the freeways back home in the States than you had of getting killed in combat in Iraq.

Well, at first that sounded plausible, and I agreed with him, but then I started thinking. Back home in the States, I'd never had somebody try to fire an RPG or rocket at me on the freeway, and I'd never had somebody point his AK-47 at me and drop a mag of 7.62 on me while I was driving home from work. Both of which had happened to me in Mosul. In Iraq, it was not a matter of *if* you'd get hit, it was a matter of *when*. Every single Stryker vehicle in my platoon, all four of them, had been a target of an attack by anti-Iraqi forces at least once, so I had to disagree with him on that one—the freeways back home are not more dangerous than the streets here in Iraq.

Bravo Victor 21

We were returning back from a countermortar mission up on OP Abrams when Victor 21 (1st Squad's vehicle) got hit by two 155 daisy-chain IEDs. They were the lead vehicle when they got hit. I was sitting down in the back of our vehicle, which was the trail vehicle, and Horrocks and Spc. Benitez were up in the air-guard hatches. The explosion was so loud that I actually thought it was our vehicle that got hit.

We then raced to the airfield, because there were a couple

casualties and we had to drop them off at the CSH (combat support hospital) over at the airfield. Sgt. Williams received shrapnel injuries to the neck, Sgt. Thompson, who had been sticking out of the TC hatch, received shrapnel to the arm, and Spc. Scroggins received severe whiplash injuries. Once we got to the CSH we sat around and waited for more than two hours while they received medical attention.

While waiting, I went over and checked out Victor 21 to see what kind of damage those two IEDs did. Amazingly, damage was very minimal, in fact I hardly saw any at all, just three flat tires and a couple minor dings here and there on the armor, that's about it.

The driver for Victor 21, Spc. Cannon, was outside the vehicle chain-smoking with his CVC (combat vehicle crewman) helmet still on. I went up to him to see how he was doing and he was kinda shaken up by it, and he told me it was the first time he'd ever experienced somebody trying to kill him, and that was kinda weird. He told me he'd dodged a bullet on that one because he kept his hatch closed. Some drivers had the bad habit of leaving the hatch open when they were driving around, because of the heat. He pointed out to me that a couple of his periscopes were cracked from shrapnel.

What's kind of ironic is that the night before, Horrocks and I were sitting around smoking and joking outside our conex room with Sgt. Williams. Sgt. Williams is built like an NFL football player and is also one of my favorite NCOs in the platoon, like I would have loved to have him as a squad leader, and there were times when I was extremely close to asking him if I could move over to his squad. He was always looking out for the Joes, and was just a cool guy to talk to and shoot the shit with, and he'd leave you alone and let you do your thing as long as you were squared away and had your shit together.

We were all joking around, and Sgt. Williams said that if his vehicle ever took an IED he'd grab a bayonet and give himself an itty bitty scratch so that he'd get a Purple Heart. We all laughed and thought it was funny, but the guy upstairs must have been listening, too, and I don't think he thought it was too funny, because Williams got his Purple Heart all right, the very next day, and there was no need to fake it. The shrapnel to his neck was a serious injury and could have killed him.

After a couple hours of hanging out at the CSH, we drove back to the FOB, and Victor 21 drove to the mechanics' bay to get serviced and get a couple new tires. The vehicle was serviceable and ready to roll back out in a matter of hours.

Bravo Victor 22

We were doing a mounted patrol in our sector in Mosul, and for some reason, somebody gave the command decision to split all four vehicles in the platoon up, and have each vehicle patrol a different street by itself. Our vehicle pulled away from the other vehicles and into a suburban neighborhood. We stopped the Stryker, dropped the back ramp, and dismounted. Sergeants Horrocks and Warren went over on one side of the street, and Sgt. Blough and I took the other. This was the first time that we'd ever done a foot patrol as a squad-size element, and I remember thinking, Why are we doing this? This goes against everything that we were ever taught from day one, which was always stick together, that way when you're in trouble, the rest of the platoon is nearby to help you out.

As we were doing our foot patrol down this residential street, I looked over at Sgt. Horrocks and gave him this look, like, This is totally fuckin' stupid, and he returned the look. I then looked over to Sgt. Blough and said, "Why are we doing this? Shouldn't we all be together when we patrol the streets?"

He told me that I was right, and he didn't know what was going on.

We then heard a loud explosion, which didn't really surprise any of us. And shortly after, we were all told to "Mount up!" Which we did. We heard Sgt. Castro calling over the radio that 22 had gotten hit with an RPG. So we drove to where 22 was, dismounted on a nearby street, and pulled security. From where we parked our Stryker, we couldn't see 22, but we could definitely see the thick cloud of black smoke coming from it, and we could hear explosions from ammunition and explosives that we'd tied on top of the vehicle.

Our squad leader then took off to find out what was going on. I don't know how many times in the motor pool while smoking a cigarette I'd looked up at the top of the Stryker and asked myself, Why in the world would they tie down a bunch of explosives and ammunition on the outside of the vehicle like that? Our squad leader ran back to us like a chicken with his head cut off and asked for a fire extinguisher. We all just looked at each other like he was absolutely crazy.

The top of the Stryker had enough explosives on it to blow up a small house, and as far as I was concerned, human life was not worth trying to extinguish a fire on a highly explosive war-fighting vehicle with an itty-bitty fire extinguisher. None of us humored him or even toyed around with the idea of trying to help our squad leader extinguish the fire. It could burn down to the ground for all we cared. He took off with the small fire extinguisher. I seriously thought to myself that that was going to be the last time we would ever see him. I told Sgt. Blough that and said, "Watch, he's going to get himself killed."

A couple seconds later, the forty-pound cratering charge went off, making a thunderous explosion, and I looked over at Blough and said, "I told you."

My squad leader came running back with the fire

extinguisher. (The cratering charge blew up before he had a chance to get to 22.) The CO then showed up to assess the situation, and Blough and I went with him to walk down to the area where the Stryker was completely on fire. He saw where the Stryker was, saw how it got hit trying to drive by itself down this valley, and that there was a busy freeway behind it, and that no other vehicle was around when this happened, and he just started shaking his head and I heard him say, "This was a textbook ambush."

An Iraqi fire truck then showed up, and the firemen all got out of their little fire truck and started hosing down the fire. While they were putting the fire out, Sgt. Blough, Spc. Webber, and I kicked down doors to the house that was right by it. I still have no idea why we cleared that house. I think the only reason we did was because it was right next to where the Stryker was burning.

By this time, the Stryker was almost completely burned to the ground, and we were now waiting for some combat engineers to show up so they could drag the Stryker's dead carcass back to the FOB. When we walked back to where our Stryker was parked, the driver and TC for 22, Spc. Neitherton, and Spc. Strong were there by our vehicle. They were both a little shaken up, but at the same time kinda pumped that they had survived the attack.

When the battalion commander, Lt. Col. Buck James, showed up, he didn't look too happy. He had this stern look on his face, and you could tell that he didn't like what was going on here one bit. He walked over to where Horrocks and Warren were and took a knee beside them and pointed his finger to a nearby house and said, "I bet you that son of a bitch lives right there." Sgt. Horrocks then told the BC, "Well at least nobody got hurt today sir."

The BC replied, "Roger fucking that."

And then got up and walked away to further assess the situation.

Bravo Victor 23

In a way, it was kind of my fault that Victor 23 was a target of this RPG attack. Actually, it was my shitty photography that did it.

The day before this incident happened, my platoon was driving around our AO out on a movement-to-contact mounted patrol, and we all parked our Strykers out in front of a suspected terrorist hotel. We all dismounted to pull security while our platoon leader took a squad and went inside the hotel to investigate.

My squad leader told Doc Haibi and me to go inside the hotel with the platoon leader. He asked if any of us was any good with the digital camera, as he wanted photos of all the rooms inside the hotel. I told him that I took black-and-white photography in high school, so he handed me the camera and told me to follow him as we walked through the place. Cool, my first gig as a combat photographer.

I've seen skid-row hooker hotels, the ones with hourly rates, more sanitary and better furnished than that hotel. The digital camera was a piece of shit (yeah, I know, sure, blame it on the camera, retard), and it was hard to get an entire room to fit in the picture. I had to hold the camera with one hand out in front of me so that the room was behind me, so in every single shot it looked like I was taking a photo of myself.

My platoon leader also gave me the order to take a photo of everything I saw, so I did. I took photos of the curtains, the stairs, the bathrooms, the doors, the carpet, the roof, everything, even the guys working behind the front counter.

I later found out that that wasn't really what he meant by take a photo of everything.

When we returned to the FOB, the platoon leader looked at the photos and thought that they were garbage, and I guess he thought I did it as a joke to be funny, so we had to go back out again the very next day to that hotel for a retake.

Take two.

Of course, this pissed everybody in my platoon off because that day was supposed to be our day off. So we went back to the hotel, and they got somebody else to take the photos of the rooms while I waited outside and pulled security and had to listen to everybody say, "Thank you, Buzzell."

On the way back to the FOB, we were informed that there were some old artillery rounds just sitting out in the middle of an open field over by the traffic circle. We drove up to the location and sent a couple squads to go find them, which they immediately did, just sitting there in the open.

We called it in and waited for EOD to show up and blow it up, which they told us could take anywhere from thirty minutes to an hour.

So we all sat around in the sun and waited, and waited, when all of the sudden we heard a loud explosion. I was leaning up against the berm next to Sgt. Horrocks when the explosion went off and we both kinda looked at each other and said, "Wow, that was quick, usually EOD takes forever to show up and blow up UXO." Usually they'd give us a heads-up prior to blowing up the UXO, for some reason they forgot to do that this time. We then got word that it wasn't EOD, that they weren't even anywhere near our location yet, that it was actually an RPG that was fired at 3rd Squad's vehicle, Victor 23. The RPG fell short and blew up on a berm right in front of the Stryker.

We ran to our vehicles and secured the area, searched some

nearby buildings, found nothing, and then returned to the FOB, of course everybody thanked me for this.

The guys in Victor 23 used the exploded RPG shell that had been aimed at them as a vehicle decoration. They tied it onto the front like a hood ornament. I was kinda tripped out for a while on this attack, because if somebody had gotten killed, I would have blamed it on my photography. But since nobody in the platoon got killed or hurt, I just again reminded myself *never* to volunteer for shit again.

Bravo Victor 24

It was on an early-morning IED sweep with the combat engineers that our vehicle got hit.

At the time, early June, they were working us to death, two or three missions a day, and I was completely racked out from the lack of sleep and physical exhaustion in the back of the vehicle with the rest of the squad, when all of the sudden I was woken up by a loud explosion, and the steel birdcage surrounding our vehicle was vibrating like it just got hit by something big maybe.

I opened my eyes, looked around, noticed that everybody was still alive in our vehicle and that nobody was hurt, and the first words out of my mouth that I semiconsciously said were, "Hell, yeah! We're going back to the FOB, dude! Whoo-hoo!" and I closed my eyes and tried to go back to sleep.

Every time a vehicle got hit and/or received some kind of damage, the mission was called off and we had to return immediately to the FOB so that the vehicle could get repaired and serviced, thus the squad usually got the rest of the day off, or remained off until the vehicle was serviceable again. Like I said, we were being overworked at the time, and this was an early-morning mission, so I was extremely tired and not in the mood to play soldier.

My squad leader yelled, "*Buzzell!* Wake the fuck up! What the hell is wrong with you? We just got hit!"

So I reluctantly woke back up and just sat there, bored, waiting for further instructions.

At the time there was some confusion as to what exactly hit us. Sgt. Hoerner was calling in over the radio that it was an IED, but Sgt. Horrocks, who was sticking out of the back air-guard hatch, was reporting down to us that it was an RPG or a rocket of some kind, because after the explosion we drove past an RPG fin laying down on the ground.

We stopped the vehicle, dropped ramp, and dismounted the guys to secure the area and assess the damage. I was hoping that the damage would be severe so that way we'd maybe have a couple days off. As soon as I stepped out of the vehicle I noticed that we were almost in the exact same location where Victor 22 burned to the ground when they took that RPG.

After about a half hour of just standing around, we all loaded back onto our vehicles and drove back to the FOB. The only damage we sustained was a blown tire that whatever was fired at us detonated on. The tire was located directly behind where I was sitting. If I had been driving around in a Humvee that day, my wife probably would have been $250,000 richer.

We later found out that it was a remote-detonated rocket that hit us.

Sleepless in Mosul

Had another all-night mission. Took a bunch of caffeine pills before we rolled out so I could stay awake all night. This one was a huge joint operation with the ING and ICP, where they cleared a huge sector of Mosul. Our job was just to be there in case anything happened.

Right about the time the sun was coming over the horizon I heard two loud explosions from off in the distance. No idea what the hell that was all about or what was going on. Then at the crack of dawn, I heard the faint crack of an AK-47 fire off a ten-round burst from behind me. Several of the bullets whizzed by over my head, so I picked up my M240 Bravo machine gun (which weighs 27.6 pounds according to FM 23-68), pointed it toward where I heard the rounds fired, and pressed the safety button from safe to fire. I scanned the area, but I couldn't see shit. Not a single thing. I yelled at my assistant gunner, Pfc. Pointz, asking if he saw anything, because that was kinda his sector to be looking at, and he said no.

Off to the right a little bit from where I was looking I could see several Iraqi Army soldiers carrying an ING soldier who was shot in the leg area into a white ING truck. A squad leader in my platoon and a combat medic went over to administer first aid to the individual. Shortly after, a white ambulance with one of those red crescents on it showed up and kinda drove around in circles, but finally it got to him and drove him off to a nearby hospital. No word if he made it or not.

The other day, two rockets were fired at our compound, one landed near the chow hall and the other one blew up in the air. A Stryker vehicle was also RPG'd in downtown Mosul as well.

Dear Mom and Dad

PROBLEM: Soldiers failing to write to family and loved ones back home notifying them that they are okay and still alive.
SOLUTION: Once a month, all soldiers must fill out a white index card like it's a postcard and write a message on the back

of it, to be mailed home back to their parents or wife telling them that they are okay, and that index card must be handed to a squad leader or higher.

I'm fucking serious, what happened was a lot of soldiers were failing to contact their parents and let them know that they were okay, and these worrywart parents were contacting the chain of command saying that their little Johnny wasn't writing to them enough. So to fix this problem, once a month we all had to form up and each of us was handed an index card to fill out to a parent or wife to tell them that we were okay, doing well, still alive, and hand it over to the squad leader who double-checks and makes sure that everybody fills one out, and he then personally goes over to S-1 and drops it off in the mailbox.

I was writing to my wife all the time, so the first postcard I filled out to my parents, in the best kindergarten dyslexic letters I could:

> **DeAr mOM aNd dAd,**
> **I Am fInE, I aM 27 YeArS Old AnD ThEy ArE TrEAtiNg mE LiKe I aM 6. wEhAvE tO fIlL tHeSe CaRdS 0uT NoW bEcAuSe PeeplEZ ArNt wriITiNg t0 MoMMY aNd DaDDiE EnUff, sO nOW thEy mAke uS. LoVe.CoLbY**

My dad, who spent twenty years in the Army, fully understood that this was how the Army solves problems and laughed when he received the postcard. My mom on the other hand didn't quite get it and my dad had to explain it to her, and when my mom asked why I wrote all pre-schoolish, he said that I was just being a smartass again, which she fully understood.

FREE ADVICE

I get a lot of e-mails from people just joining the military, and people already in the military asking me of all people for advice on what to look out for once they get here to the great two-way live fire in the Middle East. Instead of answering every single e-mail, I've decided to just post some of the advice up here on this site.

- If you're a new guy to the unit, learn as much as you can as soon as you get there. If they hand you a TM or FM, memorize it in its entirety. A lot of people will want to help you out when you get here, take advantage of that. Stay the fuck away from people that have negative attitudes. Avoid these bad apples like the plague. For example people who brag about how many Article 15's they have, or guys that start off every sentence with: "Man, this is bullshit . . ." or "Fuck the Army . . ." or "I ain't doin shit . . . " or "Fuck this shit." I had a probation officer tell me that once you start hanging out with shit, you're going to end up smelling like it. (In other words, don't hang out with me if you get assigned to my platoon.)
- Remember, if the enemy is within range, so are you.
- Whenever you find an IED, weapons cache, or a stack of old artillery rounds that are just sitting there in plain sight, automatically think it's a decoy and be prepared to be ambushed.
- It's not a question of if you'll get RPG'd or IED'd here in Iraq, it's a question of when. When it happens, look around and make a mental note of every single person you see standing around. Try to memorize those faces. Because the next time you get hit, and you see the same faces standing around watching, that should tell you something. Tell your chain of command:

"Hey, those same guys were hanging around at the last place we got hit," and detain those guys ASAP for questioning.

- When you get hit with an IED, expect to be ambushed with small arms and RPG fire immediately after.
- The number one advice I have for people coming to Iraq is become very good friends with your interpreters. They will help you out a lot out here. Learn as much as you can from them. They know this place better than anybody else, they have their ears to the streets, they will tell you where the dangerous neighborhoods are, what to look out for, what to do and what not to do. Listen to them.
- Learn as much Arabic as you can. You can get a Speak Arabic in 10 Days crash course CD off Amazon. Constantly practice your Arabic as much as you can, on the interpreters, contractors, shop owners, whoever.
- On patrols, they're constantly going to tell you to scan rooftops for possible attacks. But also be aware that they also like to fire RPGs from the corners of the buildings and disappear in the streets. Be aware of that.
- Know the maximum effective ranges of your enemy's weapons, and be aware of that when you're scanning. When on patrols, reverse the situation in your head. Think: If I was going to attack us, where would I do it from and how? These people are geniuses when it comes to playing dirty, they've been fighting like that for years and years.
- Always assume that somebody is watching you, because they are. And always assume you're going to get hit, and in your head think: If something happens right now, where would I go and what would I do? Always be at least one step ahead.

- Always expect the mission to last way longer than it's supposed to and plan accordingly. If you smoke always bring at least a carton. That way you don't have to worry about running out of smokes, and when everybody else runs out and starts turning into nicotine-addicted crack addicts, you can charge 10 to 20 bucks a pack. And yes, people will happily pay that for a pack of smokes in the field.
- This one is going to be a hard one to explain, but I'll do my best. Everybody here owns an AK-47. One way to help tell if the person holding the AK-47 is Friendly (like an ICP or ING) or Foe is by his body language. Example: the "bad guy" with an AK-47 will be crouched down in an attack position, sneaking around with an AK up ready to fire. He's in a threatening position, being sneaky. An ICP or ING won't move his body like that. He'll usually be in a standing up position, more relaxed, walking around. I can explain this one better verbally and in person.
- Situational awareness. Always be aware of your surroundings.
- Not everybody here is a bloody terrorist. (This doesn't mean put your guard down and think everybody here is your fuckin' friend either, they're not.) Target identification is key. One time a different platoon in my company was doing a raid on a house, and they blew the front door up with some explosives and it woke up some Iraqi who lived down the street, who was a police officer during the day. And he came out in civilian clothes and an AK-47 to investigate what the hell was going on. He lived, but he almost didn't. I'm not going to tell you what to do in a situation like that, that's up to your chain of command, but make sure you know

your platoon's SOPs and ROEs inside and out for situations like this, so when you get here, you know exactly what to do if they come up, because they will.
- It's still Iraq. It's just as dangerous now as it ever has been. People are still getting killed here every day, and every time you leave the FOB you're still entering the concrete jungle that's filled with people who would love to kill you, by any means necessary. Always have your guard up, and never get complacent.

One learns survival, by surviving.

—Charles Bukowski

Posted by CBFTW on August 2, 2004

TO HELL WITH OBSERVATION POSTS

Had an all-night mission last night with the INGs. I was popping caffeine pills all night like they were Tic-Tacs to stay awake. We returned to the FOB at around 11:00-ish just to roll right the fuck back out to do a fuckin' OP. Right at the hottest time of the day.

An OP is an Observation Post. A dum-dum retard explanation of an OP is when we go somewhere and hide out and wait for hours and hours for "the bad guys" to show up and do something, if they do something, we're there to send them to Allah and engage them with everything we've got. Sounds pretty cool, huh? Sounds exciting and fun, right?

If you want to know what an OP in Iraq is like, here's what you do: Go put on some boots, long pants, long sleeve T-shirt, some skateboarding knee pads, gloves (mandatory in my unit, don't ask why), grab your high school football helmet, and a huge backpack. Not no first day of school backpack either, grab one of those outdoorsy heavy duty ones, like what the European hostel kids carry around.

Now that you've got all that shit on, go down to the nearest fitness center, like a 24-hour nautilus. Go to the weight room and throw a 45-pound weight in the backpack. No wait a minute, let's make this accurate, the machine gun I carry weighs 27.6 pounds, I carry about 400–600 rounds of 7.62, that's like say, 25-pounds (it's probably more than that), the body armor which are two ceramic plates weighs about say, 10 pounds each, and you have your pistol, knife, first aid kit, camera, night vision, and whatever crap you need to carry, let's just say it all comes out to: 80 pounds. So throw in your backpack a 45-pound plate and a 35-pound plate. Don't forget water, grab a gallon of water and throw that in your backpack as well.

Okay, now that you have all that in your backpack and you have your football helmet on, go walk into the sauna. Every good gym has a sauna. Once you're in the sauna, crack open a *National Geographic* magazine and rip out the centerfold of the Third World country landscape that's inside every issue, and tape it to the wall of the sauna. Now sit there, with all that crap on, and stare at that centerfold photo for two, four, or six hours. Now if you really want to make this realistic, bring a jar full of mosquitoes, flies, and as many different exotic malaria-carrying insects and bugs as you can find and open up that jar in the sauna and let them loose.

This is what an OP in Iraq is like.

Posted by CBFTW at 3:26 p.m., July 19, 2004

OP Abrams

OP Abrams is this huge hill that sits in an agricultural part of Mosul which we did countermortar missions from. It's located right next to the Tigris River. Alongside the Tigris is a dirt road, and it makes a complete loop, so we call the dirt road AO LOOP.

The Tigris River runs right through Mosul and it reminds me a lot of the Sacramento River back home in California. My dad used to take me and my brother there a lot when we were little kids to go fishing. Caught my first fish there, a medium-sized striper. I thought about those times, especially one day when we drove past an Iraqi man and his son slowly floating down the river in a small boat fishing. It looked like a Steinbeck novel. The kid calmly waved as we drove by. I waved back with my nonfiring hand. The sunset was out, and so were a lot of Iraqi families, all hanging out along the river, enjoying themselves, swimming and picnicking. A lot of them would wave and cheer as we drove by.

Even the stray dogs by the river looked to be at peace. And peasant farmers were herding their herds of oxen and cows into the river, so they could cool down in the water. Kinda cool, seeing a bunch of these monstrous black oxen with huge horns, just sitting in the river with only their heads sticking out of the water, looking content.

I myself would never in a million years eat a fish caught from the Tigris, let alone even think about doing the backstroke in that thing. Every mile or so, you'd see a large sewage truck dumping God knows what into it. The tree-hugging environmentalists back in California would have a heart attack if they witnessed this catastrophic crime going on on the Tigris, and even a person like me, who could give two shits about the environment, was getting nauseous watching this.

Whenever we drove along the Tigris I was always reminded of the soldiers that were lost in that thing, and in fact to this day I will still be scanning the river in hopes of finding one of their bodies floating on the surface. I don't know the specifics of what happened, but when we first arrived in Mosul some soldiers tried to cross the river, and something happened to them, and several of them ended up drowning. A helicopter showed up to try to rescue them and somehow the helicopter ended up crashing in the river. We had a bunch of Navy SEALS go swimming in that river to try to find their bodies, but they never found anything.

On the other side of the river sits a palace that once belonged to Saddam Hussein. Since Saddam is no longer in power and is unable to adequately maintain his palaces, we gladly took over the lease and converted it into a forward operating base called FOB Freedom. If you ever find yourself over at Freedom, you might as well just walk around with your saluting hand taped to your PC (hat), because there's nothing but brass and high-ranking military officials walking around up in that bitch.

Not only is FOB Freedom a beautiful palace, but it is also a beautiful target to mortar and RPG. For a while, they were getting hit, and hit hard, every fucking day, mostly because it's in a really shitty location. It's across a river, there's a busy freeway that runs alongside it, it's kinda up on a hill, basically the whole FOB screams, "Shoot me!" in Arabic.

Well, since Freedom was getting attacked, and our job as American soldiers is to protect and defend Freedom, we got tasked out to pull these mind-numbing countermortar missions up on OP Abrams, and in the hottest months of the year, too, June, July, and August, when the average temperature can get up well beyond 120 degrees, *in the shade.*

Our job was to go up there and observe the other side of the river to make sure that nobody got any crazy ideas with the mortar tube. All the platoons in my company took turns pulling shifts up there. We'd send a platoon-size element up there on their Strykers to the top of that hill, typically during the hottest part of the day, park the Strykers, drop ramp, and dismount the troops, and in full kit we'd sit there for hours, with no shade whatsoever, and burn in the scorching Iraqi heat and sun. The water that we'd bring with us was only good for about fifteen minutes, because after that the sun got the water so extremely hot that it was a pain in the ass to drink.

The countermortar missions up on OP Abrams were getting old, and getting old fast. The only thing they were good for as far as I was concerned was draining whatever morale we had in us out completely. Spc. Cummings once brought a thermometer with him up to OP Abrams, and the thing only went up to 120 degrees, and the red stuff went all the way past the top.

It was one of those normal days up on OP Abrams, where the temp was way over 120, and the sweat was just pouring down our faces, when the platoon leader went ahead and gave the command decision to let us all go swimming in the river.

Here was the platoon leader's plan for Covert Swim Ops in the Tigris: There were four Strykers in a platoon, three Strykers would stay up on top of the hill and pull 360 security while one vehicle would drive down alongside the river, dismount the guys, and let them go swimming for thirty minutes, and once the thirty minutes was up, they'd all load back up on the vehicle and drive back up to the OP and another vehicle would go down.

I couldn't believe this was happening. Do my platoon leader and the other guys in my platoon not see the sewage trucks just down the river dumping God knows what into it? I pointed this out to my AG, Spc. Cummings, and told him that this was absolutely insane. He didn't seem to care, in fact he was all pumped up and couldn't wait to jump into the river and morph into the toxic avenger.

All summer long we'd had to pull these bullshit countermortar missions in hellish temperatures right next to that river and fantasize about how good it must feel to go swimming in that thing to cool off, and this was our chance to finally have a little bit of fun and actually do it.

I tried to talk my AG out of it, but he wasn't having it. We sat and watched 1st Squad take turns cannonballing into the river. It looked like they were having a blast. Some of the soldiers took out their digital cameras and snapped photos of the swimmers down below.

Then it was our turn to swim. I bitched about this being the dumbest idea ever the whole way there, but of course nobody was listening to me. Once we got down to the river, we parked, dismounted, and all the guys in my squad took off their gear and one by one all of them dove in. Except me.

I lit up a smoke and sat there next to the pile of equipment they had all just stripped themselves of, and watched them jump into the river multiple times, and listened to them tell me how great the water felt.

Fuck it.

I thought to myself that the Hajji cigarettes that I smoke will probably kill me faster than a quick dive, so I extinguished my smoke and took off my gear and dove in with my boots and BDU pants on. The water was great, ice cold, and even though I said I would never do the backstroke in the Tigris, I did end up doing the backstroke in the Tigris, with my BDU pants and combat boots still on. It was the fastest thirty minutes ever.

Then it was our turn to get back on the vehicle and let somebody else swim. We put our kits back on and went back to pulling the OP. My pants were completely dry in less than a half hour.

When everybody was done swimming the platoon leader came around and told each one of us to keep our mouths shut and not to tell a single soul about this. If word got out that we all went swimming in the Tigris, he'd probably lose his job.

Sometimes when I was at the Internet cafe, and the Internet

would be running slow, or while I waited for service to come back up when the server was down, I'd check the hard drive to see what photos were left behind on it. When people e-mail photos to people, the computer for some reason saves a copy of it, or they forget to delete them from the computer.

I never found any photos of soldiers butt-fucking or torturing Iraqi prisoners, but it's amazing the incriminating photographs you'd find, people drinking whiskey straight from the bottle inside their conexes, naked Filipino KBR girls, one time I found a dozen photographs of this sergeant in my unit, who I'd see at the gym all the time, receiving oral favors from this low-ranking female soldier, who I'd see every now and then down at the chow hall. Both of them had the same unit patch on that I did.

I'd always post the pornographic pics of soldiers up as a screensaver on the computer before leaving the Internet cafe.

Well, a couple weeks after we pulled that OP, my platoon leader took one hell of an ass chewing from our CO when somebody in my platoon left a bunch of digital photos of us swimming in the Tigris on one of the computers at the MWR center by accident.

Our platoon leader is a good guy, he doesn't reek of "Fraternity for Men" like some of the other officers that I've bumped into while I've been in the Army. I think a big reason why I like him is because he used to be a regular enlisted soldier, and then he got out, went to college and did the whole ROTC thing, and then came back in as an officer. Thus he kinda knows what it's like to be a Joe.

My squad leader's wife got the entire squad a bunch of neoprene seat-cushion things that cushion your ass when you sit down. She got us all these because the seat cushions on the seats inside the Stryker were so terrible. One day on OP Abrams, I grabbed a seat-cushion chair thing from inside the vehicle, and I told Pfc. Pointz to also grab a seat cushion, because if we were going to sit on our ass on an OP for hours, we might as well do it in comfort. So we set our gun down and we both sat down our seat-cushion chair things next to it. Fuck it.

Our platoon leader saw that we were both maxing and relaxing on seat cushions, and he walked up to us and said, "What's next guys? A cooler full of beer?" And I said to him, "In a perfect war, sir, yes, we would be up here with a cooler full of beer."

He then smirked and said, "Carry on, men."

BRUTAL ATTACK ON A COUNTERMORTAR MISSION

It was at night, the moon was gone, and the visibility was almost zero. Had my night vision goggles on. We set our gun position down on this hill, me and Pfc. Pointz. I laid down in the prone position and scanned my sector. I was only on the ground for like thirty seconds when I started feeling a tingling sensation all down my back and up my arms. I was like, What the fuck is that?? I had my NODs on and I looked down on the ground, and at first it looked like the TV screen when the cable goes out, you know like millions of bees in a snowstorm, but once I took a closer look I realized that I was lying down on a huge pile of literally thousands and thousands of ants. I looked at my arms and there were hundreds of ants crawling all over me, in fact I could hear them crawling on me. The ants here are not like the itty-bitty house ants back home, the ones in Iraq are fucking huge, like as big as the ones at Fort Benning. I freaked out, they were all over me, crawling all up and down my back, up my arms, on my face, everywhere. I jumped up, threw my helmet off, tore my vest off as fast as I could, swearing and cussing every profanity in the fucking book, slapping and hitting myself all over trying to get them off of me as fast as I could. Every now

and then I could feel one of them biting into me and I'd grit my teeth in pain. I yelled at my assistant gunner to help me out and start slapping them off me as well.

Pfc. Pointz and Spc. Cummings both found all of this very comical. I tore my top off, my T-shirt, they were down my pants as well now. That wasn't too pleasant a feeling.

Lesson: Don't be a fucking idiot like me, and always look before you lie down anywhere, especially in this country.

On the way back to the FOB, our shocks and hydraulics completely went tits up and the vehicle was bouncing up and down like an East L.A. low-rider Impala the whole way. It was sort of fun for like the first couple minutes, but then after a while I started feeling seasick, and I almost barfed up my beef enchilada MRE. (That wasn't a racist joke, I seriously ate a beef enchilada MRE prior to this.)

Posted by CBFTW at 8:11 a.m., July 26, 2004

Mail Call

For a couple weeks on my weblog in July I had a mail-call feature, where I answered some of the readers' questions. Here are a handful of them, as posted:

QUESTION: Hi, I am a mother of a Stryker soldier. He's been in Iraq since last November. What can I do for my son when he comes home? I know when he came home for R&R he was not the same kid who left in November. Very jumpy and always looking around seeing who was there and everything. Is there anything I can do for him to help him get readjusted to being here and not Iraq? I pray for all of you guys over there and hope that you make it home okay. God

bless you all!!! Stryker Mom
ANSWER: Buy as many kegs of beer as you can, and invite as many women to the party as possible. Honestly, I don't know how to answer your question. I haven't even had R&R or leave yet, so I have no idea what it's like back in the world. He might just want to be alone, which is the one thing I'm looking forward to the most when I get back. I know I just want to spend some time completely by myself for a while.

QUESTION: My hubby told me that due to spotty connections and long lines, he couldn't get on the Internet much. You seem to be posting blogs almost every day. What's up with that? Is he just feeding me a line?
ANSWER: It's what I tell my wife when I don't want to talk to her, eerrr I mean, ummm . . . Next question please.

QUESTION: Dear sir, I discovered your blog today and I read some of your letters. I'm an Iraqi living in Baghdad. Every time I walk or pass by army troops I wonder, how do they feel? Are they convinced that they should be here? Do they hate us? Blame us? Have they expected what is happening here or have they imagined something different when they came a year ago? For me, I thought at the beginning that things would be better, there would be peace, and we would be able to look for a better future. I thought that we would be able to forget the 24 years of wars and try to benefit from our money to rebuild the country instead of buying weapons, but all these were just illusions.

I want to explain something for you: Most of Iraqis are against violence and we believe that most terrorists, or who are called resistance, are either not Iraqis or are gangsters who want to benefit from the situation here in the name of resistance. I don't believe resistance means killing innocent people or exploding a car near a police station or a church. All those terrorists want is pushing Iraq to a civil war. I think many countries are willing to put Iraq in this situation so they can go on with their plans and this is all part of a big game in which you and me are just players. I do not even drop the possibility that American politicians are behind some of the events happening. They said their war is against terrorists, but they brought the terrorists to our country to fight them here. There is even a possibility that Al Qaeda is a fake and it is really a tool for the Americans being used to help in controlling the whole world (if you have seen the movie *Wag the Dog* starring Dustin Hoffman, you will understand what I mean).

I hope these troubles will end soon and you will be able to return back to your wife and family. Before, I used to feel sorry when I hear that a soldier had died. I think about his family and children and why they had to pay for it. Now I also feel sorry when I hear that Iraqis are being killed every day leaving their families struggling to live. I pray for you and for us to stay safe in this bloody world. Yours, Zena
ANSWER: Thank you for sharing your thoughts. No, I have not seen the movie *Wag the Dog,* but I have seen the Stanley Kubrick flick *Dr. Strangelove,* which I highly recommend to anybody who lives in another country, who wants to know what our government and high ranking military officials are really like behind closed doors. The movie is extremely accurate, especially with this current Bush administration.

QUESTION: What was Christmas like in Iraq? —Mike B
ANSWER: It sucked ass. We were out in the field, Samarra, living out of the Strykers, freezing our asses off at night. Our combat medic brought a CD of the Chipmunks singing Christmas carols. God, I hate the Chipmunks, and we

listened to that CD nonstop between missions in the Stryker. Talk about pain and suffering. We all ran out of smokes too, nothing worse than running out of cigarettes in the field. They brought a satellite phone out to the field on Christmas and all of us got one five minute phone call. Anyways, Christmas in Iraq was like that Nat King Cole song they always play during the holidays, "Unforgettable."

QUESTION: Since Saddam's fall, what items are the Iraqis buying like crazy? I have heard cell phones & satellite dishes. Trying to find out the specifics on what companies are making the products that are being bought. Thanks.
Jenkins, Jason
ANSWER: About 25 meters from my room is a small shop that's owned by a couple Iraqis. I went over to them today and asked the three Iraqis behind the counter your question, and the first answer all three of them gave me was: porno. They said now you can buy porno videos downtown, and you couldn't do that when Saddam was in power. They also have worldwide communication available to them now that wasn't here before, cell phones, Internet, and there's a shit-load of European cars here now. Every day I see truckloads of European cars being brought here, and a lot of people here are now driving BMWs and Mercedes. It's weird, almost every car here looks like it's straight off the junkyard, but then every now and then you'll see some luxury European car driving down the street.

QUESTION: I check out your blog every day . . . not sure how I found it, but it's great to get a perspective that you would never get unless you knew someone in Iraq. I have two questions for you: 1) Personal question: You joke about your recruiter a lot and the duty you pull (as every military guy I ever have known does)—but do you feel like you're making a difference for Iraq? For America? We'll probably not know for years, but I'd like to know what your (and maybe the general) opinion over there is. 2) Aside from the Iraqis on your FOB, what is your view of the Iraqi citizens' opinions of what is happening and their view toward you? Do they seem thankful? Do you think they feel like they have a chance to actually make their country better? Do you sense hope? I also want to add that I truly respect what you are doing. Thanks . . . be safe. And thanks again for sharing your thoughts. —Allen

ANSWER: 1) I personally think we're making a difference for the better here for these people. I don't know what it was like here when Saddam was in charge, but all the Iraqis that I've talked to tell me it sucked. Do I feel like I've made a difference for America? I don't know. 2) Every time I leave the FOB and hit the streets here in Mosul, my cargo pockets get filled with gifts from the Iraqi people. Fruits, breads, candies, toys, whatever. Yeah, there's a lot of people who also hate us, but you don't know their story.

QUESTION: First, the vast majority of Americans are very thankful for the great job you and your fellow soldiers are doing in Iraq. Next, continue to keep your musings real. Your stories about your experiences in Iraq are great. You don't need to use error free grammar. Your writings about Iraq are more interesting than those of Dan Rather, Tom Brokaw, and Peter Jennings combined. Lastly, if you don't mind, I have a few questions. 1) Friends of mine who oppose GW Bush and the war don't have a moral problem with anti-war protesters who publicly protest during ongoing conflict. I find this to be very problematic. I think it is fine to protest before conflict begins, but I have a problem with protesters who take a public stance once soldiers' feet are on the ground. What is the general opinion of you and your fellow soldiers regarding public protestations against the war after battle begins? I don't think this type of behavior influences most soldiers to do their job with less professionalism. Yet, I can't imagine it doesn't have some negative impact on your psyche. Do most soldiers perceive these public protesters as less patriotic? ANSWER: The University here in Mosul had a huge anti-America protest a couple months ago. Hundreds and hundreds of young students protesting us being here. I asked my Kurdish friend who lives in Mosul what he thought of all the protesters and with a look of disgust he told me that the protesters are just ignorant and uneducated on what's really going on with Iraq. Sometimes I feel that way about our protesters back home. On a raid once I found some old Iraqi newspapers from back in the Saddam era, and he would always print photographs of all the anti-war protests in his papers, I guess to make it look like EVERYBODY in America was against Bush and the war. Me personally, we have the right to assemble and protest whatever we want to protest. If they want to protest before the war, go ahead, if they want to protest during the war, go ahead. It doesn't bother me and I don't think about them. I know this sounds like a total brain-washed answer, but my job is not to think about them and have them affect my job, my job is to do my job. If people want to protest the war because they think it's an unjust war, that's fine, that's what makes America America, we have that freedom to do that. A lot of the soldiers here are totally gung ho 100% for this war, which is fine, but whenever we sit around smoking and talking about the war, if I even bring up an argument that even remotely questions us being here and the legitimacy of this war, I'm usually called a liberal communist pinko from California. Which I'm not.

QUESTION: It seems like we're trying to wage a politically correct war in Iraq. We can't just bomb Fallujah and Mosul into dust. While that would certainly take a lot of bad guys out of the picture it would also evaporate the support base for the war. Do you perceive any general strategic handicaps as a result of fighting a "nice" war? And basically, what would you do? If you could say "Screw everyone" and fight any kind of way you could to win, what would you do? Also, I've been discovering and reading Iraq war blogs since I found salam pax's site a year and a half ago. Yours is by far the best soldier blog out there. BLinder—art director
ANSWER: The only time that I can think of that we should have done something different was back when we took fire from a mosque. If I was calling the shots, I probably would have surrounded the area around the mosque and dropped a MOAB [mother of all bombs] care package on them the minute we took fire from the mosque. It would have saved us a hell of a lot of ammo if we did that.

QUESTION: My question is about the Strykers. I remember before the war there were a lot of news stories about its armor, whether or not wheels (instead of tracks) was a good idea, etc. Maybe you could give a short "Consumer Reports" like review of the Strykers. How's comfort, road noise, reliability, etc. What's good about it? What would you change on it? Good luck to all you guys. —Jeff North
Huntsville, Alabama
ANSWER: I remember shortly before our deployment here to Iraq, *The Washington Times* printed a huge article on what a piece of overpriced shit the Stryker was and how the armor couldn't protect against anything. Which wasn't really an assuring thing to read prior to coming to Iraq.These people have no idea what the hell they're talking about. Here's the

deal, before deployment, if you would have asked me what I thought about the Stryker, I would have told you: No comment. In fact a lot of soldiers would have told you that. But now that we've been out here and it's been combat tested, and we've seen what it's capable of doing, and how it can withstand anything that's thrown at it, I will never say a negative thing about the Stryker again, ever. In fact, no lie I don't know of a single person in my Brigade who has anything negative to say about the Stryker anymore. Even people I know who hated it and bad-mouthed it every chance they had talk very highly of it now. Yeah, Strykers are kind of an RPG magnet, but it can take a hit, and EVERY vehicle here in Iraq is an RPG magnet. For what we're doing out here, they're perfect, they're extremely mobile, quiet, high speed, the armor works, and it's reliable. People I know who came from a light unit love it, and people who came here from 11Mike world love it. Tracked vehicles suck in urban environments, too slow, too loud, and they always break down. The big advantage with the Stryker is that it's not a tracked vehicle, which allows it to be extremely mobile and fast. Which is what you need here.

List of Improvements:

- The seat cushions suck. It's like sitting on a slab of metal. I would put thicker foam seat cushions.
- The air conditioning sucks. It's like one 5-inch fan. I'm sure if they could design bunker busting missiles, they can design an air conditioning system that works. When it gets too hot, we turn on our NBC fans, and the tube that you hook up to your gas mask with fresh air, you shove that down your shirt or pants. Helps cool you down.
- More electrical outlets. There's only like 4 or 6 outlets

in the Stryker, which is a big problem especially when we're out in the field for any long duration of time. You figure there's like 10 guys in the vehicle, that's at least 10 things that need to be recharged, like portable DVD players, Gameboys, electric razors, MP3 players, Discmans, digital cameras, electric toothbrushes, laptop batteries, crap like that. I would at least add 2 dozen more outlets.

- Loud speaker on the outside of the vehicles. Nothing motivates troops more before a mission than good motivational music. Remember in the movie *Apocalypse Now,* when they had the speakers hooked up to the Air Cav helicopters? Well, we need to do the same goddamn thing with the Strykers.

One time we had this huge joint mission with the Iraqi Civil Police, it was an early morning raid. We all met up at the FOB before the mission. The ICPs all showed up in their Toyota pickup trucks, about a dozen trucks, all jampacked with Iraqi Police. Every pickup truck had a huge Iraqi flag mounted on a pole, and all the ICPs had on brand new police uniforms, AK-47s, and they were all wearing the red and white jihad towels around their heads. It was an awesome sight. They all showed up with this aura of pride that I can't really describe. We had a couple Counter Intelligence guys ride with us on this one, and they brought these loudspeakers with them. They placed the speakers on the outside of the vehicle, and when we'd drive around town sometimes, they'd play this recording in Arabic. I'm not sure exactly what it says, but I think it says something like: Do not be scared, we are Coalition Forces, we come in peace and to help. Do not shoot us, or we will shoot and kill you. That kind of crap. Anyways, while we were driving out the main gate to the FOB to do this joint mission we had the loudspeakers blasting "Ride of the Valkyries," theme song from *The Good, the Bad, and the Ugly,* "The Star-Spangled Banner," and the *Rocky* theme song. It motivated the hell out of us all. In fact, it even motivated the Iraqi Police, I remember looking over at them and they were all getting into it big time.

QUESTION: What can we at home send in the care packages? I have been sending them for years to deployed troops (even before the war, to soldiers stateside). I know all the usual things, but what really excites the troops beyond beef jerky, powdered drink mix, and insect repellent? I went nuts on e-Bay recently and sent my son over 1,000 novelty toys to share with the local kids. I always toss in some 100mph tape, para-cord, foot care items, etc., games and books, but I am looking for some new ideas. Keep up the good work and stay safe. We are so proud of you and your fellow soldiers. —Connie
ANSWER: Sounds like you got the right idea about what to put in care packages, those are all great things to get. What soldiers like to get is the crap you need but don't like spending money on at the PX, like soap, toothpaste, foot powder, that kind of boring stuff. Junk food is also popular. Some soldiers like getting crossword puzzle books. Another popular item in care packages is old magazines. Another good thing to send in care packages (even though it's illegal) is bootlegged music and DVDs. Burned music onto a CD is a good thing to send to soldiers, and everybody loves DVD movies, because once you watch it you can pass it around to others.

QUESTION: Every time I see film of Iraq, I see white cars with orange doors or fenders. What is up with that? I'm talk-

ing about the Iraqi civilian cars. —Dave Hollenbeck
ANSWER: I wondered the same thing too when I got here, it seems like every single car here is white with orange fenders. I asked a terp that question and he told me those are taxi cabs. But I don't think all of them are taxi cabs, because I see a lot of non-cabbies driving them.

QUESTION: I'm glad you set the world straight that your road bound Stryker truck was the burning thin box on rubber tires in *SOF* magazine. While you are dumb and blind in your top-heavy Stryker truck rolling on easily set on fire tires, hiding out in a quiet part of Iraq, 1700+ M113 Gavin tracks rumble all over Iraq with infantry facing outboard ready to fire back. It's obvious which vehicle is the "joke" and which one has the actual "situational awareness" and is combat capable. (Hint: it ain't Stryker and it starts with a G. . . .) —Carol
ANSWER: Thank you for the very intelligent e-mail, "Carol." If you want to believe that the M113 Gavin is better than the Stryker, that's fine. Even Hemingway had critics.

QUESTION: In your opinion as a human being living in the heart of the storm, what is the meaning of life?
Sincerely, Chip
ANSWER: The meaning of life for me right now is to make it back in one piece.

QUESTION: I'm addicted to your blog! The first thing I do every morning is check to see if you put up a new post, whenever you don't post I get extremely worried. Don't take this the wrong way, but what if something happens to you? Like say you get hurt or . . . How would we ever know? Is there any way a family member, friend, or maybe even your

wife could post something up there to let us know just in case? —Nicole
ANSWER: I wasn't really planning on getting hurt or killed out here, so I don't really have a plan of action in case that happens.

YOU GOT MAIL
Subject: Blog
Got an e-mail from someone giving your webpage address and really enjoyed it. I am an 80-year-old vet of WWII, I was a 1st Lt. paratroop infantry, 513th. I enlisted in the NCNG (my father was the regimental commander) at age 15, when I was in 10th grade in HS, in May 1940, when he told the family that the NG would go into federal service in Sept. Served 2 years an enlisted man, OCS, then paratroops. I was severely wounded in the Bulge and spent 3 years in hospitals, a little disabled since. Was fortunate to receive a DSC [Distinguished Service Cross], British Military Cross, Bronze Star, and Purple Heart. Since you wrote a piece about the Stryker, you may be interested to know that I trained one of the two Strykers for whom that vehicle is named; he was in my platoon for two years; I was wounded before the Rhein Jump after which he was killed. Your blog is most interesting. I will come back often. Thanks for what you are doing for the USA; there are a lot of us who really know what you are doing for your country and, indeed, for the world. —Dick Manning,
Mountaintop, PA

Subject: Ever Read Ernie Pyle?
When I read your posts I can't help but think of the late, great Ernie Pyle of WWII fame. I'll bet Ernie's looking down on you and saying, "Damn! I shudda had the Internet!" He's proud of you I'm sure. —Pat

Subject : Thank you
Thank you for your reports. I called the *NY Times* to cancel my subscription. I find your blog more informative (and reliable) than their war coverage. (Since they offered me a half price rate, I kept it for another 6 months . . . just for the features, not the hard news.) Stay safe, thinking of and praying for you guys every day.

HERE'S A COIN
The temperature was way over 100 today and my platoon had a movement to contact patrol scheduled for the afternoon, but my squad leader told me I had to stay back because the Command Sgt. Maj. wanted to talk to me at 1300.

That's not good. That usually means you fucked up and are on your way to an Article 15 (disciplinary action) and some extra duty. I asked my squad leader why the CSM wanted to see me. He told me that he had no idea. I racked my brain on what I could have possibly done wrong out here, then I started getting really nervous. It's a long story (Friday night coke binge, Monday morning drug test), but there was this one time back at Fort Lewis where I was really nervous about this one drug test and I was praying to God that this meeting with the CSM wasn't about the results from that test.

What I found out at 1300 was that the Command Sgt. Maj., who is pretty much the top of the food chain in the NCO ranks here, wanted to present me, as well as a handful of other soldiers in my company, a coin for, as he said, "Going above and beyond what is expected of you out here in Iraq." He said that the platoon selected each and every one of us for this award, because they wanted us to be recognized for all the hard work we've done out here. And he presented each and every one of us a Command Sergeant Major Award Coin (note: a coin is not a big deal, it's not a medal or anything like that; a coin carries the same weight as say, a thank-you card) and shook each and every one of our hands. I thought that was kind of cool.

I've been out here busting my ass doing a thankless job and I'm being recognized for it and thanked by higher. That was a huge morale boost for me today.

> The first quality of a soldier is constancy in enduring fatigue and hardship. Courage is only second. Poverty, privation, and want are the school of the good soldier.
>
> —Napoleon

Posted by CBFTW on July 13, 2004

Learning About Improvised Exploding Devices Is Fun

CJTF-7 OIF Smart Card 4

THE IED AND VBIED THREAT

IEDs (Improvised Explosive Devices) are the largest cause of Coalition injury at current time, and the largest threat that Coalition Forces face. An IED can be almost anything with any type of material and initiator. And vehicles of every imaginable sort can become a vehicle-borne IED.

Common Roadside IED

Common roadside IEDs are explosives, usually an artillery or mortar round(s), placed near the road at the designated kill point. They may be hastily camouflaged with dirt, rocks, trash, or of items that are common along the road. Early in the operations, these devices were command detonated with usually an attack of small-arms fire or RPG rounds.

Emplacement TTPs

1. Camouflaging devices with bags of various types to resemble the garbage along the roadways or burying these devices in the roadbed.

2. Using a decoy device out in the open to slow or stop convoys in the kill zone of the actual device that is obscured along the route of travel.

3. Throwing devices from overpasses or from the roadside in front of approaching vehicles or the middle of convoys; usually done by males of all ages.

4. Emplaced in potholes (covered with dirt).

5. Employed along MSRs [main supply routes] and ASRs [alternate supply routes] targeting convoys.

6. Employed along unimproved roads (targeting patrols).

7. IEDs often used in conjunction with RPG/SA [small arms] fire as a distraction to divert attention of Coalition Forces (create a kill zone for subsequent attacks by RPG/SA fire).

8. VBIEDs used to gain access/close proximity to compounds/buildings.

9. Worn by attacker (suicide vests); possibly employed by women to gain proximity to Coalition Forces.

IEDs can be disguised to look like any object and to function through a multitude of actions. An IED is only limited by the Bomber's imagination and capabilities. IEDs are unpredictable and extremely hazardous to all, including the Bomber.

Remote Control Devices

Remote control devices of every sort are showing up. They include car alarms, key fobs, door bells, remotes for toy cars, garage door openers, cell phones, FRS and GMRS two-way radios.

The adaptation of using radios, cell phones and other remote control devices has given the enemy the standoff ability to watch forces from a distance and not be compromised.

The enemy has continued to improve these techniques, and more sophisticated and destructive devices are being discovered.

Types of Explosives Used

The most common explosives used are military munitions, usually 122-mm or greater mortar/tank/artillery.

- This is the easiest to use since there are so many munitions available in the ITO and they provide a ready made fragmentation effect
- Allows for relatively easy "daisy chaining"

Other types include putting PE4, TNT, or other explosive in container such as oil/paint cans.

Vehicle-Borne IEDs

Vehicle-borne IEDs come in all shapes, colors, and sizes. From a simple passenger car, to a large delivery or sewage truck. There have even been instances of what appeared to be generators, donkey drawn carts, and ambulances used to attempt attacks on Coalition Forces and the New Iraqi Government. To include using vehicles that are familiar to Coalition Forces.

VBIEDs have increasingly used larger amounts of explosives,

and the explosive charge has ranged anywhere from 100 lbs to well over 1000 pounds. And has included things such as mortar rounds, rocket motors, rocket warheads, PE4 explosives, and artillery rounds.

A growing technique is to have multiple vehicles involved. The lead vehicle is used as a decoy or barrier buster, once it has been stopped or neutralized and the Coalition Forces start moving to inspect or detain—the main VBIED comes crashing through and into the crowd and detonates. Thus increasing their casualty ratio.

Service members need to stay alert to signs and indicators to prevent the VBIED from reaching its destination. Of these are fake markings and plates, official symbols in the wrong location, drivers that are not familiar with the vehicle's controls, and drivers that seem to be agitated or lost in their directions.

Key to Defeating the IED Threat

- LET THEM KNOW THAT YOU ARE READY: The enemy is looking for an easy mark. He wants to get away. Show him that you are not an easy target.
- VEHICLE DISPERSION: 75 m to 100 m or greater, makes it more difficult to correctly target the convoy—this results in late or early detonation and the likelihood that the enemy will not get away.
- KNOW THE INDICATORS: Bags, piles of rocks, piles of dirt in or beside the road. If you don't like what you see, trust your instinct, stop, turn around, and go another way. Report observation through the chain of command. Let the experts check it out.
- VARY THE ROUTE AND TIME AND SPEED OF TRAVEL: We know the enemy is watching us and attempting to determine our patterns; make every

attempt to vary this pattern; never take the same route twice in two days. The enemy placed the IED there for a reason, and he is targeting you!

- ALWAYS HAVE FRONT AND REAR SECURITY OUT: Roll up or remove HMMWV/FMTV canvas, so that you can see behind you, and pay attention to where you are going. Determine who has what security responsibilities before you move, face out during movement and constantly scan assigned sectors of fire. Many ambushes are initiated with an RPG shot from the rear.
- REPORT, SECURE AND REDUCE CACHE SITES: The enemy is drawing his supply of explosives from somewhere.
- TRAVEL IN CONVOYS OF 3 OR MORE VEHICLES: The enemy may not detonate the IED if he believes that he will be caught. It is very difficult to successfully attack 3 or more vehicles if they are widely dispersed.
- VEHICLE MODIFICATIONS: Install machinegun mounts and outward facing seats.
- SANDBAG VEHICLES, WEAR IBA AND HELMETS: . . . these actions have saved lives.

Countermeasures

1. Use counter-recon and route security patrols along highly traveled MSRs and other convoy routes. Aggressive patrolling can mitigate the threat; devices have been encountered that the perpetrator had not had time to finish emplacing.

2. While traveling in a convoy, watch the sides of the roads for objects that look out of place and stay alert.

3. Increase the knowledge of Coalition Forces on IED awareness and minimize knowledge of operations to non-Coalition personnel.

4. Assume any manmade object encountered can contain an

IED. Do not drive over or step on sandbags, garbage bags, burlap material, boxes, or garbage in the road while on patrol.

5. Upon discovering an IED, assume it can be remote detonated. Be aware of any suspicious individuals in the area and secure a safe distance around the device.

6. IEDs have been found that were targeting vehicles traveling in either the left or right lanes on the highways; drive aggressively and keep vigilance when driving for the above mentioned objects.

7. IEDs currently used to target an initial Coalition activity (ex: convoy or patrol); future incidents could target a secondary activity (ex: first responders—MPs, EOD) as the devices and employment TTPs gain complexity.

CAR BOMB

Last night a car bomb was discovered along a busy freeway here in Mosul. My platoon was placed on QRF while 3rd Platoon rolled out to secure the area and blow the thing up.

Car bombs are starting to become a very popular thing here in Mosul. The car bombs in Iraq are not like the car bombs you see in the movies, where they just blow up and the car just catches on fire. The psychopaths who are making these things have got the art of car bomb making down to a fucking science, where they can produce the highest amount of casualties and damage humanly possible. It's mind blowing the amount of damage one single car bomb can do.

When they go off there will literally be nothing left of the VBIED, there'll be a huge hole in the street where the car once was. The explosions create these huge mushroom clouds of dust that can be seen miles away and the cars that were around it will all be thrown on their backs, and windows in buildings blocks away will be shattered from the concussion of the blast.

We like the cars, the cars that go boom.
—Some rap song in the eighties

Posted by CBFTW on July 18, 2004

ANOTHER DAMN CAR BOMB
At 0330 last night I woke up to a very loud explosion. At first I thought it was another bad dream, but my roommate also heard it and woke up and said, "Hey, did you hear that?!" Yeah, I told him. We stayed up for a couple minutes silently after that, wondering what the hell was that, and then we both went back to sleep. We later found out that it was an IED.

This morning we all went to breakfast and when we returned I took my weekly dose of anti-malaria medication and went to my room. Shortly after that, Sgt. L banged on my door and said that our platoon just got placed on QRF (Quick Reaction Force) and to stand by and be ready to go at any minute, today might be another 24th of June (that was the day of the Mohammed Al Noory Mosque/Sheikh Fatih police attack). The main gate to the airfield to our FOB just got hit by a vehicle-borne IED (car bomb) and there's mass casualties.

The vehicle-borne IED was a Toyota pickup with a female driver.

The airfield here also got mortared several times today.

Posted by CBFTW at 8:11 p.m., July 26, 2004

AND ANOTHER DAMN CAR BOMB
I'm getting pretty good at guessing just from the noise an explosion makes if it was a mortar impact, vehicle-borne IED, or a controlled detonation. This morning I went to

breakfast at the chow hall. Had the usual—eggs, sausage, side of bacon. And as I was leaving the chow hall with my morning dose of coffee in my hand, I heard a loud explosion off in the distance and observed a huge cloud of dust. I thought to myself, damn, that was probably a car bomb. Guess what? It was.

Posted by CBFTW at 9:53 a.m., August 2, 2004

Sandbagging It

When we got to the Middle East we spent the first month in Kuwait, at Camp Udari. I was one of the lucky ones that got selected to do the backbreaking detail of filling up sandbags to line all the floors of the Humvees and trucks.

To this day I cringe in pain whenever I think about that detail. Hours and hours of filling up sandbags in the Kuwait sun and placing them on the floors of Humvees and LMTVs, cursing my recruiter the whole time. (This wasn't in the brochure!) We were lining the bottoms of the vehicles with sandbags so that when they got hit by an IED, the sandbags would absorb some of the concussion and shrapnel.

Months later when my unit was sent to Mosul to replace the 101st Airborne Division, I was doing gate guard duty at one of the main gates to the FOB, and the engineers were driving their huge trucks in through our gate. One of the trucks was carrying what I thought was a huge chunk of charred scrap metal. When I took a closer look at what they were dragging in I made out what looked to be a frame of a Humvee. I later found out that the engineers were dragging in the remains of a Humvee that belonged to the 101st that had been hit by an IED earlier in the day.

I thought to myself, Damn, all those hours spent filling up those damned sandbags were for absolutely nothing.

CLEANING UP THE STREETS OF MOSUL

An IED sweep is a mission where we roll out with the combat engineers and sweep the filthy streets of Mosul clean of Improvised Exploding Devices.

Here's how an IED sweep works:

The combat engineer's job is to find the IED and once it is located, defuse it, or better yet blow it up, and our job as 11 Bang-Bangs is to tag along behind them, usually several hundred meters behind them, provide security, and to be there as a Reaction Force in case they come into contact. If they do come into contact, we're there to come up and flank the assaulting force, and kick the shit out of whoever is fucking with the combat engineers.

We usually do these IED sweep missions bright and early in the morning, and we'll usually drive around the main supply routes here and there in Mosul looking for them, usually for a couple hours at a time, while the combat engineers search until they find an IED, or one physically blows up on them, which is, I guess, one way of finding an IED here in Iraq.

The combat engineers roll out with two Stryker vehicles, a Humvee, and a 22-ton six-wheeled vehicle that's twenty-seven-feet long, heavily armored, and looks like something out of the first *Star Wars* movie, called a "Buffalo."

These Buffaloes are pretty much indestructible, but they look extremely awkward, and if you don't know what it is and what it does I guess it looks like a target, and thus the anti-Iraqi forces always try to hit it.

Today was a successful IED sweep; we found three rocket launchers, two with rockets in them. We found them right there on the side of the road, not even hidden, just lying in

front of a playground. We stopped our vehicles and pulled 360 security around the area and had the combat engineers blow them up with some explosives.

Whenever UXO is put in plain view like that, it might be a lure for an ambush. Like that one time we found a bunch of artillery rounds sitting over by the traffic circle, just sitting there, and while we were waiting for EOD to show up, somebody decided to fire an RPG at one of our Strykers.

Posted by CBFTW at 5:07 P.M., July 14, 2004

Care Package

My wife sent me a care package for my birthday. Inside was a scrapbook that she made me which had a bunch of little cut-up photos of me and her together over the last couple years, and next to each photo she wrote a brief message about why she loved me. But the best items in the care package were the two smuggled twenty-two-ounce bottles of Guinness beer.

So on my birthday, July 17, I gave one of the beers to Sgt. Horrocks, and we turned the light off to our room, locked the door to our conex, and slowly drank them together. It was like we were both thirteen again and we were drinking beers that we stole from our father's stash. The beer was the first we'd had in a long time, and both of us just sat there, fully enjoying every little swig and making a comment about how good it tasted every time we did so.

It brought back a lot of good memories of when we were drinking buddies back at Fort Lewis, and we'd go out every weekend to bars in Olympia and Seattle and we'd both get completely trashed. Fun times.

About halfway through the beer, Horrocks asked me,

"Hey man, are you feeling it?"

"Dude, I think I am man."

He started laughing and said, "Me too, dude!"

We both laughed.

Then I made the joke that maybe we should take it easy because if we slammed the rest of it, maybe we'd get all drunk and start getting wild and start breaking shit in our conex room and start tossing things around for the hell of it.

We then finished the beers, and I threw the bottles away in the dumpster located over by the National Guard conexes across the street from us, and when I came back I went to bed.

And that was probably the best birthday, and beer, I've ever had.

"MASSEM?"

Today my squad had gate guard duty.

My platoon had a countermortar observation post up on OP Abrams to attend during the afternoon. My squad on the other hand lucked out and had gate guard duty. When the guys exited our gate they all cursed at us and flipped us off as they drove by. We all just waved and smiled at them. Suckers. They were just jealous that they didn't have gate guard, instead of an OP. I don't blame them, anything is better than an OP. We have a lot of Iraqis working on our FOB, building shit and doing stuff. We had an Iraqi come up to us in the heat of the afternoon with two large bags of ice. With a smile he said that he wanted to help us, because we were helping them. That was very cool of him.

Pfc. Evans and I ripped open one of the bags of ice and started cooling ourselves off with it, rubbing our foreheads with it and stuff. Pfc. Evans then looked over at me and said, "Damn, that was the nicest thing I've heard from an Iraqi the whole time I've been here."

Later on in the afternoon, another Iraqi contractor came up to our gate and kept on saying, "Massem? Massem?"

What the hell is "Massem"?

After a couple minutes of trying to figure out what the hell "Massem" was, we finally realized that he was asking us if we had a *Maxim* magazine.

Every Stryker pretty much has a *Maxim* inside of it, it's like required reading or something here in the Stryker Brigade. The ceilings of some of the Strykers are actually covered in pinup girls from *Maxim*. So we lent him the latest issue, and he just sat there turning the pages with an ear-to-ear smile, wide-eyed and saying, "Good! Good!" every time there was a photo of some girl in skimpy underwear looking all sexy. After flipping through the *Maxim*, he handed it back to us, thanked us, and walked off.

Happy.

Posted by CBFTW at 4:01 P.M., July 20, 2004

Money

Spc. Callahan, one of my good ol' drinking buddies back at Fort Lewis, posted on a website an ad saying that he was a soldier in Iraq in need of booze. First he asked his mom, dad, family, girlfriend, and friends if they could hook him up, but none of them would comply. Within twenty-four hours Callahan received two responses. He e-mailed his address to them and told them all about how he was stop-lossed, got his leave canceled, and was having problems with his girlfriend, and a shipment of booze would really raise his morale and all of his buddies' morale as well, too, because by this time, none of us had had a drink in like seven months (except for the beer that me and Horrocks shared).

One of the guys that e-mailed him back was an old-school punker from back in the early eighties and from the way he talked, it seemed like he was pretty well-off financially because Callahan offered to send him money for the bottles but he insisted that money was no problem.

A few weeks went by and Callahan received a care package from the guy, and it was bottles of Bacardi, vodka, tequila, and whiskey. And not the cheap shit, either, the expensive good shit.

So the night that Callahan received this care package, he came over to my room and whispered (because he didn't want Sgt. Horrocks to know about this) that he was having a party in his room tonight, and it was just him, Sgt. Vance, and me. At the time our platoon was having a weeklong rotation of Force Protection, which was just to pull six-hour tower-guard shifts, each squad pulling a shift, and we didn't have to go out on any missions the next day, so I figured why not, how much harm could one drink do? I told him I didn't want to get wasted, or get into any trouble, and that I would stop by just to hang out and have a drink, maybe two.

When I later stopped by Callahan's conex, in my PT uniform, and I knocked on his door, he unlocked it and let me in. They were playing a Social Distortion CD (*Prison Bound*), and Callahan and Vance both had on civilian T-shirts of random punk bands, and they were both passing around the bottle and smoking.

I was extremely hesitant to take a sip, because getting busted drinking in Iraq is like a capital offense. So I debated whether or not to even take a sip. After a few minutes, I said, "Fuck it." Callahan handed me a bottle and I took a small sip, and it instantly warmed me up, and my exact quote was, "Man, that feels so good, especially once it hits your lips." (I was quoting Will Ferrell from *Old School*.) After that first sip, that was it, I kept on taking sips, and was all for chugging as much as possible. All three of us polished off a bottle and then some, and we then decided to step outside, feeling extremely tipsy, but I didn't think I was drunk at this point. All three of us then sat down on these plastic lawn chairs, lit up our smokes, and started talking about the stuff that we usually talked about when we were all together—punk shows, the bar-room brawls we got ourselves involved in back in Washington, and all the things that we were all planning on doing once we got back to the States.

While we were outside we had Social Distortion blasting from Sgt. Vance's CD player from inside his room. A sergeant from 3rd Platoon then walked over to us and asked us how we were doing and was telling us a story about how he saw Social Distortion play at the Roxy back in the day. I tried to talk to him about the Roxy, one of my favorite clubs in Los Angeles, but I found that I was inadvertently slurring all my words as I tried to do this. Sgt. Vance walked over to me and advised me to go to my room. That's all I remember after that.

The next day I woke up in my bed with a throbbing headache and extremely thirsty for some ice water, and I noticed that my shoes were still on my feet. That scared the shit out of me, because I never go to bed with my boots on and I couldn't remember a damn thing about the night before.

As I was slowly waking up and coming to, Sgt. Horrocks started to wake up as well, and from his bed he said, "Dude, you're a fucking idiot!" That also wasn't a good sign, definitely something that I didn't want to hear after a night like that.

I didn't want to know why, but I asked him anyway, and he said, "Dude, you don't remember what you did last night?" I told him no, not really, I remember I went to Vance's room for a couple drinks, but I don't really remember much after that.

He then filled me in on what happened. I guess after Sgt.

Vance told me to go to my room, I tried to make my way to my room, and Sgt. Horrocks was on his way to the latrine, and he saw me swaying and hardly able to stand up straight, and he told me to go to my room before First Sergeant catches me walking around like a skid-row bum. He then told me that I told him to "Fuck off," and that I didn't care if First Sergeant found me drunk, and in fact I was going to run over to First Sergeant's room, bang on his door, show him that I was drunk, and tell him how "money" I was (to use a reference to *Swingers*, a favorite movie that was passed around the barracks a lot).

I then told Horrocks, "Bullshit man, you're lying, I wasn't going to bang on First Sergeant's door and tell him how money I am, no way."

He then told me that I really did try to do that, and it took a couple soldiers to restrain me and get me into my room, and the whole time I was yelling how "money" I was.

Now I was completely embarrassed, because I didn't remember a damn thing about it.

Horrocks then chewed me out for being a retard, and he was also a little bit hurt that he wasn't invited to the party.

My guard-tower shift wasn't till 1300, so I laid around in bed and tried to sleep it off the best I could till it was time to show up. When Spc. Cannon and I showed up to Guard Tower 16 to relieve Sgt. Vance and Spc. Callahan, they both greeted me with a huge smile and jokingly asked me how I was feeling today. I told them I felt fine, and I also apologized for the night before. They both said that it was no problem and then left the guard tower to go back to their rooms to sleep. Spc. Cannon and I both then sat down and began our shift.

I lit up a smoke and looked over at one of the walls inside the tower and noticed that somebody had written the words "Buzzell is a Lightweight!"

Bastards.

Continue to Monitor the Situation, Over

Each guard tower has a radio, and every hour, each tower must do a radio check with "Front Line Yankee."

Example:

Front Line Yankee, this is tower one six, radio check, over?

Then Front Line Yankee calls back over the radio and says something like, "Tower one six, this is Front Line Yankee, read you Lima Charlie, over." (Lima Charlie is military jargon for loud and clear.)

And also, if you see anything suspicious going on from your guard tower, you're supposed to call it in to Front Line Yankee.

The following is an actual radio transmission that happened out on tower guard duty, as told to me by Spc. Callahan:

"Frontline Yankee, this is Tower—[hesitation in the female's voice], I think I see guys setting up mortar tubes on a roof, over."

"Tower—, this is Front Line Yankee, can you tell me if they have weapons, and can you positively identify a mortar tube? Over."

"Front Line Yankee, this is Tower—, negative, I can't tell if that's a mortar tube or what, and they don't have AKs, over."

"Tower—, this is Front Line Yankee, continue to monitor the situation, over."

"Front Line Yankee, this is Tower—, roger, out."

[Ten seconds go by.]

"Front Line Yankee, this is Tower—, roger, it's definitely a mortar tube. I can see them shooting onto our FOB. Time: now, over."

[Explosions from mortars hitting our FOB.]

"Tower—, this is Front Line Yankee, have you engaged the mortarmen, over?" [More explosions from mortars hitting our FOB in the background.]

"Front Line Yankee, this is Tower— [shocked, like, you want me to shoot?], umm, that's a negative, over." [Explosions from mortars hitting out FOB in the background.]

"Tower—, this is Front Line Yankee, roger, do you have positive ID on the target, over?"

"Front Line Yankee, this is Tower—, they're packed up, and they're gone now, over."

> Hey, 296, if you see a Hajji setting up a mortar tube could you please shoot them? I would like not to be mortared on the way to chow hall. Thank you.
> —Graffiti in a port-a-shitter stall over by the chow hall

STRYKER SOLDIERS HAVE SMALL DICKS

I feel like Matt Drudge right now reporting a Joe rumor on the blog that I heard on "Joe Radio" (Joe Radio is what we call the rumor mill here in the Army), but this is a humorous Joe rumor.

Every couple months, the Army does a mandatory drug test, even out here in Iraq. We've had several of them out here so far. Well, the rumor that's circulating around the conexes is that there's a memo being passed around the chain of command that says, "Stryker Brigade Soldiers Have Small Dicks," and the rumor is that higher just received the results from the last drug test and it looks like a lot of soldiers in my brigade have been taking penis-enlargement pills. And those pills showed up on a lot of soldiers' last drug test results. Not that I have ever looked into it, but as far as I know, penis-enlargement pills are not in violation of any Army policy or reg.

Story developing . . .

Posted by CBFTW at 8:39 p.m., July 22, 2004

BLOWING SHIT UP BECAUSE IT'S FUN

> If it's natural to kill, why do men have to go into training to learn how?
>
> —Joan Baez

Today we drove out to the range to fire our weapons and blow shit up with some explosives. Once we got to the range, which was way the fuck out in the middle of nowhere, we had our platoon sergeant teach us a class on explosives.

Like almost every guy I've ever met in the Army who's demo qualified, my platoon sergeant loves to blow shit up, it like gives him a hard-on or something. He taught us all a class on C4 explosives, breaching, and how to blow up a bridge and/or house with some det cord and some C4.

It was a cool class. Timothy McVeigh would have liked it. I even got to play around with some explosives. I got several sticks of C4, cut them into smaller squares, got some det cord, and made some charges. Felt kinda like arts and crafts class.

The ranges in Iraq are not like the ones back home. They're a little bit more "liberal" here. On the range was a small abandoned cement brick house that looked half dead, so we decided to place a charge inside each corner of the small house, and I was the lucky guy that got to pull the charge and blow the house up. That was awesome. Everybody stood around with digital cameras getting footage of the explosion. That was the first time I ever blew a house up with some C4. We also got to shoot our AT4 anti-tank rockets, fire the .50 cals, and throw some hand grenades around. Always training here in the Army, even during combat deployments.

At the range there were six Iraqi guys about a hundred meters away from us just chilling on a small ridge watching us shoot and blow shit up the entire time. Once we boarded our vehicles and left the range they all got up and ran around the range picking up all the brass shell casings like they were hundred-dollar bills.

They sell the brass downtown, and they melt the brass to make pots and pans and shit like that. Right after that my squad had gate guard where nothing eventful happened. Airfield got mortared today, that's pretty much it.

Posted by CBFTW on July 23, 2004

COMBAT ZONE PT TESTS

Had another late night mission last night. This time I stayed away from the stimulants. We went out, did our shit, and then came back early in the morning. We all got three hours of sleep, then rolled right back out.

Even though we're deployed in a "combat zone" we still do a lot of the same bullshit that we do in the rear. Like we even do PT tests out here. A PT test in the Army is a timed two-mile run, push-ups and sit-ups, timed, two minutes, do as many as you can, to see how good shape you're in. Do you think the guys in Nam took PT tests?

But then again, maybe the guys in Vietnam didn't have to take PT tests, because if you look at all those old black-and-white photos of the guys that were there in the shit during Vietnam, they all looked extremely skinny and rugged and physically exhausted. And then you look at some of the photos of the soldiers coming out of this war, and a lot of the soldiers you'll see are like these fat fucks with pot bellies and blubber butts. Like a lot of the National Guard guys that I see walking around on FOB Marez, it's like that's all they do here is hang out at the chow hall and try to see how fat they can get.

It's totally embarrassing to the uniform.

So maybe it is a good thing we have PT tests.

Posted by CBFTW on July 23, 2004

LIQUOR STORE

We had a patrol bright and early this morning. It was in a neighborhood way the fuck out there, on the other side of the river. We've never been to this neighborhood before, so it was a nice change of scenery for us.

On the way to this location we drove past a couple white guys in multi-colored spandex bicycle clothes, riding along the side of the freeway on their ten-speeds. I did a double take at them and looked over at Sgt. Williams, who was in the air-guard hatch next to me, and said, "Holy shit! Did you just see what I just saw?!" He said yeah, and told me that it must have been some Delta Force guys or something getting some PT done. Weird.

We had to scope this neighborhood out for an upcoming raid, so we parked our vehicles in this field that was covered in garbage and had some filthy dirty ducks walking around in it, and dismounted the guys. I stayed up in the vehicle as the rest of the dismounts in the platoon took off to go check things out.

I noticed something bizarre.

The women in our AO that we patrol through on a daily basis usually wear the traditional dresses with scarves around their heads, and they hardly ever make eye contact with you, and when they walk they usually look straight down or not at you. In this neck of the woods, a majority of the women didn't wear any of that stuff. In fact all the women here wore T-shirts and summer pants and sandals.

These women were extremely friendly, almost too friendly, it was like they were flirting with us. They'd all smile and wave like crazy at us as we drove up. After about thirty minutes of sitting in that field, watching the ducks eat some of the trash that was scattered on the ground, we got the call to go meet up with the rest of the platoon that was located down the street. On the way there I noticed a little liquor store on a street corner. (!!!!) I've NEVER seen a liquor store here in Iraq before, ever.

The outside of the liquor store had several beer advertisements of European brands I've never even heard of. I had to do a double take to make sure I was seeing what I was seeing. The shop owner in the store saw my wide-eyed reaction and he chuckled.

It seems like every street in Mosul that has shops usually has a store that sells tombstones. There's a high death rate here, so the cemeteries here are huge, and the demand for tombstones is high.

Well, a couple shops away from the liquor store was a small tombstone shop, and on a couple of the tombstones outside the shop were bright red engravings of a Christian cross. Then I pieced it all together and I realized that we were in the Christian neighborhood of Mosul. I've heard about this place, but we've never been here.

When we stopped the vehicles to pick up the rest of the guys in the platoon, Sgt. Horrocks was telling me how the most beautiful Iraqi girl he's ever seen was flirting with him. I didn't believe him, and he told me to ask our interpreter, and "Zee" told me that it was true, that many of the women in this neighborhood liked the American soldiers.

We then drove around for a bit, and drove off back to FOB Marez.

As we were driving away from this neighborhood a bunch of little kids chased us, waving, smiling, and cheering.

Posted by CBFTW at 2:48 p.m., July 25, 2004.

THANKS, BUT NO THANKS

In a brief bout with insanity I thought about extending my tour out here. The Army has my ass stop-lossed till the end of February '05, and we're supposed to be back at Fort Lewis around the holidays, November '04. Even if we do get back by Thanksgiving, I'm still in the Army till 28 February 05.

I've spoken before several times to our recruiting NCO about reenlisting, because I haven't decided yet what exactly I want to do when I get out of the Army, and to be on the safe side, I thought maybe I'd look into the Reserves, just to hear them out, see what they're all about and if you do twenty years with the Reserves you can get retirement checks. The recruiting NCO broke it down to me that he could get me into a reserve unit, but with the way this war is, they're calling up every single National Guard unit to pick up shifts out here, I'd probably be coming right back to Iraq. So I said "later" on that idea.

The Army is hurting really bad for soldiers right now. They have all sorts of crazy reenlistment plans and programs going on to entice soldiers to reenlist or extend. One of them is extending for another one-year tour out here with the guys that are replacing us.

Rumor has it that you get an extra tax-free grand a month if you do.

I wouldn't do another year here for an extra thirty grand a month, tax-free. They asked me, Well, what plans do you have for when you get out of the Army? Do you know how hard it is finding a job now? I honestly have no idea what the fuck I'm going to do when I get out, but one of my favorite movies is *Taxi Driver* with De Niro, so I told them I thought about maybe being a cabdriver in NYC, maybe for some veterans cab association or something, grow my hair out, wear my field jacket with my Combat Infantry Badge sewn on it, drive around the bad parts of NYC with a fully-loaded Glock in the glove box, chill out, etc.

A lot of the cabbies in America speak Arabic, so maybe I could be down with them and shit.

They looked at me crazy and told me good luck.

But now they have a thing where you can extend for an extra three months doing something with some big shot and they'll give you an extra grand a month. I thought, what's an extra three months? I'm in the Army till February 2005 anyways, might as well get an extra three months of tax-free combat pay to go along with that extra grand thrown on top, and maybe if I extend they can guarantee me a leave slot so that I can go back home and see my wife. So just out of curiosity I flirted with the idea of extending and went to find out more about what exactly the job was.

Sgt. Blough (who reenlisted in theater) was the guy who put the word out to us about this program, so I went up to him and I told him that I might be interested in that, and asked if there was any more info on it, and he told me, "Oh, we need people to drive around town in a Humvee and . . . ." Stop right there, I said, no need to tell me any more, I'm not interested, all you had to say was Humvee. I've seen way too many blown-up Humvees out here.

I don't know how the hell those guys can do it, like the MPs and shit. Anybody who drives around Iraq in a Humvee, even a so-called "up-armored Humvee," should get like a special medal or something. I remember how nerve-racking that was driving through Baghdad in the back of First Sergeant's Humvee on our convoy up here from Kuwait. The whole time I was like, Please God, don't let us get RPG'd or IED'd, I swear to God I'll never jerk off again for the rest of my life.

In the Strykers we operate out of now, an IED feels like a speed bump, and we have pretty good armor to protect us from RPGs and those rockets they like to fire at us, and I feel relatively safe driving through Iraq in the back of one. But driving around Mosul in the back of a Humvee would be like Russian roulette.

Posted by CBFTW on July 25, 2004

I'M NOT EVEN SUPPOSED TO BE HERE TODAY

Last night at around 0100, I was at the Internet cafe, right about to check my e-mail, when a sergeant stormed into the Internet cafe and yelled that everybody was to report back to their squad leaders and back to their rooms, time: NOW.

So I logged off and went back to my room, and checked in with my squad leader. I asked him what the hell was going on and he told me that they wanted to get 100% accountability on everybody because, they don't know if it's true or not, but there was a report that three US military personnel were just taken hostage, and they wanted to make sure it wasn't any of us.

These next couple of weeks are going to be a little bit hard for me. Today was the day I was supposed to be on a plane to go be with my wife during my two weeks of mid-tour leave, so morale is kinda low. After surprisingly granting me leave, they canceled it, something to do with stop-loss, they say I might still get to go home, maybe, but I'm on the bottom of the list with the rest of the guys who are stop-lossed, and there's a bunch of people in front of me.

This sucks, all day today I was thinking, damn, I could have been on a fucking plane right now, getting sloppy drunk on airline drinks until the stewardess cut me off, and on my way home to be with my wife who I haven't seen in almost 10 months. The last time I saw her was at the SeaTac airport right before I left for Kuwait. I remember exactly what she was wearing and everything. It was weird today, all day I was thinking in the back of my mind that if I was going to get hurt, it would be on a day that I wasn't even supposed to be here.

It's like that Kevin Smith movie, *Clerks,* where the guy has to work on his day off and all that crazy shit happens and he keeps on saying, "I'm not even supposed to be here today." And you think about the guys from the 101st who were on their way to go home on leave on a helicopter and right when they left the airfield, they shot the helicopter down, and all the guys died. The guys that got IED'd on the way to the airport to go on R&R. The other day at finance, the guy in line in front of me told me that this guy was going home on leave and the day before he was supposed to go a mortar killed him, or that civilian contractor who got killed and had his letter of resignation and plane ticket literally on him. The guy that got the Red Cross message and was able to go home on emergency leave, but stayed here with his men instead and died a couple days later. I could go on and on with stories that I've heard, of people getting waxed the day before they were supposed to leave or on a day they were here instead of there. I'm not superstitious or anything like that, but it kinda fucks with your head when you start thinking what-if type scenarios.

If this was Vietnam, I'd probably have FTA (Fuck the Army) inked in black pen all huge on my helmet in protest of having my leave canceled, but since this isn't Vietnam, I decided to put a black and white peace pin on my flak jacket in "peaceful" protest of getting my leave canceled instead. I bought the pin at a head shop on Haight Street the last time I was in San Francisco, and I brought it with me here to Iraq, but haven't worn it yet because I haven't yet found an appropriate time to pin it on till now. It's the exact same pin that Private Joker wore in the Vietnam movie *Full Metal Jacket.*

As soon as I walked over to the motor pool with my machine gun slung over my shoulders like I always carry it to the motor pool, my squad leader, who's an ex-marine, said, "Is that some kind of sick joke?"

He saw the humor in it, and didn't tell me to take it off, which kinda surprised me. Of course everybody who saw the pin on me before the mission today came up to me and started spitting lines out of *Full Metal Jacket.*

> Well I'm in another state, another state of mind, / I wish that I could be there right next to her / This road leads to this, this one leads to that, / Her voice sends shivers down my spine. These scars in my flesh, / I'm bruised and I'm bloodied / Only she knows the pain that I've been thru. / Talk to her a thousand miles away, / There's tears in her eyes. / If I make it back I'm gonna show her, / she's the only one for me.
>
> —"Another State of Mind," Mike Ness, Social Distortion

Posted by CBFTW at 10:28 p.m., July 27, 2004

WAR IS HELL

I had to pull radio watch in the War Room last night, which is our conference room where the war gets planned, and somebody left a copy of an April edition of *People* magazine there. I read how *Survivor*'s Rob and Amber are in love, Kelly Osbourne is in rehab, Omarosa has a surprising past, and Reese Witherspoon and hubby Ryan Phillippe bought a house in Los Angeles for $4.9 million.

And for a split second, I was actually glad I was here in Iraq.

Posted by CBFTW on July 13, 2004

I DON'T WANT TO LIVE ALONE

The entire time I've been here, I've been behind an M240 Bravo machine gun. On raids my job is to cover my platoon's ass while they assault the target house. If all hell breaks loose I'm there to provide a rain of 7.62 cover fire. I have an AG and AB working with me. The assistant gunner's job is to be my second set of eyes and to point out targets to me, tell me rates of fire, sectors of fire, etc. He carries the tripod, spare barrels, and a shitload of ammo. My ammo bearer's job is to carry a chunk of my ammo, and he pulls rear security on my gun position, makes sure nobody sneaks up behind me and shoots me in the back. For this raid, one of the line squads (3rd Squad) was missing a guy due to leave (lucky bastard), so they handed me an M4 rifle and placed me with a line squad with a bunch of trigger pullers, and put my AG behind the M240. I requested a shotgun for this raid. Request: denied.

So they moved me over to 3rd Squad, which was totally fine with me because I was pretty good friends with almost everybody in that squad. I was a lot closer to them than I was to the guys in my own squad.

Sgt. Vance and I were extremely close. We were pretty good friends and hung out together prior to deployment, but we really bonded once we got here. Every night, we'd hang out, either in his room or mine. And because of Sgt. Vance I was close friends with Spc. Callahan. They had been stationed together in Germany prior to both coming to Fort Lewis. So since I hung out with Vance a lot, I hung out with Callahan a lot, too, and we became sort of a clique.

We all had similar interests, listened to the same music.

For this raid, our team would be Sgt. Vance (team leader), Spc. Callahan, and me.

The best way to describe a raid to somebody who knows nothing about these sorts of things is, in a nutshell: We show up, surround the house, blow the fuckin' front door up with explosives, or knock it down with a battering ram, storm into the house, throw a bunch of flash bang grenades around, apprehend the target individual or individuals, blindfold them and zip tie 'em, search the house, throw the detainees in the back of the vehicles, drive off, and take them in for questioning and/or a one-way, all-expenses-paid trip to beautiful Guantanamo Bay, Cuba. Badda bing, badda boom.

We received a warning order for this raid yesterday, and today we received the OP order. This one was a pretty big mission, with a very high profile target. The guy that we are to apprehend is supposedly the mastermind behind all the attacks that happened in Mosul on the day we attacked that mosque.

So after dinner chow, we performed rehearsals. That's where we all get together and practice the raid as a team to prevent any possible confusion and make sure everybody is 100% on the same page on what each person's job is. We go over the raid countless times and through multiple scenarios.

I never take uppers like caffeine pills, Hydroxycuts, Ripped Fuels, Red Bulls, or any of that heart attack crap before a raid, because as soon as you show up to the target house and that ramp drops and you dismount from the back of the vehicle, your heart is going a thousand rpm's and you're wide awake from the adrenaline. You have no idea what the hell you're about to get yourself into, how chaotic it's going to be, if the house is booby trapped, how many people are armed in the house, how hostile the situation is going to be, if the target individual is in the house, or even if you're going to enter the right fucking house.

Before the raid, you do a personal PCI (pre-combat inspection) on all your gear. Make sure everything is up to standard. Check your NODs, make sure they have fully charged batteries. Make sure you have a full combat load of ammo (I always pack a little bit more). Clean your weapon, oil the bolt, tie down all your sensitive items, and perform function checks. You go over the OP order in your head until it's memorized. Your squad leader will come over and double, triple check your shit, to make sure that everything is up to standard, and quiz you on the OP order.

Horrocks and I will usually brew up a nice pot of gourmet PX-bought coffee before we roll out on night missions. Horrocks will usually blast a CD of Sgt. Barry Sadler's "Ballad of the Green Berets" to get pumped up and I usually like to listen to mellow music before a raid on my iPod while I'm doing PCIs on my equipment in my room. Today the soundtrack was the Cure, the Smiths, and a little bit of the old school U2, and then shortly before we go out on the mission, I'll switch it over to the "Stryker Soundtrack" and blast some of that for a while.

This was to be a pretty cool raid. Second Platoon would be the main effort for this raid and the squad I was placed in, 3rd Squad, was to be the assault team once the front door was taken down by another squad. Since I'm kind of a big guy, my job was to carry the fifty-pound battering ram.

Anyway, it was at night when we arrived at the target individual's neighborhood and the target house was in a way old-school neighborhood, a lot of the buildings looked like they were from ancient biblical times, which they probably were. Way cool. We crept silently through the dark shadows in these really narrow mazed alleys for almost a half hour before we finally located the target house. My shoulders were killing me from carrying the battering ram, but I didn't care at all about that, I was psyched that I was with Vance and Callahan and this was my first raid going in with them as an assault team and I was pumped. As we prowled silently through these narrow alleys, I could hear the faint buzzing of a Predator unmanned reconnaissance plane flying far up above as well as people inside their houses watching TV and talking to each other in Arabic as we passed them, totally unaware that we were outside creeping around in the dark like strangers in the night. We communicated to each other with soft whispers and hand signals. We finally found the house, and quickly stacked outside the main door, and once that door was taken down, we stormed in there as fast as we could, weapons up, Sgt. Vance went in first, then Spc. Callahan, and then me. The rest of the platoon followed. As soon as we entered the house, the attack helicopters showed up out of nowhere.

The trick to clearing rooms is Violence of Action. Once you commit and you're going in the building on a raid, there's no going back and you go all out, which is something Sgt. Vance always stressed to me. And you want to be quick and forceful so they don't have time to react to a damn thing. These people never knew what hit them. We busted in when they were sleeping. Scared the living shit out of them. Half a dozen little kids, a woman in traditional black Arabic clothing, and the target individual, all sleeping on the ground in the outdoor part of the house. The kids were screaming in fear and crying and so was the lady, who was probably the guy's wife and the kids' mother. We separated the target individual in another room, tied his hands with a plastic zip tie, and put a blindfold on him. Had our platoon leader and interpreter question him as we searched the house for hidden weapons. We had a bunch of people with us searching and investigating the house with all sorts of crazy toys that would make the guys on that TV show *CSI* jealous. One of these items was a "vapor sniffer," which can detect if you have handled explosives and exactly what kind of explosives you have been around. Say you played around with a bunch of dynamite a couple days ago and washed your hands several times since, the vapor sniffer could still detect the explosives. They put the vapor sniffer up to the target individual's hands, he had no idea what the hell was going on, and the test results showed that he came up positive for several types of explosives. So we had our guy.

There were tons of fucking cockroaches crawling around in this house, and all over the cement walls. These people lived like Gandhi, they hardly owned any worldly possessions at all, no TV, no futon, no stereo, nothing. All this dusty old house had inside of it was tubs of rice, a small foam mattress that lay on the dirty cement floor, and a small dresser drawer. That's it. Once we got our guy and finished searching the house, we left. On the way out, I walked past the kids and the Iraqi lady who was now hysterically hitting herself in the chest repeatedly and sobbing something in Arabic out loud. I asked the interpreter what the hell she was saying, and he listened to her for a second, and then told me that she was saying, "Don't take him away!" and "I don't want to live alone!" that sort of stuff, over and over again.

I felt sorrow for that lady and her kids, and wonder what's going to happen to them now. But this guy that we got was a real piece of shit, killed a shitload of innocent people, and their families are forever changed and a lot of Iraqi people are spending the rest of their lives alone because of this scumbag. Bottom line is Iraq is now a way safer place now that he's off the streets. But regardless, you still feel kinda sorry for the lady and the kids, and wonder what the hell is going to happen to them now.

> We sleep safe in our beds because rough men stand ready in the night to visit violence on those who would do us harm.
>
> —George Orwell

Posted by CBFTW at 2:05 p.m., July 29, 2004

ONE ENEMY KIA

On Pvt. Malcolm's wall, by his bed, he has an 8 × 10 photograph of his family farm in the Midwest, and a bunch of inspirational quotes from the Bible taped up next to it.

He's been in the Army just as long as I have, but he's been cursed and damned with bad luck the entire time, getting kicked out of this squad and that squad, which is why he's still a private. In fact the first time I saw him, it was on some training exercise back at Fort Lewis, right about the time I first got to the unit. Malcolm was lying down in the front lean-and-rest (push-up) position knocking out push-ups for punishment for something he'd done wrong. Most of the time I saw him, he was in that position. And on this training exercise, Malcolm couldn't handle all the stress, and he actually refused to train.

"Refuse to train" is when somebody breaks down, can't handle it anymore, and decides to quit. It's pretty common at basic training, but he was the first person I'd ever seen refuse to train at their unit. After that field problem, they sent him over to Supply.

When we got to Mosul, he showed steady improvement as a soldier, so they decided to send him back to a line squad, and moved him over to 1st Squad, where he was constantly teased and made fun of, thus he had another breakdown, and was put on a 24-hour radio guard shift in the war room with Sgt. Anderson, and at one point during the radio guard shift he decided to step outside for a cigarette break. Sgt. Anderson denied him that request and informed him that he was only allowed one smoke break every other hour. So Malcolm asked instead if he could go take a piss, which Sgt. Anderson allowed him to do, but instead of going to take a piss he went over to a mortar bunker, lit up a cigarette, and pulled a paperback out of his cargo pocket and just started reading. A half hour went by and Sgt. Anderson went outside to look for him and found him in the bunker smoking a cigarette, still reading, and yelled at him, at which time Malcolm told him, "I'd rather get an Article 15 than sit in the war room with your ass."

So he received an Article 15 for insubordination.

So then they decided to send him over to weapons squad, and when Sgt. Blough first brought Pvt. Malcolm over to me to tell me that he was now on my gun team, Malcolm had his M4 rifle tied down with some survival cord that was tied off and wrapped around his waist. He had left his weapon unsecured somewhere, so as corrective training and punishment he was told that he had to have his rifle tied to his body everywhere he went until he learned not to go anywhere without his weapon.

Like I said before, if there's a problem, the Army finds a solution. Sgt. Blough then briefed me on why his weapon was tied to his waist and told me to do my best with him and straighten him out if I could.

I told him Roger.

I then told Malcolm to step into my room, and then I basically told him the deal, which was that I was now his new team leader and that I would try to help him out as much as possible so that these last several months would go by easy. I told him I wasn't going to yell at him and punish him for stupid shit as long as he didn't do anything stupid and stayed out of trouble. And then I told him to go clean his weapon, and to meet me in the motor pool 30 minutes before we leave tonight for our mounted patrol and OP, so that I could give him a brief class on the M240 Bravo machine gun, how to load it, clear it, and fire it, so that he understands the basics.

Since we're missing a couple guys on leave, they're having me operate the .50-cal on our vehicle for the next couple days, and for now I'm having Pvt. Malcolm pull air guard and operate the M240 out the back of the air-sentry hatch on our vehicle.

Tonight is my first night as a TC.

In the motor pool I taught Malcolm how to mount the gun on the back of the vehicle, and went over all the basics with him, and then at the end I asked him if he had any questions, he told me no. But I could tell there was something disturbing him, he was smoking his cigarettes very nervously and he looked kinda pale. So I pulled him over to the side and asked, "Hey man, are you all right?" he paused for a while, and then without making eye contact with me he said softly, "I'm not all right. I don't want to pull air guard."

What? He doesn't want to pull air guard? WTF?

So I asked him, "Why man, what's up?"

He said, "I'm scared to be out the hatch. I don't want to do it. I was in 21 Victor when we got hit with those IEDs and ever since then I don't pull air guard because I'm too scared."

Malcolm was inside 21 Victor the day it got hit, and I had no idea that he's been creeped out ever since. I didn't know what the fuck to say or do in a situation like this. I've never dealt with a soldier who was too scared to do his job.

Damn.

In the movies the guy always has something way cool in a situation like this to say to his soldier, but I had no idea what the fuck to say. And I gave it a try and the big brother in me kinda stepped in and I told him, "Look man, you'll be all right, we're not going to be out too long, and nothing's gonna happen to you." And then I told him, "I know how you feel man, fuck, I feel the same way too sometimes, but you just gotta do it man. You'll be all right, nothing's gonna happen, OK?"

I hate telling half-truths to people. But it worked, he looked a bit more relieved. He paused and thought for a second about what I just said, and with a blank stare he hesitantly told me that he didn't want to do it, but he was going to do it anyways. I told him not to worry about a thing, and if he had any questions or anything to talk to me.

We then all boarded our vehicles and exited FOB Marez, and while we were driving around Mosul, I constantly looked back to see how he was doing. He looked nervous as hell, but overall, he looked all right. We drove around a bit, and then when it got dark, we drove over to this one area of Mosul that had a bunch of houses under construction and pulled an OP.

We parked our vehicle, dismounted the guys, and I began my shift by lighting up a smoke and scanning my sector with the .50-cal. Shortly after, I overheard on the radio the squad leader from 1st Squad, Sgt. Williams, whisper over the radio:

"We have a man creeping up on us, break,
He's wearing a white man-dress, break,
And he has a loaded AK-47 in his hand, over."

It was impossible for me to see the guy from where I was positioned, because 1st Squad was in a different location than we were, so I didn't have a shot at him.

We mounted up all the guys in the back of our vehicle and raced to the location where 1st Squad was at to find out what the hell was going on, and by this time they already unloaded on the guy and he was KIA. When we pulled up to the scene, they said that they needed a body bag.

Now in video games and the movies, when soldiers kill people, they just leave the body there and Charlie Mike (continue mission). Not us. We don't work like that. No, we police up our dead. We secured the area, and the guys went and put the guy in a black body bag and threw him in the back of our vehicle so we could drop off the body at the Mosul police station. As soon as they threw the body in the back it filled the vehicle with a very unpleasant aroma of bad personal hygiene. The zipper on the body bag was busted, and blood was drooling all over the place. The guys who carried the body in had blood smear marks here and there on their BDUs.

One thing I've noticed about me since I've been here is that I've developed that really disturbing warped, sick war humor about everything. Like a week ago, I was flipping through the photos on Spc. Martinez's digital camera, and when I came across the photo of the dead guy they killed in the mosque, without even thinking about it, I just busted up laughing, because the way the guy's eyes were open, and how his tongue was sticking out and his mouth was all agape, it just looked comical to me.

I had a headset on my helmet that allowed me radio communication with the driver. Here is the conversation me and the driver had on the way to the police station while we had the dead guy laying down in the back of our vehicle:

DRIVER: Hey, did you ever see those old *Police Academy* movies?

ME: Yeah.

DRIVER: Remember that one where they put the body in the body bag and he comes back alive?

ME: Yeah!

BOTH OF US: (Laughter.)

ME: Hey, you remember that Chris Farley movie, the one with him and David Spade where they're driving that car, and they hit a deer, and they both think it's dead, so they put it in the backseat of the car and they drive off, and then all the sudden it comes back alive and goes psycho and fucks the car up?

DRIVER: Fuck yeah, that shit was funnier than hell!

BOTH OF US: (Laughter.)

ME: That'd be funny if the dead Hajji came back alive and started thrashing around the back, wouldn't it?

BOTH OF US: (Laughter.)

Though I was making jokes with the driver on the way to the police station, I was concerned about Malcolm. I was sticking out of the TC hatch and I looked back to see how he was doing, but he wasn't up in the back air sentry hatch behind the M240 anymore, there was someone else up there now.

I then ducked back down from the hatch and looked at the back of the vehicle and Pvt. Malcolm was sitting down in the back of the vehicle on the bench, with the dead guy on the ground by his feet. I could tell right away from the expression on his face that he was all fucked up.

Fuck, goddammit, I didn't want him sitting down in front of that body bag. Why didn't somebody switch out with him?

But it was too late, we were almost at the police station. When we got there we dropped the back ramp, grabbed the body bag, and handed over the dead body to the ICPs as well as the weapon that he used, which was an old busted-ass AK-47 that was completely missing the buttstock and handle. Totally ghetto.

After killing that Iraqi and dropping his dead body off at the ICP station, we were all feeling a little bit hungry so we all decided to drive back to the FOB and head over to midnight chow for some grub.

I wanted to make sure I sat down next to my guy, to make sure he was okay. I looked all over for him, but I didn't see him anywhere. I found my acting squad leader, Sgt. Blough, and sat down next to him. I asked him, "Hey, where the hell is Malcolm at?"

Sgt. Blough then told me that when we parked the vehicle to go to chow, he said that he wasn't hungry and didn't want to eat, and he just wanted to go to his room, so he left as soon as we parked our Stryker, and walked all the way back to his room from the chow hall by himself.

When an infantry platoon goes to the chow together, the entire platoon will usually sit semi close together in a certain area of the chow hall. It's this unexplainable bond thing that happens in the infantry. The platoon leader will usually sit with the platoon sergeant, and 1st Squad will sit all together at one table, 2nd at another, 3rd at another, and then weapons squad (my squad) will usually sit together at another table.

First Squad was all sitting together at their table, going into minute detail stand-up comedy acts on how the guy "danced" when they all unloaded on him. In fact I overheard one of the guys in 1st Squad even crack the joke that he didn't even think that he was a bad guy, in fact he said, "I betcha anything the guy was just a janitor!" Which received laughter among the squad that shot him.

Now, from what I knew of the situation so far from Sgt.

Blough, this guy, who was creeping up on them with an AK, got close, saw that it was American soldiers, started yelling at them in Arabic, charged his weapon, pointed it at them, and started firing.

We've pulled many OPs here in the past, and at various times of the day, and a lot of times the landlords would drive up and just make sure nobody was stealing any of the wood or cinderblocks from these construction sites. Some would say in Arabic, or broken English, something along the lines that "Ali-baba, steal, just checking."

So I was thinking that this guy that they shot up was probably just some poor guy working the night shift to feed his wife and kids, and that the landlord hired him to watch the houses being constructed and to make sure nobody steals anything. And this guy probably just looked over and saw some movement by one of the houses that he was guarding, and he probably just walked over to investigate it, and next thing you know, he gets smoked.

But then again, I wasn't there, so I wouldn't know.

Pfc. Cortinas and Spc. Oaks, both from 1st Squad, the squad that ended this guy, were leaving the chow hall at the exact same time as I was. Cortinas is a gunner, and Oaks is the squad's designated marksman. I congratulated Cortinas on his kill, and shook his hand.

Me and Cortinas used to be really close friends back when he was in my squad, but when we got to Mosul they moved him over to 1st Sqd. I asked him about what happened, and he told me about how the guy crept up on them, and they were all up on the roof of that building, and Cortinas peeked up a little to take a look, and he pointed his weapon at him, at which time another soldier from the squad who was also up on the roof shined his IR (infra-red) floodlight on him (the IR floodlight is a light that you can only see through night vision goggles), and saw that he was carrying an AK-47, and then he fired at them.

So they all lit him up.

I looked over at Spc. Oaks, who was walking back with us, and I could tell that he wasn't really 100% agreeing, so I asked him what he saw. He told me that he was up on the roof, and had eyes on the guy, who was over at the lot next to them smoking a cigarette, and there was a bunch of stray dogs around him, and they weren't barking, which means that the dogs were probably used to him and comfortable being around him, and the guy came over, and next thing you know he fired at them, so he and everybody else fired back.

All I know is that I would have done the same thing they did.

Posted by CBFTW on August 3, 2004

MEN IN BLACK
Thursday, August 04, 2004

This is what CNN wrote on their website about what happened 04 AUG 04 here in Mosul:

MOSUL CLASHES LEAVE 12 DEAD
Clashes between police and insurgents in the northern city of Mosul left 12 Iraqis dead and 26 wounded, hospital and police sources said Wednesday.

Rifle and rocket-propelled-grenade fire as well as explosions were heard in the streets of the city.

The provincial governor imposed a curfew that began at 3 p.m. local time (7 a.m. EDT), and two hours later, provincial forces, police and Iraqi National Guard took control, according to Hazem Gelawi, head of the governor's press office in the Nineveh province. Gelawi said the city is stable and expects the curfew to be lifted Thursday.

Now here's what really happened:

I was in my room reading a book (*Thin Red Line*) when the mortars started coming down. Usually when we get mortared it'll only be one, maybe two mortars. But this mortar attack went on for almost 20 minutes. Each one impacting the FOB every couple of minutes. Something was up.

Sgt. Horrocks ripped open the door and yelled, "Grab your guys! And go to the motor pool! The whole BATTALION is rolling out!" Holy shit! The whole battalion?! This must be big. So I closed my book and ran over to my guys' rooms and ripped open their doors and yelled, "Get your fucking shit on and head down to the motor pool! Time: Now!" I ran back to my room and grabbed my shit and started running as fast as I could to the motor pool, hearing small arms fire off in the background. By now every swinging dick was running to the motor pool. Some putting their clothes on while they were running.

At the motor pool, everybody was strapping on their kits and getting their shit ready as fast as they could. One by one the Strykers were rolling out of the motor pool ready to hunt down whoever was fucking with us. Soldiers in the hatches of the vehicles were hooting and hollering, yelling their war cries and doing the Indian yell thing as they drove off and locked and loaded their weapons.

You got the feeling that whoever was attacking us had just now stirred up a bee's nest, and now they're getting the swarm. As I turned on all our computers and radios inside our vehicle to get ready to roll out, I heard on our radio that the shit was hitting the fan all over Mosul, large amounts of AIF (anti Iraqi forces) were attacking us with small arms, IEDs, and RPG fire, and there was a bunch of people wearing all black armed with AKs all over Mosul.

Fuck.

I then heard one of our interpreters, a Kurdish guy, say in vengeful broken English, "Give me gun, I want to kill these motherfuckers!"

As we rolled out the main gate, our FOB was getting attacked and we had soldiers lying down in the prone position up against the berm on the outer perimeter of the FOB firing their weapons. I've never seen that done before here at FOB Marez.

I'm usually an M240 Bravo machine gunner in my platoon, but because we were missing some of our guys on mid-tour leave, I had to cover down as a TC (truck commander in Stryker world). This was only my second day as a TC, and honestly, I didn't even know how to operate any of the shit inside the vehicle.

We headed north up Route Tampa and drove right past several HETs (heavy equipment transporters) that were entirely engulfed in flames in the middle of an intersection where they were ambushed earlier with RPGs and small arms fire. As we drove past the burning HETs, I thought to myself that there was no way anybody could have survived that attack.

I was sticking out of my hatch, behind the .50, and shortly after we passed the burning HETs, I glanced over to the left side of the vehicle, at which time I observed a man, dressed in all black with a terrorist beard, jump out all of the sudden from the side of a building, he pointed his AK-47 barrel right at my fucking pupils, I froze and then a split second later, I saw the fire from his muzzle flash leaving the end of his barrel and brass shell casings exiting the side of his AK as he was shooting directly at me. I heard and felt the bullets whiz literally inches from my head, hitting all around my hatch and .50-cal mount making a "Ping" "Ping" "Ping" sound. I ducked the fuck down in the hatch, and I yelled, "We're taking fire! 9 o'clock!!!" I traversed the gun around towards where the guy was and fired a burst. Since we were in a moving vehicle, the target was now at 7 o'clock, and when I fired the burst it was right over our back air guard hatch, where First Sgt. Swift was sticking his head out and shooting his M4. First Sgt. yelled down, "Tell him to stop fucking shooting over my head!!!" Shit. My bad.

My platoon sergeant who was sticking out the left hatch right next to me a couple seconds ago was now collapsed and on his back. He looked like a boxer who had just got knocked the fuck out by Rocky or something. Dazed and confused, he yelled, "I'm hit!" I looked at his helmet and a bullet had gone right through his Kevlar CVC (combat vehicle crewman) helmet and exited through the other side. Holy shit! I didn't see any blood on him. He took his CVC helmet off and examined the holes. No fucking shit; the bullet entered and exited, missing his upper forehead by like a quarter inch. A fuckin' miracle. He was standing right next to me, that's how close those bullets were to hitting us. My platoon sergeant then put the CVC helmet back on, with the holes, and got back up in the hatch, and we Charlie Mike'd (continued mission) to Bridge 5, where there were a large concentration of Anti Iraqi Forces. Our job today was to locate and kill them. Or as our battalion commander would say, "Punish the Deserving."

We were driving down Route Tampa when all of the sudden all hell came down around us, all these guys, wearing all black, a couple dozen on each side of the street, on rooftops, alleys, edge of buildings, out of windows, everywhere, just came out of fucking nowhere and started unloading on us. AK fire and multiple RPGs were flying at us from every single fucking direction. IEDs were being ignited on both sides of the street.

I freaked the fuck out and ducked down in the hatch and I yelled over the radio, "HOLY SHIT! WE GOT FUCKIN' HAJJIS ALL OVER THE FUCKIN' PLACE!!! They're all over goddammit!!!"

Bullets were pinging off our armor, all over our vehicle, and you could hear multiple RPGs being fired, soaring through the air every which way and impacting all around us. All sorts of crazy insane Hollywood explosions were going off. I've never felt fear like this. I was like, this is it, I'm going to die. I cannot put into words how scared I was.

The vehicle in front of us, Bravo 21,was getting hit by multiple RPGs. RPGs were flying right over our vehicle. I kind of lost it and was yelling and screaming all sorts of things (mostly cuss words). I fired the .50-cal all over the place, shooting everything. My driver was helping me out, pointing out targets to me over the radio. They were all over, shooting at us. My entire platoon was being ambushed. We were stuck in the middle of a kill zone.

With RPGs still flying, our driver floored it, pedal to the metal, and redlined the vehicle right through the ambush as fast as he could. The street we were driving on had three- to four-story-high apartment buildings on each side. The first floor were storefronts. As we were driving away I saw 100's and 100's of bullets impacting all over these buildings.

Finally we fired our way out of the kill zone and made our way to Bridge 5. We parked the vehicles there and dismounted. I lit up a smoke and started to scan my sector. The Pepsi bottling plant across the street was all up in flames.

Then after a couple minutes, we were told to load up and go back to where we got ambushed. I'm not going to lie, I didn't want to go back. Fuck that shit, I don't want to get killed. That was the last place on earth I wanted to be. I was scared to death. But we had to go back, and we did.

Third Squad mounted our vehicle and we started back. I was up out of the hatch, scanning. I saw a lot of people running down the side streets with AK-47s. I didn't have a shot at them with the .50 because we were going way too fast. I pulled out my Beretta 9mm and fired several shots. We rolled back to the area where we'd just dodged death, and we were taking fire from all over. I fired and fired and fired and fired and fired. At EVERYTHING. I was just 360-ing the .50-cal and shooting at everything. We were taking fire from all over, and every single one of us had our guns blazing. At one time, I saw a dog try to run across the street and somebody shot it.

Sgt. L and Sgt. Vance were out the back air guard hatches with both M240 Bravo machine guns, just laying waste to whatever they were shooting at. Sgt. Horrocks, Spc. Callahan, and Spc. Reyes were all in the back of the vehicle frantically tearing open ammo boxes and linking all the belts of 7.62 ammo that we had stashed for the gunners who were firing the 240s.

At this point, I had the .50-cal traversed as I was trying to kill these two guys shooting at us up on a rooftop with AK-47s, and I was shooting right above the heads of the guys who were in the back air guard hatches on our vehicle, Sgt. Vance and Sgt. L. Sgt. Horrocks, sitting inside the back of the vehicle, grabbed my arm, which startled the hell out of me. I quickly jerked back and looked at him and he yelled, "Hey!! Get that gun to the 12!!! Let that one go!! You're doing good!" He told me later that when I jerked back around to look at him, I had this crazed wide eyed look in my eyes that freaked him out.

I could now hear the Kiowa helicopter hovering up above us, which is a beautiful sound to hear in situations like this. Earlier in the day they were engaging targets.

We were running low on .50-cal ammunition at this point, and my platoon sergeant, Sgt. Hoerner, told me to reload the .50-cal with more ammo. I had no idea where we kept the extra .50-cal ammo, so I asked Sgt. Hoerner over the CVC radio, "Sergeant, where the hell is the ammo for the .50-cal located?" He told me that the ammo was strapped down on the outside of the vehicle, over on the right side. Why the fuck would the ammo for the .50-cal be on the outside of the vehicle?

With my hands I did the sign of the cross on my chest, said a prayer (please God, I don't want to fucking die), and as my platoon sergeant laid down some suppressive fire with his M4, I got up out of the hatch, got my whole body completely out of the vehicle, and went over, grabbed a couple green metal boxes of ammunition located on the outside of the vehicle, and got my ass back to the hatch as fast as possible. I was shaking and scared out of my fuckin' mind as I did this. While I was on the roof of our vehicle I could hear the sounds of sporadic gunfire and a couple explosions going off somewhere, scaring the living shit out of me every time one cracked off.

When I returned inside the vehicle and ripped open the ammo boxes, to my complete disappointment, I realized that I had grabbed the wrong ammo boxes. (These ammo boxes that I grabbed were 7.62 caliber, I needed .50-cal.) As I cursed my bad luck (GODDAMMIT!) I once again got out of the hatch and walked on top of our vehicle to find a box of .50-cal ammunition. I found the .50-cal boxes, but of course they were strapped down, so Sgt. L, who was sticking out of the back right air guard hatch, helped me out by cutting the strap off with his Gerber knife which allowed me to grab a couple boxes. Sporadic gunfire was going off, and every time I felt a chill run down my neck and I was saying to myself, "HURRY the fuck up!" Once I got back inside my hatch, I threw the ammo boxes down, and reloaded the .50-cal, thinking to myself that having the ammo located on the outside of the vehicle has got to be the dumbest fucking idea in the world, and whoever thought of that idea should be fucking shot.

Then we dropped the back ramp of our vehicle and dismounted the guys from 3rd Squad.

We were parked kinda close alongside these buildings, so I decided to close my hatch, in case somebody up on a rooftop wanted to throw a grenade down on us. I wasn't taking any chances today.

Third Squad had with them both M240s and an AT4 rocket. I laid down as much suppressive fire as I could at the surrounding buildings to allow them the ability to maneuver to a nearby street corner, which had absolutely no cover whatsoever. I saw a crowd of people suspiciously peeking around a corner at us, I pointed this out to Sgt. Hoerner, and asked him what I should do. As he was shooting nonstop from his hatch, in the heat of the moment, he told me to just fucking shoot them, and he briefly explained to me that these people have no fucking business out on the street whatsoever. So I pointed the crosshairs right at them, but then I moved it to right above their heads and fired a burst, which got them to disperse in a hurry. I could tell that they were just spectators.

Sgt. L, who had his squad dismounted and out in the open, grabbed a refrigerator that was standing there and slammed it down on its side, to give them some much needed cover. The Stryker that was in front of us, 65 Victor, backed up so that their vehicle could give them more cover. Strykers were also launching TOW missiles at Anti Iraqi Forces.

Down in the hatch, I was frantically scanning my sector when suddenly about 300 meters away from us, over by the traffic circle, I saw two guys with those red and white jihad towels wrapped around their heads creeping around a corner. They were hunched down hiding behind a stack of truck tires. I could tell by their body language that something was up. I placed the crosshairs right on them and was about to fuckin' waste them, but for some reason I didn't pull the trigger. These guys were not dressed in black like the guys earlier and from what I could see they didn't have any weapons on them. Something told me that I should wait for just one, maybe two more seconds. Then I saw another guy come creeping around that corner with an RPG in his hands. As soon as I saw that I screamed as loud as I could, "RRRPPPPPGGGGGG!!!" into the CVC. My crosshairs were bouncing all over, so I gathered my composure as fast as I could, put the crosshairs on them, and engaged them with a couple good ten-round bursts of some .50-cal, right at them.

Nobody moved from behind those tires after that.

A couple minutes after that the Stryker that was parked 10 meters in front of us, Bravo 65 Victor, took an RPG that came from a building that looked like a parking garage that was diagonally across the street. It scared the fucking shit out of me when they got hit. Once that happened we all pointed our weapons to that building and started lighting it up with everything we had.

Bravo 65 immediately reported casualties, "We're hit! This is Bravo 65 Victor! We have wounded!!! We need CAS Evac, Time: Now!" came over the radio.

Lt. Armeni, who was inside that vehicle, got severely injured and needed medical attention immediately. The RPG penetrated right through the armor and sliced Lt. Armeni's guts completely so that they were hanging out of his stomach.

Victor 65 pulled out to drive back to the FOB. We were now pretty much out in the open and the next target in line for an RPG. Sgt. Hoerner, knowing this, then threw out about five smoke grenades onto the street in front of our vehicle, thinking that the smoke would somehow conceal our position, as well as 3rd Squad, who was dismounted and also wide open at this time.

The smoke added to the confusion for me. As I was trying to orient myself, a loud explosion took place and it scared the shit out of me, because now it was apparent to me that we were next in line for an RPG, and somebody out there was definitely gunning at us. An RPG was fired at our vehicle from the building to our right, but it missed and landed about ten meters in front of us. I couldn't see where it came from, so I just pointed the gun towards the building where I thought the RPG had come from and just started pulling the trigger. Sgt. Vance, who was behind the refrigerator, fired an AT4 anti-tank rocket at the window where he thought the RPG had come from.

I then saw a man, dressed in mostly white, with no weapon on him, run for his life, out of the building, and right in front of our vehicle. I lowered the .50 cal at him and tried three different times to hit him, missing him every time. Several other people tried shooting at this guy as well, and somehow the bastard got away.

Third Squad, which was now completely out in the open again, since Bravo 65 was no longer there to provide them cover, ran back to our Stryker and tried to get back on since there were still RPGs being fired, and they were all out there like targets. When they got back on our vehicle, Sgt. Hoerner told them, "You guys shouldn't be in here!! We're a fucking RPG target right now!"

Spc. Callahan then told him, "But sergeant! We're an RPG target out *there*!"

This gunfight had been going on for 4½ hours when the INGs showed up to the party (about fucking time) in their ING pick-up trucks, all jam packed with ING soldiers in uniform armed with AK-47s.

Third squad then dismounted from the vehicle again, and Sgt. L directed them and the INGs to the building where RPGs were being fired from. They breached the front door with a shotgun and the INGs went in first followed by 3rd Squad. We then drove down the street beside the building.

While I was sitting down in the hatch scanning my sector with another lit cigarette in my mouth, I heard my platoon sergeant collapse next to me. At first I thought he was shot again, but I didn't hear the cracks of any gunfire. I leaned over to find out what the hell was wrong with him. At first I thought he was a heat casualty, because it was an extremely hot day. So I grabbed a water bottle and offered him some water. Half out of it and dazed, he told me that he had just lost consciousness from the concussion he received earlier from the bullet impact that had gone completely through his CVC helmet. He had chew all up in his teeth as he was telling me this. I offered him some water, which he declined.

Then all the sudden, mortars started impacting. These bastards were now dumping mortars on us!

The Kiowa helicopters that were flying up above reported that they saw several individuals fire several mortars and take off to a nearby mosque, which was southwest from our position. The CO then directed our platoon leader, 1st Lt. Montoya, to take his platoon and secure the area. We then got the call to go out and try to find the guys that were firing the mortars. We had a couple truckloads of ING soldiers, about two ING Squads, to follow us as we drove over to the mosque.

On the way, we passed a watermelon stand, and all the watermelons were blown to bits and had bullet holes in them. In fact, everything on that street had bullet holes in it, the cars, the buildings, the noncompliant Hajjis, everything. There were thousands and thousands of brass shell casings littering the streets. Even our vehicle was completely covered inside and out with brass shell casings and links.

Once we got to the suspected location, we parked the vehicle and the INGs started clearing the area, and a couple of them went inside the mosque to check it out, and we had a couple Kiowas flying overhead to provide eyes in the sky.

The INGs didn't find shit.

We had to return to FOB Marez, as we were running extremely low on fuel, ammo, and water. It was hot and my entire DCU uniform was completely soaked wet from sweat and filth. So we all mounted up and drove back to the FOB. Once we returned, we parked near the motor pool to get more fuel for our vehicles and for a resupply of ammunition and water. Sgt. Woolridge, the TC for Bravo Victor 65, ran up to our vehicle holding all his gear and his kit and he asked, "Hey, you guys rolling back out? Do you have room for one more?"

Sgt. Woolridge was pretty much begging for us to take him back out with us, though he had been in the vehicle right in front of us earlier that had been RPG'd. We had no room for him in our vehicle, we were jam packed. Since we couldn't take him, he gave us all the ammo and water he had on him, and told us, "Go get 'em."

While we were waiting for the word to roll back out, we sat around and exchanged war stories over plates of food from the chow hall. I sat down on an ammo crate while Sgt. Vance sat down on a water cooler, and he told me all about 3rd Squad's heroics on the ground that day, about their vehicle that got shot by at least three RPGs the first time through Route Tampa. Each one that hit the vehicle knocked him down from the air-guard hatch. One of the RPGs took out the engine to their vehicle, and Spc Callahan, while it was still rolling, grabbed a fire extinguisher and tried to put out the fire. When they got to Bridge 5, Vance and Callahan were vomiting out of fear.

Sgt. Horrocks came up to us to see how we were doing. He smiled and told us all about how he was reunited with "Maxine" and when 3rd Squad was dismounted on the street, he fired her from the hip, John Wayne-ing it, and took out a guy on a rooftop.

By now it was night, and at 2300 we were ready to roll back out. All the Strykers were filled with fuel, water, and ammo. I was exhausted, and wasn't really in the mood to go back out and risk getting killed again, but you don't have the option to not go back out in situations like this. When they say go, you go.

We all loaded back onto our vehicles and actually started to leave when over the radio they told us to go back to the motor poll and to stand by till further notice. No problems there.

So we drove back and parked, dismounted the guys, and waited. Some guys took all their kits off and stretched out on the concrete to try to catch some rack, while others smoked cigarettes and talked.

I was smoking like a chimney, one right after another. My nerves were completely shot and I was emotionally drained and I noticed that my hands were still kinda shaking. The stars were now out over Mosul, and I decided to go sit by myself up against the tires on the side of the vehicle and stare at them for a while. I was thinking how I was lucky to be alive. I've never experienced anything like the fear I felt today. A couple times today I thought about that guy who jumped out from the corner of that building with that angry look on his face when he pointed the AK at my head and pulled the trigger.

The attacks on my platoon up to this point had been just chickenshit hit and run bullshit, an IED here, a solo RPG or rocket there. Every time we'd get hit, they'd be nowhere in sight.

These guys today were on the offensive, had held their ground, and showed no fear whatsoever.

Sgt. Vance saw me sitting by myself, and he came over and sat next to me. He asked if I was OK. I thought about that one for a second and I told him, "I don't know." He bummed a smoke and said, "Are you sure?" I told him how I wasn't really in the mood to roll back out for another inning with these guys, and I also told him that I was kinda tripping out about how not everybody that I engaged today had a weapon in their hands. And that I wasn't really too sure about what happened to some of those people.

Vance started telling me a little bit about his father, who had been in Vietnam, and who had given him sound advice about situations like this, "Put all the things that bother you, and keep you awake at night, and clog your head up, put all those things in a shoebox, put the lid on it, and deal with it later."

As soon as he told me that, the battalion commander walked into the motor pool and came up to us and asked how we were doing, and congratulated us on a job well done. Then he informed us that there were organized attacks all over Iraq today, but that we got the worst of it, and held our own. We asked about casualties, and he told us that Lt. Armeni and Sgt. Paul Schmitz were both in critical condition.

I knew that Lt. Armeni had been hit, but I didn't know about Sgt. Schmitz till now. Sgt. Schmitz was a good guy, I don't think I've ever seen that guy without a smile on his face. He then told us again that we all had done a great job, and that he was proud of all of us. Shortly after that they told us to go back to our rooms. I walked back to my room, thanked God, and passed out on my bed.

Note: I don't think CNN's report of only 12 dead is accurate.

Posted by CBFTW at 5:23 p.m., August 5, 2004

I've put the events of that day in a shoebox, put the lid on it, and haven't opened it since.

Here's What the Army Said

Task Force Tomahawk Press Release
Release # 08-13

FOR IMMEDIATE RELEASE

Coordinated attacks in Mosul leave 14 civilians dead; Iraqi Security Forces stand their ground against attackers, return stability to the city.

MOSUL, IRAQ (August 4, 2004) –A series of coordinated attacks in Mosul today targeting Iraqi Police, Iraqi National Guard and multinational forces left more than fourteen Iraqi citizens dead and 31 wounded. Iraqi Police and Iraqi National

Guard soldiers responded quickly and returned stability to the city. No Iraqi security forces were killed in the attacks.

The attacks occurred over a three-hour period of time and began at approximately 11:30 a.m. when terrorists fired on the Al Karama police station in eastern Mosul. No damage or injuries were reported in that incident. Ninety minutes later an Iraqi Police patrol was engaged with small arms fire and rocket propelled grenades in southern Mosul. The police returned fire and reported no injuries in that incident.

Attackers also attempted to disrupt the power and health care system in the city by attacking the Mosul Power Plant and the Al Jahmouri hospital in west central Mosul with small arms fire and rocket propelled grenades.

Iraqi security forces repelled all of the attacks, killing eight terrorists and capturing two. The two terrorists who have been detained are being held by Iraqi Police pending further investigation.

Multinational forces served in a supporting role, providing additional support where and when the Iraqi leaders involved in the attacks requested it. No multinational forces were killed in today's attacks.

Ninevah Province Governor Duraid Kashmoula imposed a citywide curfew that began at 3 p.m. today and will last until 6 a.m. August 5. In an evening address to the people of Ninevah Province, the governor stressed calm.

"I am asking from you my beloved people of Mosul to stay calm and do not be afraid because we will do our best to stop anyone who might bother you," Kashmoula said.

He also condemned the attackers and praised the Iraqi Security Forces for stopping the attacks.

"What has happened today, destruction by burglars and criminals, this proves that they are not real Iraqis. The Iraqi

Police, the National Guard and the Facilities Protective Service personnel faced them and killed or arrested many of them," he said.

During today's attacks, police confiscated a large cache of weapons that contained rocket propelled grenades, rifles, mortars, explosives and munitions, reported [Mosul police chief Mohammed] Barhawie.

"This operation proves that we will not bow to our enemies and with the help of God, we will defeat them," said Barhawie. "Mosul will remain a symbol of the unity of Iraq and a symbol of the fight against terrorists."

Terrorists are targeting security forces as well as facilities that provide for the health and well being of citizens of Mosul. These attacks underscore the desperation of terrorists in their attempts to halt the progress of democracy and prosperity in Iraq.

Since the transfer of sovereignty on June 28, Iraqi Security Forces continue to assume the majority of the responsibility for maintaining the overall security of the region.

"GREEN" GUNNER

B. Abell Jurus, coauthor of the book *Men in Green Faces,* which is about Navy SEALs in Vietnam, forwarded me an e-mail she received from Ed Fitzgerald, one of the original Green Berets. He also read my "Men in Black" blog entry, and had this to say about it:

That "green" gunner captured vividly the total confusion, the terror of that situation he was suddenly thrown into. He shows us clearly something that is very true—the fact that in the middle of a firefight like that, you only can track about 1⁄10 of what is happening. (Maybe ¼ of what is going on for the most experienced and coolest guys on the scene, those with

many previous firefights.) So often in fiction (and in the bullshit tales told by people who were never in a real firefight) we read these accounts where the "hero" both "sees" and tells you step by step in minute detail every single thing that is taking place—in a situation where he could easily be killed or horribly maimed. Mostly, that's just crap. The way this guy described it (with all the warts—not sure what he is hitting most of the time, shooting too close to his own men, etc.)—that is indeed how it is in a situation like that.

Too often, even in otherwise very well-written action books, there is no hint of that confused desperation which hits people when they are suddenly in it up to their eyebrows, with death or serious injury an all too real possibility. Loved the way that "green" gunner captured the reality of that kind of firefight—he nailed it right on the money. —Ed

Posted by CBFTW at 9:14 p.m., August 7, 2004

Lt. Armeni

The day following the ambush, I went directly over to the Internet cafe to check my e-mail and to search the Internet for any information and/or press about what happened. I found little to no press about the firefight, just a couple paragraphs here and there, just stuff along the lines of what CNN wrote on their website. It kinda made me wonder what else goes on here in Iraq that never gets reported to the people back home. I then logged into my e-mail account and started sifting through my e-mails, and then I came across this e-mail:

Subject: Mosul Fight dated 5 August
Date: Fri, 6 Aug 2004 22:17:54-0700

Thank you for your site. I was able to read a little more into the event that left my son Lt. Damon Armeni wounded and in critical condition. I am a retired officer and served in Vietnam, Panama and the first Gulf War. Being able to read a little more into the events that lead up to his injury helps. I am so very proud of him. Thank you to the young soldier that left those remarks, they said my son was cussing the Iraq people as they were taking him away, oh God this hurts so much. But again thank you and God Bless. Please excuse this spelling and such I am still a little upset.
Dan Armeni

——Original Message——
To: Dan Armeni
Subject: RE: Mosul Fight dated 5 August

I've been praying for Lt. Armeni for the last several days. I know as a fact that there are at least 5 guys still alive today because of him. I was in the Stryker right behind him when he got hit. We are all very concerned about him and praying for him here. If there is anything I can do please let me know, he was one hell of an officer, and down to earth, which made him well liked among the men. I pray for him and his family.
—cb

I then posted this up on the weblog:

Before we came here to Iraq, we had a bunch of OCs (Observer/Controllers) from the Joint Readiness Training Center in Fort Polk, Louisiana, come up to Fort Lewis to help us out with our training. We were doing some simulated combat training to help get ready for Iraq, and in one of our training scenarios, Lt. Armeni engaged a lone sniper with a TOW missile. Which gave the OCs a hard-on; they said that that was fantastic, because it was like smashing a fly with a sledgehammer.

Lt. Armeni brought that same smash-your-enemies tenacity out here to Iraq which inspired all of us. Right now Lt. Armeni is in critical condition in Germany. He was wounded on that attack on 04 AUG 04. I received an e-mail from his father thanking me for this site which allowed him a little more insight to the event that critically wounded his son on that day. I am asking everybody to please include the Lt. and his family in their prayers. It would mean a lot. To me, and everybody else here. I know of at least five guys here who are alive today because of his actions on that day.

His father then e-mailed me:

Thank you very much. We need those prayers. Damon is flying to Washington D.C. even as we speak and my wife and Damon's wife are flying together to link up. So far he has lost his spleen, two ribs have been completely removed, a lung was collapsed so he has chest tubes, he has two bags connected to his intestines and his colon was punctured. He is on a vent that is breathing for him. They also have not been able to close his wound because of the swelling. Probably the best thing you guys can do is pray for him, but also make those bastards pay. I know that he is mad because they managed to get him and he thought they were cowards and you guys were the best. He was very proud of your unit. Make their lives miserable CB, and as a TC watch out for your men. Damon was always concerned about you guys. I will join my wife and daughter-in-law with Damon's two-year-old once they have him off the vent. We sure hope that

is soon. Take care son, all our prayers are with you guys and we look forward to the home coming. My wife, who is an advanced critical care nurse practitioner, insists that she will have Damon there for that home coming. If you guys need anything, anything at all, my family is more then willing to send some boxes your way.
Thanks so very much.
Dan Armeni

AL QAEDA
Today we had a company formation and our CO came out and talked to us. He told us we all did an incredible job and was proud of all of us. He said we all executed our jobs perfectly. He also informed us that the people that were wearing black were actually insurgents from Iran, members of Al Qaeda.

Captain Robinson then said the Army estimated that there were at least 100+ of them out there attacking us. The CO also compared the ambush to what those Rangers went through in Mogadishu. Our CO said he stopped counting the number of RPGs fired after the number 12. He also said that if there was ever going to be a movie about the Strykers, the other day would be the perfect story for it.

He then went on to say that after what went down esterday, he better not hear any of us complaining or crying about how we haven't earned our CIBs. Which made everybody bust up. The CIB is a Combat Infantry Badge, it's awarded to soldiers with the 11 Bravo MOS who are assigned to an infantry unit, brigade or smaller, that engages in active ground combat. The CIB is a pretty big deal in the infantry.

We all got our CIBs at the beginning of the year, shortly after we arrived in Mosul, and at the time, a lot of us felt that we didn't get shot at enough times, or hadn't engaged the enemy enough times, to deserve to wear a CIB. I've even overheard soldiers say that they were never going to wear theirs, because they felt that they hadn't done anything to deserve one.

When my father was in the Army, he was an artillery officer, and in Vietnam he was a forward observer attached to the infantry. He had to be up close to where all the action was so he'd be able to call in some arty on Charlie's location. He carried a shotgun with him in Vietnam, because as he told me, with a shotgun you didn't really have to be a great shot, all you had to do was point it in the direction of the enemy and you'd hit him.

Since my father's MOS was artillery, he wasn't awarded the CIB. So when I received my CIB, I felt like mailing it to him with a letter that said, "Dad, here's my CIB, I want you to have this, because you probably deserve this more than I do." But I never mailed it to him, because the post office was over by the airfield, and every time we went over there I'd forget to bring my CIB. And my dad might have thought it was corny for me to do something like that.

We (infantry guys) all received the CIB, and all our combat medics received a CMB, and we had both the CIB and CMB ceremony together over by the motor pool. A CMB is a Combat Medic Badge, and all it means is that you were a medic in a combat zone.

At the ceremony, it's Army tradition to award the youngest soldier first. So we had the youngest infantry and combat medic come out and get pinned first. We were all shocked, and a lot of us kinda chuckled, when we saw that a medic there to receive the CMB was the guy who was the main reason why we all now have to lock and load our weapons in the motor pool prior to rolling out, and have our squad leaders inspect our chambers immediately when we roll back in from missions, to make sure that none of us has a bullet chambered.

What happened was, the medic was in his conex room, and his 9mm pistol accidentally went off and the bullet whizzed right through the wall and nailed the soldier who was in the next room right in the arm. The medic that shot the guy in the arm then immediately went over to the guy who was shot, and treated him.

We also had the chaplain walking around yesterday, checking up on us and available for us just in case we wanted somebody to talk to. There was no need for me to talk to him, I did enough talking to God the other day.

Today was spent cleaning our vehicle inside and out, which was no easy task. No matter how well we cleaned it, we were still finding brass shell casings and links somewhere. We also fixed whatever was broken. I cleaned the .50-cal inside and out. I discovered the remains of a smashed-up impacted 7.62 bullet that had my name on it by my hatch. I put that in my pocket. If I ever have kids, and I get all old and have grandkids, I could show them the bullet that Al Qaeda tried to kill me with. Have them bring that in for show and tell at school. Later on in the day we had an OP. I was super-paranoid exiting the FOB, flinching from the smallest thing, and I was totally looking for anybody dressed in black. What's up with the black wardrobe anyway? Are these guys like "Goth" or something? Whatever. Once we got to our OP, I was feeling kinda hungry, so I grabbed an MRE from the top of the vehicle, and there was a bullet hole right through it. My platoon sergeant who took that bullet right through his helmet the other day is still in the hospital. He was wearing a CVC helmet, which is made of Kevlar. He got a major concussion from it, and they're keeping their eyes on him at the hospital. The TC for 23 Victor, who took some RPG shrapnel to the face, is okay now and should be back to work any time now.

Posted by CBFTW at 4:35 p.m., August 6, 2004

PURPLE HEART CEREMONY

Today at 1515 we had a company mass formation for a Purple Heart ceremony for the firefight that happened several days ago. My platoon sergeant was one of the soldiers today to receive a Purple Heart. This Purple Heart ceremony was by far the largest we've had so far here in Iraq, a lot of people were getting them today, about a dozen. Most of the Purple Hearts awarded were for RPG shrapnel and grazed bullets from AK-47s. When they put out a time to be at a formation, like 1515, what they really mean is be there at 1500, you always have to be at a formation 15 minutes early, then at 1515, you stand at parade rest till the big shots show up. Today it was the Battalion Commander, the Command Sergeant Major, and the Full Bird. They didn't show up till almost 1540. So for about 40 minutes we had to stand in the hot sun, sweating our asses off in our DCUs.

For completely selfish reasons, I always hate award ceremonies, because you get to watch other people receive medals, and you're standing there in formation with a bunch of guys who are thinking the same thing you're thinking, "Hey, how come I didn't get one?" At award formations every now and then when somebody gets pinned a medal, you'll hear somebody in the formation cough the word "bullshit" under their breath, or whisper "What the fuck? *That* guy?!" But that childish behavior never happens at Purple Heart formations, in fact, that's the one awards ceremony where I'm glad I'm not one of the guys out there getting a medal.

Finally an Army captain came out, and we all stood at attention as he said his "Attention to Orders, these men are awarded the Purple Heart . . ." speech. I only got to watch about 20% of the ceremony, because it was *so* damn hot and we were standing in the sun for *so* long that the sweat that was pouring down my face was getting into my eyeballs, and the sweat was all salty and stingy because I've never washed my hat. (Gross, huh?) So when they pinned the third guy in the long line of awardees, I had to shut my eyes. You can't move your body at the position of attention, so I couldn't wipe the sweat from my eyes and face. I couldn't keep them open. So for about 80% of the ceremony I had to stand there with both my eyes closed. Finally, when everybody was pinned, they told us to stand at parade rest and I was able to touch my face again and wipe the sweat from around my eyes and be able to see again. Our commander then gave a brief speech. I couldn't hear what he was saying, because he didn't really talk that loud and I was way in the back. All I heard was "You guys whooped them" or something. When he was done talking, it was all over and they released us. And exactly when they released us a sergeant ran up and yelled "QRF has been activated! Third Platoon, get your asses to the motor pool!"

When they activate QRF (quick reaction force) that means something's going down in Mosul and they need U.S. forces to be there. As the guys from 3rd Platoon ran off to the motor pool to go deal with whatever, I overheard one guy say, "You guys don't get hurt, I don't want to stand around in another Purple Heart Ceremony."

Posted by CBFTW at 8:56 p.m., August 7, 2004

MAKE A WISH

Last night I was sitting down smoking a cigarette outside my room with Pfc. Pointz. And I was staring up into the stars over Mosul when I saw a flash of white streak across the night sky, and I freaked out and yelled, "Oh shit!" and stood up. I thought it was a mortar or a rocket, but instead it was just a shooting star. Pointz just laughed at me.

Posted by CBFTW on August 8, 2004

Becoming the Media

From: Mike Gilbert
Subject: your blog
Date: Mon, 9 Aug 2004 16:39:22-0700
CB,
Thanks for writing your story. Your stuff is the best—the best—of the soldier blogs, hands down. I don't know if we met when I was over there with the brigade. I think maybe we did; I spent some time with B Co., Capt. Robinson and his crew. In Samarra mostly, but a little bit in Mosul too. Got a cool picture of Armeni that I gave to his mom, him riding high in the TC hatch with an M240B. OK. Stay safe. Keep writing. Let me know if there's anything you think I can do.
Mike Gilbert
The News Tribune
Tacoma, Wash.

Right after I read that e-mail, I received a dozen or so e-mails from readers who all wrote to me to let me know about an article that they all saw that appeared in some Tacoma, Washington, newspaper. They all said that the article quoted the hell out of me. So I did a Google search, found the article, read it in disbelief, and then realized that the guy who wrote the article was the same guy that sent me the "good job" e-mail, Mike Gilbert.

Stryker Brigade Slammed by Insurgents

MICHAEL GILBERT; The News Tribune

It didn't get much media coverage, but troops from the Fort Lewis-based Stryker brigade say fighting last Wednesday in Mosul was the heaviest and most sustained combat they've seen in their nine months in Iraq.

Insurgents with mortars, rocket-propelled grenades, AK-47s, and improvised bombs fought a series of coordinated, running attacks against Stryker and Iraqi troops. One estimate put the number of attackers at 30 to 40, another at more than 100.

Either way, U.S. and Iraqi forces killed an undetermined number of them—the official estimate is at least a dozen—while suffering no losses themselves.

About a dozen Stryker troops were wounded; all but two returned to duty, said Lt. Col. Kevin Hyneman, the brigade's deputy commander.

The two more seriously wounded include Lt. Damon Armeni, 25, of Tacoma, a Wilson High School and Pacific Lutheran University graduate, who is reported in critical condition and is awaiting surgery at Walter Reed Army Medical Center for shrapnel wounds, his family said Monday. There was no information available Monday about the other wounded soldier.

A soldier in Armeni's company—Blackhawk Company of the 1st Battalion, 23rd Infantry Regiment—said the lieutenant was injured by a rocket-propelled grenade blast after maneuvering his Stryker in to protect five infantrymen under fire.

"Needless to say, we are proud of our son's actions but hurt so very much for what he is going through, praying that he'll pull through," said his father, Dan Armeni.

In an interview Monday, Hyneman said the fighting took place on the east and west sides of the Tigris River, which bisects the city, and at a hotel near the northernmost of the city's five major bridges. The insurgents also attacked a hospital and a power plant, and ambushed Stryker convoys as they rolled past multistory buildings on the way to the fight, according to other sources.

Insurgents in Mosul typically attack Iraqi authorities and American troops with car bombs, sporadic mortar fire into U.S. camps, and small-scale ambushes with small arms and RPGs.

"Anti-Iraqi forces tried a pretty widespread offensive action, uncharacteristically," Hyneman said. "I think they were surprised by how the Iraqi National Guard and the coalition fought together as a team."

The official version as reported that evening in a news release by Task Force Olympia, the Fort Lewis-based command for northern Iraq, said "multinational forces served in a supporting role, providing additional support where and when the Iraqi leaders involved in the attacks requested it."

Hyneman and the task force spokesman, Lt. Col. Paul Hastings, said the fighting drew in virtually all the troops in the brigade's two infantry battalions in Mosul, as well as elements from other brigade units in the city.

One soldier described what it was like on his Web log on the Internet. The soldier, who identifies himself as CBFTW, is attracting readers with his absorbing, personal account of Army life in Mosul.

"We were driving there on that main street, when all of the sudden all hell came down all around on us, all these guys wearing all black . . . a couple dozen on each side of the street, on rooftops, alleys, edges of buildings, out of windows, everywhere just came out of . . . nowhere and started firing RPGs and AK-47s at us," he wrote.

CBFTW described how a bullet passed in one side of his buddy's helmet and out the other without hitting his buddy—

he suffered a concussion, is all.

"Bullets were pinging off our armor all over our vehicle, and you could hear multiple RPGs being fired and flying through the air and impacting all around us. All sorts of crazy insane Hollywood explosions . . . going on all around us," he wrote. "I've never felt fear like this. I was like, this is it, I'm going to die. I cannot put into words how scared I was."

"My platoon was stuck right smack dab in the middle of the ambush and we were in the kill zone," CBFTW wrote. "We shot our way out of it and drove right through the ambush."

Hyneman said about a dozen Strykers were damaged, mostly the tires and some sections of slat armor that protects the vehicles from RPGs. All were repaired and returned to service within two days, he said.

Chaplains and mental health counselors were sent around to check with soldiers the next day.

CBFTW said he and his buddies also spent much of the next day cleaning up the brass shell casings out of their vehicle, fixing broken parts and cleaning their weapons.

"I discovered the remains of a smashed-up impacted 7.62 (mm) bullet that had my name on it by my hatch. I put that in my pocket," he wrote. "If I ever have kids, and I get all old and have grandkids, I could show them the bullet that al-Qaeda tried to kill me with. Have them bring that in for show and tell at school."

- To read CBFTW's account of last week's Stryker brigade battle in Mosul, go to cbftw.blogspot.com.

Now that this article was out, I knew that my days of writing about my experiences in Iraq were going to be numbered, and that my weblog would soon be the next casualty of war.

Spc. Buzzell's account caught the attention of the *News Tribune* in Tacoma, Wash., the newspaper that covers Spc. Buzzell's home base of Fort Lewis. Noting that the attack got scant coverage by bigger media, the local paper drew heavily from Spc. Buzzell's anonymous account. The Pentagon's internal clip service picked up the *News Tribune* story and it landed in the hands of commanders in Iraq.

Within hours, Lt. Col. Buck James, the battalion commander, ordered Spc. Buzzell to his office.

—Christopher Cooper,
"Army Blogger's Tales Attract Censors' Eyes,"
Wall Street Journal, September 9, 2004, p. B1

I'M *SOO* FUCKED

I was just returning from the chow hall when I saw my platoon sergeant outside my door waiting for me and he said, The colonel wants to see you, hurry up and go shave, I'll be back in 15 to take you down there. My heart sank. Shit. I know exactly what this one is about. It's like that feeling you get in high school when you'd fuck up, and they'd call your name over the loudspeaker and tell you your presence was needed in the principal's office, and you know the police are there in the principal's office waiting for you. Not good. I stepped inside my room, and my roommate was inside and he said, "Shit man! The BC was just here looking for you!!" Fuck. I'm dead. The battalion commander AND the colonel want to see me?!

A couple days ago at the Internet cafe, I looked over at the person next to me and he was reading my blog, totally unaware he was sitting next to the author. So I saw this one coming. The Full Bird Colonel wasn't around so my platoon sergeant walked me down to the BC's office, and all I could

think about was latrine duty, being a private again, loss of pay, or worse. On the way to the BC's office, my platoon sergeant asked me if I knew what this was about, and I told him, "I think I have a pretty good idea why he wants to see me, Sergeant."

When I got to his office I was sweating a lot from being freaked the fuck out. My heart was beating at an accelerated rate as well now. The BC is a pretty intimidating guy, with an intimidating name, "Buck James." He's done more time in combat zones than I've done in the Army and he's like Patton meets Vince Lombardi with a little bit of Knute Rockne.

The battalion commander is a total hard charger kinda guy. The kinda guy infantrymen love. As I stepped into his office (I scanned the room for MPs), he told me to take a seat and I did, nervous as all hell. My platoon sergeant sitting right next to me. The BC looked at me, offered me a cup of coffee, I declined, and then as he walked to his desk he said, "You're pretty well read. I can tell right away that you're a reader." Now I'm really shitting my pants. First off, he knows about my writing, second, I know from numerous experiences and run-ins with judges, probation officers, principals, and police officers how something like this works, they always start off with a nice compliment, and then they throw the book at you and fry your ass. He said, "You're a big Hunter S. Thompson fan, aren't you?" (Pause.) At first I didn't know how to answer that one, I'm sure this meeting wasn't about chitchatting about literature. I said, "Uhhh, yes sir." He said, "Me too, but I thought the movie was just pure garbage. Didn't do the book justice." I didn't feel like contesting that, and as I'm sitting there waiting for the guilty death penalty sentence to come out of his mouth, he asked me if I ever read such and such by such and such. I was *so nervous* and had so many thoughts flying in my head I wasn't even registering what he was saying to me at this time, so I lied, "No sir, I've heard of him, but never read him." And then he said, "I'll let you borrow a copy of his book sometime, you'll really like him."

Then he sat down behind his desk and on his desk he had a huge file that looked to me to be about as thick as *The Rise and Fall of the Third Reich.* With his right arm that had his Ranger Battalion Combat Patch sewn on it, he started turning the pages. I could see the painting of *Guernica* on the first page as he flipped through it, and every single page had something I wrote highlighted in bright yellow ink and a bunch of weird forms attached to it and a bunch of papers. I'm pretty sure those highlights and notes weren't in regard to pointing out my spelling and grammar mistakes, and I could feel the sweat dripping down my face as he was flipping through the pages. He calmly looked up and told me that my shit was really good, and he liked reading my stuff, and that I was a good writer. He even mentioned something about including it in the unit's history and archives. That didn't relieve me one bit, like I said, it made me more freaked out. I'm waiting for him to say the word "but" followed by a couple Article 15s.

Then we discussed things: Operational Security, how the enemy could use what I wrote on my blog as useful information, he told me not to mention weapons capabilities and the use of TOW missiles in firefights and to not mention any names, like Lt. Armeni, that these terrorists could use that information to harass the family back home and possibly put them in danger, and specific locations like Bridge 5 or the Pepsi bottling plant, and he told me that the process that I used to load the .50-cal during a firefight could be information that the enemy could use against us.

I agreed with 100% of everything he was saying, and I agreed to take all that information off the blog immediately. He was totally right. And the final conclusion from what he told me was that I could continue writing, but maybe have my platoon sergeant read my stuff before I post. He stressed that he didn't want to censor me and that I still had the freedom of speech thing, as long as I wasn't doing anything that would endanger the mission. I totally 110% agree with him on that one. I thanked him and I told him that I would not want to do anything that would endanger anybody here or back home, which is of course true. Finally I walked out of his office, with a feeling that I had just dodged a full mag of AK-47 bullets. I went back to my room, and my roommate (Sgt. Horrocks, who I told about the blog just the other day) was waiting for me all wide eyed and said, "Well, what did he want?!?!?! What happened?!?! You busted?!" I told him all about what happened. And then I said, "Well, the positive thing is at least he knows who I am now." And Horrocks looked at me and said, "That could be a good thing, or a bad thing."

These words I write keep me from total madness.
—Charles Bukowski

Posted by CBFTW at 6:18 p.m., August 10, 2004

SNIPER FIRE (?)
The other day, we went somewhere, and did something (counter-mortar mission). Once we got there, we dismounted from our vehicles, and our squad leader placed us where he wanted us to be, and then told us our sectors of fire. Me and my AG went down and set in behind this berm. Today, my AG brought a new toy with him. An expensive mini handheld

digital camcorder he ordered off the Internet. He just received it the other day in the mail, and he was extremely excited to have one now. Like a kid with a new toy on Christmas he kept on playing with it, filming the sky, the dirt, his boots, his weapon, the things around us, and then with a smile he pointed the camera at me and enthusiastically said, "Say hi to the camera!" I looked at him and gave him my best expressionless face that said, "Put that toy away." He got the picture, said sorry, folded his camera up, and put it back in his cargo pocket.

We sat there for a while staring silently at Mosul, when all the sudden we heard, kinda off to the distance, about to our 7 o'clock, two cracks of gunfire. The bullets kinda skimmed close to where all of us were at, and hit this old ancient-looking building that was about 200 meters away from us. We heard the bullets impact the building and make a ricochet noise. We looked at each other, paused for a second to see if any more shots were going to be fired, none did, and then I said, "Hey, was that fired at us?" Neither of us knew. So I cautiously walked over to my squad leader and asked, "What the hell was that?" He had the radio up to his ear, and said, "Wait, I'm finding out right now." Nobody knew. So one of us fired a warning shot in that area to see if they'd fire back. The area where the shots were fired was about 500 to 600 meters away, and had a bunch of trees and shrubbery. Nobody saw a thing and no shots were fired after that. Some of us thought maybe it was sniper fire (if it was, the guy had extremely pathetic aim) and some of us just thought maybe it was just some guy who wanted to test fire his weapon. Who knows?

Time went by and we then loaded back onto our vehicles, and we drove off to a different location, dismounted, and did the same thing. Sat and waited. The sun was long gone now, and the moon was out to take its place. We were overlooking a huge section of Mosul and you could see the lights of the houses and mosques in the city. We all sat and stared at the city for a while. Every now and then a neighborhood's electricity would go out, and several complete city blocks would be in complete darkness for a while, and then a couple minutes later the power would go back up, and the lights in that neighborhood would turn back on. This is a very common thing here. Lights on, lights off. Another very common thing that happens here in Mosul is tracer fire being fired in the air as well as the sounds of gunfire and loud explosions going off somewhere in the city. I remember when I first got to Mosul I'd see that and be like "Holy shit! People are trying to kill each other." Now, when I see it I think "Gee, I wonder what's going on over there."

Posted by CBFTW at 10:06 p.m., August 12, 2004

MAD MORTARMEN GOOSE CHASE

Today we went somewhere and did something (movement-to-contact mission). All of us in the back of the vehicle brought a book to read during this ride. I brought George Orwell's *Homage to Catalonia.* The *New Yorker* refers to it as "perhaps the best book that exists on the Spanish Civil War." I never read anything by Orwell before, and this book was sent to me by a reader of my weblog, who suggested that I check out Orwell, because he was a good one, and a soldier who turned writer, and he suggested that I do the same someday.

Our combat medic brought a thick ass book called *The History of Western Philosophy,* Spc. Cummings had with him a George Carlin, and Fritsche brought a paperback vampire ghosts and goblins book by his favorite author Anne Rice.

The medic was telling us that Anne Rice novels all have suggestive "gay" overtones to them, which is kinda hard to imagine, two vampires going at it sucking face. I've never read Anne Rice so I wouldn't know, nor do I care. To me books on vampires are right up there with sci-fi romance novels. Not really my cup of tea.

I got a lot of good reading done on this ride, all of us sitting in the back of the vehicle quietly reading away, when all the sudden we all heard a loud explosion, which made all of us stop reading and bookmark our places to find out what's going on. Over the radio, they said a huge air-burst mortar went off over the FOB. Then a couple minutes later, they called in that the FOB just got hit with four mortar rounds. We had Pvt. Fritsche up in the back air guard hatch, and he shouted down to us that he heard the direction where the mortars were fired from, so we turned the vehicles around and headed full speed to that direction. I asked him if he wanted to trade places from the air guard hatch, just in case we come into contact. He just smiled at me and confidently said, "I got this one."

Cool.

We were now in hot pursuit to catch some crazed mortarmen. So I opened up my book and continued reading. I was on page 92, the part where Orwell was frantically chasing down a fascist with a bayonet fixed to the end of his rifle and was about to engage in some close quarters combat. Read for a bit, then when we got to the area where we thought was the point of origin for those fired mortars, I stopped reading and bookmarked my place in the book with an Iraqi dinar that had Saddam's face on it (dinars make for great bookmarks), and we dismounted in this really shitty Third World area of Mosul that had this really bad stench of rotten milk lingering in the air. Tons of trash all over the place, and a bunch of cows and stray chickens roaming around freely. Lots of little kids also came out of nowhere to stare at us. We talked to some of the locals to see if they had seen anything. Then over the radio they said to be on the lookout for a red vehicle or something they said was heading east on this one road, so we all raced back onto our vehicle and burned rubber outta there.

The same way a cop races to an armed robber call in his police car, the only thing that was missing was the theme song to the television show *COPS* ("Bad Boys") blasting from our Stryker radio speakers.

I opened up my book and continued to read. I wanted to find out if Orwell ended that fascist that he was chasing down with a bayonet fixed rifle, but the guy got away. Damn. So I then continued reading and I got to the part where the fascists were closing in on Orwell, and while under heavy enemy fire he was now about to fuck some dudes up with a hand grenade or some kind of bomb of sorts, and was ready to blow them to bits, when all the sudden we stopped, and I had to close the book back up because the back ramp dropped and we were told to dismount.

Me and Doc Haibi took a knee and watched as the guys from a different squad pulled over this red car with four middle aged Iraqi men inside, all wearing that white traditional dress thing that they wear, and began searching them. These guys were extremely cooperative and they gladly let us search their vehicle, we didn't find shit, then another red car came by, and they pulled them over, and while they were searching that car, a couple red cars drove by, and then they pulled over another red car and searched that car, didn't find shit in that one either. Then we said fuck it, and loaded back up and went to the location where the mortars were fired, and then we stopped and dismounted.

I looked around and noticed that we were now in the same area where a couple months ago we had a mounted patrol, and we were driving around slowly, and we were the trail vehicle, and my AG and I were sticking out of the back air guard hatches. And we were being followed by literally hundreds of little kids, they were hooting and hollering, clapping and saying stuff in Arabic. So my AG looks over at me and with a mischievous smile says, "Watch this!" and then he starts chanting: "U-S-A! U-S-A! U-S-A!" over and over again, next thing you know all these little kids, hundreds of them, start chanting "U-S-A!!" Over and over again, each time a little louder. We were both laughing and thought this was all funny until I saw the reaction on the older people's faces. They didn't look too thrilled about that, and once I noticed that, I said, "Dude, that's not cool! Make them stop yelling that shit!" But it was too late, these kids were having too much fun chanting U-S-A! Next thing you know I saw an older Middle Eastern lady wearing all black pick up a rock and throw it at us. Of course that causes a huge chain reaction of rock throwing and they're raining down all over the vehicle and all over us. Our guys inside the vehicle are yelling, "Hey what the fuck is going on out there?" As I was delivering a situation report on what the fuck was going on, a rock hit me on the side of the helmet. I got the rage. I said, "Fuck this shit—I'm firing warning shots!" Sgt. Horrocks, who has rank on me, was inside the vehicle when all the rocks were being thrown at us, and he yelled for me not to fire a warning shot at them (like I was trained to do in situations like this), but to instead throw shit back at them. Like fucking what? My dog tags?

Usually I bring a pocket full of metal marbles and my trusty slingshot with me for crowd control situations like this, but like a dumb ass, I forgot them today. And as always, the day I forget the slingshot is the day I need it the most. But after we all argued for a while about whether firing a warning shot was a good idea or not, we just turned around and beat it the hell out of there. Lesson learned.

Anyway, we were now back in the same neighborhood where the infamous U-S-A incident took place. We dismounted and searched another car, didn't find shit again. Tons of stray kids hanging out on the street corners observing us with watchful eyes. Every kid here in Iraq looks like the kids you see on those TV commercials where they say, "For only 99 cents a day you can help feed this starving child." A real depressing part of Mosul. My squad leader was trying to talk to a crowd of little kids, asking them if they saw or heard anything, and while he was asking them, this one kid comes running up to us with an old empty brass 105 artillery shell, and then this other kid comes running up to us with another expired artillery shell. Both demanded money for their discovery. "Give me dollar!" they said.

Then this other kid came running over to us with an RPG fin and a handful of dirty .50-cal bullets. These kids were just finding this crap off the streets. Amazing. Then all the sudden this really skinny Iraqi kid comes running up to us with a fucking HAND GRENADE in his hand. "HOLY SHIT!!! DROP THE FUCKIN' HAND GRENADE!!! DROP IT NOW!!!" We all started yelling. The little kid, still with this proud smile on his face that said, "Look what I just found," just dropped the grenade on the ground, and walked over to my squad leader and said, "Give me money!" It was an old pineapple grenade that was all dirty and rusty, it looked like something left over from the Iran-Iraq war. We asked him where he found it, and innocently he pointed to this old abandoned house that was in the middle of a field that looked like a junkyard. We secured the area and searched the house. Didn't find shit.

Then the kids pointed to another house, this one owned by a wife-beater-undershirt-wearing Iraqi with a massive facial beard and more body hair than Teen Wolf. We searched his house, again didn't find shit. Finally four blue-and-white ICP trucks showed up packed with Iraqi Police dressed in blue khakis and strapped with AK-47s. They dismounted and asked where the hand grenade was, we pointed them to where it was, and they went over, picked it up, and they like kinda laughed at us, like "You're kidding, you guys called us over here for this?!" I could hear one ICP say in broken English, "This no good." They took the grenade and drove off. And we did the same. My squad leader then explained to me that when the 101st was here they would give the little kids in that area money and/or MREs if they found weapons and UXO, which is why every time when they see US forces they always drag over shit like that and say, "Give me! Give me!"

I then pulled *Homage to Catalonia* out of my cargo pocket and continued reading. I kinda dig this Orwell guy, he's not half bad.

> This is war! Isn't it Bloody?
>
> —George Orwell, *Homage to Catalonia*, p. 95

Posted by CBFTW at 11:40 p.m., August 15, 2004

FOB Arrest

Our battalion commander was out on business in Tall Afar, which was totally overrun by insurgents at the time, with Alpha and Charlie Companies when they called me in to see the battalion commander for 1-14 Cav, who we are now attached to and under their command.

It was right after I posted my "Mad Mortarmen Goose Chase" piece on my weblog, which pretty much pissed off somebody high up in the chain of command.

I was walking back from the chow hall when my squad leader informed me that the battalion commander for 1-14 Cav requested my presence ASAP at their war room, which was located up the street from us, over by the chow hall where I had just come from.

My squad leader told me to report to my platoon sergeant first before going over there. I walked over to my platoon sergeant's room and apologized to him for getting into all this trouble with the chain of command, and wasting his time on all this, and he told me that it was okay, and to go over to the 1-14 Cav war room right now, and he and the First Sergeant would meet me there shortly.

I walked over to the nearby bus stop and waited for the bus to come around and pick me up. When the bus showed up and the doors opened up, my First Sergeant and Lt. Iverson stepped out. I thought for sure that First Sergeant was going to chew me out, but instead he was extremely cool about it, and told me to just go over to the war room, and that he would meet me there in a little bit, and not to worry about all this.

Lt. Iverson, who was with him, then said, "Hey, you're the guy that does that blog?" I told him "Roger, sir," and he said that he really liked it, and that my writing was pretty good, I thanked him and walked onto the bus, kinda shocked, and at the same time embarrassed that the XO read my blog. As soon as I sat down, a Pfc from 1st Platoon sat across from me, and he looked over at me and said the same thing, "Hey are you the guy that does the blog that everybody's talking about?"

I wanted to lie to him, because I didn't really like people

knowing that I was the guy, it made me feel uncomfortable and like kind of a geek, but since he was standing next to me when the XO asked me if I was the guy that did the blog, I couldn't lie to him, so I told him that yeah, I was the guy.

On the bus ride to where I had to go, the Pfc told me that he thought what I was doing was a great thing, because according to him, all I was doing was telling the truth, and it's about time somebody fucking told the truth and was telling our story here in Iraq, since nobody else was, and he went off on the media, and how they don't report shit, and how the Army should worry about more important shit.

Once we got to my stop, I thanked him for sharing his take with me and exited the bus. My platoon sergeant was there waiting for me, I immediately apologized to him again for all the trouble that my stupid blog was creating for him, he then told me again not to worry about it. We sat and talked for a while as we waited for First Sergeant to show up, then we all walked over to the 1-14 Cav war room together, to see the man.

I was supposed to see their battalion commander, but he wasn't around, so instead I spoke with their sergeant major, who looked a lot like a TV movie version of the sergeant major in *We Were Soldiers.* I was expecting them to just tell me, Look, you crossed the line and you can't write anymore, what the fuck were you thinking, get down on your face and start pushing, that kinda crap, which I would have been totally cool with. I was kinda over the whole blog thing by now anyway.

I also wasn't a big fan of my blog now being monitored by the Army, who were probably dissecting my every word, and couldn't wait for me to slip up. I also wondered if my presence was being requested because of my "Hello to Military Intelligence" thing that I wrote a couple days ago:

I would like to take this time now to say a nice warm *Mar-Haba* (that's "Welcome" in Arabic) to all my new readers down at MI who are now reading this site and have this bookmarked on their computers. Glad to have you all aboard, and I hope you all like the site. Hopefully you'll find this site more entertaining than most of that other boring crap I'm sure you guys have to sift through all day.

I started getting déjà vu as soon as the sergeant major started talking to me, because everything that he was now saying was an exact carbon copy of what my battalion commander, Lt. Col. Buck James, had told me a couple weeks before when I got called in to see him.

They both told me that as a soldier I still had the right to freedom of speech, and then he went on to say that as far as he could tell from reviewing the website himself, he didn't see any violations whatsoever in operational security in any of my writings or on the website, the only thing that he could maybe see as bad was that if somebody was to read the entire site they could maybe see a pattern of how we do our missions, and then he said that this was not his decision, but that this had come down from *way* higher: that I was not being punished, that I still had my freedom of speech and that I could still write, BUT I was to be confined to the FOB, and that I was not allowed to go on any missions outside of the FOB until further notice.

Nothing further.

I didn't even try or want to contest this or ask why. I just replied with a "Roger, Sergeant Major." He then reiterated that I was *not* being punished, and again that I still had the freedom of speech thing, and that I could still write whatever I wanted to write on the blog, but I could no longer go on any missions whatsoever with my platoon outside the wire.

My First Sergeant, who surprisingly was on my side for all of this, then asked him again why and for how long, to which the sergeant major had no answer, and First Sergeant asked him to physically show him where on my website that I violated operational security, so that he would know and this would be corrected. Again, the sergeant major had no answers for him.

First Sgt. Swift then explained to him that I was a good soldier and that our platoon was short-manned right now, and that they needed every single swinging dick out there on missions, and I was one of their most experienced machine gunners in the platoon, and they needed me out there.

The sergeant major had no answers for him.

The sergeant major then looked at me for a second, sized me up, and asked me if I went to college, and if I was a writer before I joined the Army.

I told him that I didn't, and I wasn't.

Then in disbelief he said, "Wow, you're a good writer, that stuff you wrote is pretty fucking good."

I thanked him, and all three of us returned back to the conexes.

First Sergeant told me not to worry about all this and he would try to get me back to going out on missions ASAP.

Of course when I returned to the conexes, the word was already slowly getting out that I was again in trouble with the chain of command. Spc. Scroggins, a man who would rather be anywhere else but Iraq, was one of the first guys who asked me what happened. I told him I was confined to FOB because of my blog and would be unable to go out on missions till further notice; he then called me one lucky bastard and joked, "Shit, man! I'm gonna start a blog, too, man, and talk hella shit about how fucked up this war is and just say that this is all bullshit man, and get my ass confined to the FOB, too!"

Now to most people, being confined to the FOB and no longer allowed to go on any life-threatening missions outside the wire might be considered a blessing of sorts, but I didn't view it like that. Even though they said I wasn't being punished, confining me to the FOB was the worst possible punishment they could have thrown at me. It completely embarrassed me.

The next day my platoon was placed on QRF, and at around lunchtime they all got called up because mortars were being dropped on civilians at a busy marketplace in downtown Mosul. They all left to go deal with that, while I sat in my room.

Pissed.

Several hours later they all came back and Sgt. Horrocks told me all about it, how there was blood all over the place, and he even saw a huge chunk of skull just sitting there in the middle of the street in a puddle of blood.

I didn't get an order to stop writing, but it came in loud and clear to me that somebody didn't like what I was doing and that if I wanted to go out on missions again that I was going to have to stop. And since I wanted to go back out on missions ASAP, that is what I planned to do.

About a week before I was confined to the FOB, I did a brief interview from one of our phone centers with a *Wall Street Journal* Pentagon reporter who found out about me through my blog. The interview was for a story that they were doing on soldiers voting in this election.

I didn't even know that the *WSJ* article came out until I was sitting at the chow hall, by myself (because my platoon was out on a mission without me), and my CO came up to me and said, "Congratulations, they quoted you in the *Wall Street Journal* today, good job."

Which shocked me because for some reason I thought I was going to get busted because I did the interview without getting it approved first and I didn't go through the Army public affairs office so they could brief me on what I could and could not say to the media. And I was also a little nervous about the

"I'm voting for Ralph Nader" comment that I made.

After my CO notified me of the *Wall Street Journal* article, I walked over to the Internet cafe to check out the article for myself and to read my e-mails. The journalist who ran the story sent me an e-mail thanking me for the interview, so I responded with, No problem, anytime, by the way I'm confined to the FOB and can't go out on any missions with my platoon till further notice.

He immediately e-mailed me back telling me to call him collect ASAP. So I did, and I told him all about it, and he said he was interested in the story, and that he would send some e-mails around and find out what the hell was going on, and get back to me.

He was a cool guy, I told him that I wanted to get back with my platoon ASAP, and he told me that maybe if he sent a couple e-mails to a couple people, and asked a couple questions, that might put some pressure on them to get them to allow me back to my platoon.

The next day he forwarded me the e-mails that he received from General Ham, and my battalion commander, who like I said earlier was out in Tall Afar on business and had no idea that I was confined to the FOB. (Tall Afar at this time was becoming a really hot spot for insurgents.)

General Ham stated that I was confined to the FOB because I posted something on my blog that command felt jeopardized operation security, which was news to me, because nobody told me anything about that.

Here is the e-mail that the BC, Buck James, then sent to Chris Cooper.

——Original Message——
From: buck james
Sent: Wednesday, August 18, 2004 7:44 AM
To: Cooper, Christopher
Subject: RE:
Chris,
I don't mean to be short, but I am very busy right now. Spc Buzzell is not being punished nor is he confined in any way to my knowledge. There is an ongoing commander's inquiry to determine if there was a breach of operational security anywhere in his "blog." I am unaware if there is a specific policy that refers to "blogging," but the rules on what can and cannot be made public are very clear—regardless of the medium used to transmit. I counseled Spc Buzzell along with his Platoon Sergeant on these points and ensured that he understood that anything he was unsure about should be reviewed by his chain of command. I can tell you that Spc Buzzell is an outstanding soldier who has performed gallantly on many occasions. I am proud to have him and men like him in my unit.

LTC Buck James
Tomahawks!
Punish the deserving!

Immediately after, Chris Cooper, a reporter from a newspaper that has a paid circulation of over two million, asked General Ham and my battalion commander a couple questions about this whole thing, I was instantly released from house arrest and able to go back on missions with my platoon. I then immediately posted:

STAY TUNED

Amendment I
Congress shall make no law respecting an establishment of religion, or prohibiting the free exercise thereof; or abridging the freedom of speech, or of the press; or the right of the people peaceably to assemble, and to petition the government for a redress of grievances.

story developing . . .

posted by CBFTW at 6:04 p.m. Thursday, August 19, 2004

I'm not stupid. I know soldiers don't have freedom of speech. But I posted the First Amendment because I wanted it to be my middle-finger salute to whoever was confining me to the FOB. I also dropped the *Fear and Loathing* subtitle to create speculation that the Army was telling me what I could and could not write, which kinda worked because it created a buzz on the "blogosphere," as they call it.

If the Army wanted to play fuck-fuck Army games with me, fine.

Game on.

NPR, one of the most listened-to radio stations on this planet, with twenty-two million weekly listeners, contacted me via e-mail about possibly doing an interview for a story on their *Day to Day* program about military blogs in Iraq. Again, they contacted me. I did not contact them. Being a huge fan of NPR, I was totally cool with this.

Soldiers' Iraq Blogs Face Military Scrutiny

Day to Day—August 24, 2004
Military officials are cracking down on blogs written by

soldiers and Marines in Iraq, saying some of them reveal sensitive information. Critics say it's an attempt to suppress unflattering truths about the U.S. occupation. NPR's Eric Niiler reports.

A blogger with the pen name CBFTW, stationed near Mosul with the 1st Battalion, 23rd Regiment, says he began his My War weblog to help combat boredom. "I'm just writing about my experiences," the soldier says. "I'm pretty much putting my diary on the Internet—that's all it is."

CBFTW says he has avoided describing sensitive information, such as U.S. weapons capabilities, weaknesses, and scheduling. But earlier this month, CBFTW was lectured by commanders about violating operational security. Two other popular blogs run by soldiers have been shut down recently.

Lt. Col. Paul Hastings, a spokesman for the unit CBFTW belongs to, said the soldier's blog now has to be reviewed by his platoon sergeant and a superior officer. In an e-mail to NPR, Hastings said the popularity of blogging has increased the chance that soldiers may inadvertently give away information to Internet-savvy enemies.

But some critics worry that military officials are trying to muffle dissent from troops in the field. "I really think it has much less to do with operational security and classified secrets and more to do with American politics and how the war is seen by a public that is getting increasingly shaky about the overall venture," says Michael O'Hanlon, a senior fellow at the Brookings Institution in Washington.

Over and Out

Ever get the feeling you've been cheated?
—Johnny Rotten's last words at
the Sex Pistols' last gig, 1978

I then decided it'd be smart to keep a low profile after the NPR interview. I figured if the Army found out about it, they'd probably get pissed and shut my blog down, so I decided to go ahead and do it for them, before they gave me the order to do so. I took every single post that I had ever written down from the blog and posted a Johnny Rotten quote up on there, and left it that way for a couple weeks. I needed a break from the whole blog thing for a while. It was becoming more of a headache now than anything else.

The people keeping CB from posting are the same people that kept him from skating the Ralph's parking lot back in the day . . . that is all you have to know about liberty and freedom, the politics of skateboarding.

—DL

(Comment written and posted by reader.)

Everybody Knows

The whole time I was in Mosul I didn't meet a single embedded reporter while I was there. Not a single one. And a couple days after I posted the Men in Black entry on my blog I came across a sergeant from a different platoon who I've never spoken to before, and he came up to me and asked me if I was the guy who did the blog that everybody was talking about. I wanted to tell him no, but at this point, everybody knew I was "the guy" so I told him yes. He extended his hand and said, "I just want to thank you for what you're doing. Nobody back home knows what it's like here and you're telling the story for us and I just want to thank you for that."

I shook his hand and thanked him for thanking me. Then he told me how his friends and family ask him all the time what it's like here and he just forwards them my web address and says, "Read this, this is what it's like here." And they e-mail him back to say they're shocked and had no idea that it's like that here. Then he told me about his father, who's a big fan of the blog and follows it.

My father was also shocked when he found out about my blog. He found out about it when he was listening to NPR in his car and the reporter said "Army Specialist Colby Buzzell" over the air. My dad told me he almost crashed his car when he heard this, and knew right away that this was his son they were talking about and that he was in trouble again.

I didn't want my wife finding out about the blog the same way my father did, so when the blog started getting attention in newspapers and magazines left and right, I decided to go ahead and tell her about it. She works for a big-name financial company in Manhattan and I didn't want a coworker to tell her, someone who might come up to her pointing at the photo of me in the *Wall Street Journal* ("Army Blogger's Tales Attract Censors' Eyes") posing as a bad-ass with an AK-47 and a cigarette in my mouth, saying, "Hey, isn't this guy your husband?" (Which of course they all did when it ran.)

Before the ambush on August 4 I was receiving a lot of e-mails from people, and I'd just scan over them briefly. I didn't have the time to respond to every single one of them personally, but I did read every single e-mail that was sent to me. But then, when I posted the "Men in Black" entry, my blog blew up like an IED on Route Tampa. I was getting e-mails from people all over the United States, Europe, Canada, South America, as well as soldiers in Kuwait, Afghanistan, and Iraq. Soldiers I didn't even know at FOB Marez were e-mailing me. Fuck, even the helicopter pilots that flew above us on missions were e-mailing to thank me. That's when I knew the blog was huge, once I started getting e-mail from helicopter pilots.

A lot of people were e-mailing me saying that they heard about the site from someone else, and then after they read it, were now going to e-mail everybody that they knew about it, and those people then told everybody that they knew about it, and it just completely took off from there.

Most of the e-mails I got were what I call "pat on the back" e-mails. People just e-mailing brief messages that went along the lines of "we support the troops, appreciate what you're doing there," and thanked me for serving. Of course, every now and then I'd get one that said things like, "Thank you for serving, I enjoyed reading your articles until you took off with the bad words. I for one am sorry that I won't be able to read about your experiences anymore. Wouldn't it be better to reach all the people instead of the few that will go ahead and read your articles?"

I always ignored and deleted those kind of e-mails from people. Fuck 'em. If they don't like swear words, they could go read somebody else's fucking blog.

About a week or so before this, in the back of the Stryker during a mounted patrol, Spc. Cummings asked me if I knew anything about a soldier in Mosul who had a blog. Haibi and I just looked at each other, and I asked Cummings why, and he told me that his parents e-mailed him saying that they were avid readers of the blog and asked him if he knew who the author was. Haibi and I just laughed, so I told Cummings all about it, and he told me all about how his father saves all the entries that I write on a separate file, and he goes through it all and meticulously deletes all the swear words and vulgar language out of it, and then hands the PG-13 (for violence) profanity-free version of this site to his mother to read. He told me that this has been a very arduous task for his father, deleting the many profanities that are littered throughout a majority of my writings.

I told Sgt. Horrocks about my blog, just because he was my roommate and he had started getting suspicious, and knew I was up to no good once I started hanging out at the Internet cafe all the time, updating my blog and responding to the huge amount of e-mails that I was receiving. He asked me why I didn't tell him about it earlier, and I told him I didn't want anybody to know about it because it was kind of dorked-out and I didn't want to get in trouble for it. He checked the blog out, and later told me that he thought my blog was a good thing because he felt that it was getting our story out there since the media sure as hell wasn't. He e-mailed his sister about the website and after she checked it out she told him to tell me to "save the profanities for the movie!" She did the same thing as Cummings's parents, delete the explicit language out of my shit, so that her ten-year-old son can read it, so he can get a good idea of what his uncle had to go through out in Iraq.

The e-mails I got from people telling me to watch my language usually just made me chuckle, because honestly I didn't even realize that I was swearing as much as I was. But sometimes I got an e-mail that hit close to home, that didn't make me laugh, that put everything into perspective. Like the e-mail I received from a mother who had lost a son here in Mosul several days before he was to return home on R&R. She was directed to my site a couple days after the "Men in Black" post, and after reading my site she sent me an e-mail and thanked me for writing about what was going on, because as she said, "I read many entries that day and felt blessed, comforted in a way, as you have given me a peek into what my son had experienced in Mosul." And she said, "You have thoughts like he would have had, I think. I just wanted to thank you for sharing in this way. God works through people by stirring their hearts and sometimes people never know how they are helping others. I thank you, pray for your safety and your safe return home."

I read her e-mail, and then I just sat there and stared at the computer monitor for a moment, and I didn't know what to say. What do you say to someone who's lost a son here? I don't know if I did the right thing or not, probably not, but I never wrote her back. I didn't know what to write, but I also never forgot about her.

GGGOOOAAALLL!!!

Now that I am confined to the FOB and can't leave because of my stupid weblog, my platoon finally gets a mission that requires us to remain here on the FOB. But not a cool mission, like a kick down the front door raid on a suspected terrorist house, but a goddamned countermortar Observation Post, not out on OP Abrams, but right here at FOB Marez up on the water tower.

Since this was a mission that's on our FOB, I was able to go on it. Lucky me. The water tower here at FOB Marez is about four stories high, and it's a huge steel ball that's painted gray, and has our unit patch painted on it, as well as the 101st, and the Iraqi National Guard logo. The Platoon had the OP broken down into shifts, two soldiers would go up there at a time, each one for only a couple hours. Tonight, it was me and Pfc. Fritsche.

There's a steel ladder that takes you all the way to the top of the tower, and I climbed up to the top first, and when I got there, I took a look at the spectacular view of Mosul, which looked kinda pretty at night, for a shithole that it is. I then

noticed that Fritsche wasn't up there yet, so looked back down to see what the hell was taking him so long, and I saw that Fritsche was only halfway up the ladder, but he froze, and wasn't moving at all.

I asked him what the hell was going on, and he told me that he didn't want to go all the way up to the top because he was scared of heights. Oh my god. I then asked him if he was serious or just fucking with me, and he told me that he was totally serious. I then told him to stop acting like a wimp and to keep going, and that it's not that bad up here. He told me again that he was too scared to climb any higher, and asked if he could pull the OP from where he was at, and I told him to stop being ridiculous, and to get his ass to the top. He still didn't move, he kept on looking down at the ground, so I told him to stop looking down, and to just climb the ladder, one step at a time.

He still didn't move, so I yelled again for him to get his ass up here, and he slowly, one step at a time, made it to the top. We then took a seat, and once Fritsche got himself adjusted to being up there, and chilled out, we both took our helmets off and quietly stared off into the city.

And I started to remember back when I was a civilian. I lived in Los Angeles for a while. On random nights I used to go up to the historic Griffith Observatory up in the Hollywood Hills (usually on some mind-altering stimulant), and I'd sit up there for hours and hours and stare off down at the illuminating lights coming from the urban streets and buildings down below. For some reason I always thought L.A. looked really cool from way up there. Good from afar, but far from good (kinda like Mosul).

Now years later, I'm constrained up in some fucking water tower in Mosul, Iraq (itching for stimulants to help me cope with the boredom), staring off at the night lights radiating from this ancient Islamic city, with a guy who's scared of heights.

In Los Angeles, I used to look out onto that city at night and think to myself, Damn, I wonder how many people out there are fucking right now? In Iraq, I look out onto Mosul, and I think to myself, Damn, I wonder how many AK-47s are stashed out there, or Gee, I wonder how many people out there would love to kill an American?

Working a countermortar OP up in the water tower is a lot like working a guard tower on Force Pro. It sucks. There isn't shit to do up there except stand there and stare off into that city and fight boredom as best you can. You always have to make sure that you bring at least one full pack of smokes with you up in the towers. You're in a world of pain if you run out of smokes up in the guard tower, because there is absolutely nothing to do up there except chain-smoke cancer-causing cigarettes one right after another until your lungs physically hurt and you get sick from having way too high a toxic level of nicotine flowing through your bloodstream.

Thinking about shit is also a good way to stay alert and pass time up in the towers, I usually spend my time thinking about what the hell I'm going to do with myself once I get out of the Army, and if this dream gone bad is ever going to end. Even though I've spent countless hours here thinking about that very subject, I have yet to come up with a good answer.

At one time tonight I tried to blur my vision with my eyes while I gazed out onto the city, to pretend like I was staring out at Los Angeles again, but it just didn't work. No matter how hard I tried to pretend that I was somewhere else, I was still in Iraq.

At night here in Mosul, you can hear the faint barking of loathsome stray dogs coming from the city, and every now and then, all at the same time, this somewhat creepy recording in Arabic is blasted from all these shitty Radio Shack–quality speakers mounted on various mosques scattered randomly throughout Mosul. It's kind of eerie hearing these recordings, which is someone reading verses from the Koran in a monotone voice. Every time I hear those recordings I'm hit with the realization that I'm on the other side of the planet far away from home, and that I'm a stranger in a really strange land.

Like I said before, the sound of gunfire is also a pretty common thing to hear coming from the city at night. Every now and then you'll also witness a burst of green tracers being fired up into the air. It's no big deal when it happens. After a while here it becomes one of those things that you just accept, and think absolutely nothing of it.

Another thing I remembered about Los Angeles was on New Year's Eve once, I was walking back home from the hidden bars tucked away in the Los Feliz hood of L.A., completely inebriated, and I looked out over to the neighboring sector of Los Angeles and I remember hearing celebratory gunshots being fired up in the air. The Iraqis do the same mindless thing here too, but it's every fucking night here. Religious holidays, Muhammad's birthday, Saddam's birthday, weddings, sweet 16's, job promotions, or just for the hell of it, they celebrate by firing a burst of AK-47 rounds in the air.

Well, tonight I was just chilling up in the water tower, lighting another Miami cigarette with the lit end of the cigarette I just consumed, when all the sudden came the sounds of gunshots being fired from all over the city. Me and Fritsche looked at each other and wondered what the fuck was going on. They were like everywhere. Far and near, left and right, over here, over there. I was like, Holy shit, what the fuck is going on tonight?!?! Is this like a signal or call sign for the start of some kind of all out fight to the death holy jihad on FOB Marez or something?

Bang, bang, bang, bang. So I started counting all the bursts of gunfire that I heard being fired: one, two, three, four, five, six . . . Finally after a couple minutes the shooting dissipated. I was unable to count every single gunshot I heard fired, some overlapped, but the final unofficial score that I came up with was 67 bursts fired. I remember a while back, maybe a couple months ago, I was up in guard tower 16 when it was some Islamic holiday here, Muhammad from the Koran's birthday, and there weren't nearly as many celebratory gunshots fired up in the air that night as there were tonight.

Then, down by the bottom of my tower, where our Stryker vehicle was parked, Sgt. Blough poked his head up from the TC hatch and yelled up to us, "Hey, I just heard over the radio that Iraq is up! One to nothing!"

Holy shit, that's right. I completely forgot about that. The Olympic soccer games are going on, and these people here are just as fanatical, if not more so, for their soccer team than they are for their religion.

And I thought Raiders fans were bad.

Posted by CBFTW on August 22, 2004

I Quit

I wrote the "Goal!" entry on my laptop computer, saved it on a disc, and went over to my First Sergeant's door and banged on it to tell him that I had my "blog" post available for him to read. I don't know why, but I always feel like a fucking geek whenever I say the word *blog*.

I could tell that he was busy and that he had more important shit to do than to read one of my blog posts like it was my English homework. That was when it hit me that this was all completely stupid.

Here we are, inside some FOB in butt-fuck Iraq, surrounded by thousands of people that would love to kill Americans, and I'm handing over what I've written for review for the green light before I can post it on the Internet. I signed up to be an infantry soldier in the United States Army, whose job is to locate, capture, and kill noncompliant forces, not be some writer or some wannabe Ernie Pyle.

That was when I said, You know, this is lame, I quit.

I then handed over the disc to my First Sergeant, and he placed it in his computer and started reading it. I watched him for facial reactions as he was reading, at times he cracked a smile, and then he kept his military bearing and went back to First Sergeant face, and he said to me that he saw no OPSEC issues in what I wrote at all, and he then called over my CO, Captain Robinson, and he came along and he did the same thing, he read it, and at parts cracked a semi-smile, but quickly reversed himself and then agreed with First Sergeant, and he saw nothing wrong with it, and he quickly got up and left because he had more important things to go deal with.

So I went ahead and posted that entry on the blog, and shortly after that I posted an official statement there that I was no longer writing. I decided to officially quit writing altogether because I wasn't a real big fan of wasting my chain of command's time by having them review all my writing for "OPSEC" concerns prior to me posting it on the World Wide Web.

At least, *I* wouldn't be writing anything on there . . .

Operation Black Typhoon

Guide-ons, guide-ons, guide-ons.
This is Tomahawk Six.
We are about to initiate Operation Black Typhoon.
Shoot first,
shoot straight,
protect the innocent,
and
punish the deserving.
God be with us.
Tomahawk Six,
OUT.

—Our battalion commander's message to us minutes before we started Operation Black Typhoon

Tall Afar was completely taken over by insurgents. All of us were waiting inside our Strykers in full kit at the motor pool, minutes away from leaving the FOB for Operation Black Typhoon in Tall Afar, when that message came out over the radio. As soon as we all heard the words, "Tomahawk Six, OUT," I looked around at everybody inside my vehicle and I could tell that it charged everybody up. His message sent chills down all our spines, and all you could hear were wild cheers coming from bloodthirsty soldiers from inside all the other Strykers that were parked around us waiting to leave. There's probably not a single soldier here that doesn't think that God put our BC on this planet to lead men into combat. He's that inspiring.

The message itself was short and sweet, but it had the power to energize all of us to *want* to go out and "punish the deserving."

I was behind the M240 machine gun, and my squad leader was out the other back hatch. I was a little bit nervous about this one because they put out that the only road into Tall Afar, code name: Route Sante Fe, was to be heavily lined with IEDs, and that the enemy had fortified positions in four spots along the road, so expect to be ambushed on the way there.

Fuck it.

While we were staging in the motor pool for this mission, this message came over the net:

> "All stations this net, this is Tomahawk Yankee, break.
>
> Be advised that the Sapper Element has made contact, break.
>
> They have made contact with six to ten individuals on both east and south side of Route Santa Fe, break.
>
> They have received both small-arms fire and RPG fire, break."

The whole drive to Tall Afar was pretty nerve-racking, the entire time I was like, hurry the fuck up, let's hurry up and get there and get this over with.

Once we got near Tall Afar, at around 0200, we stopped all the vehicles on this road that was just on the outside of the city, and waited. Hovering way up above us was a C-130 Specter gunship, equipped with a Gatling gun and a 105mm cannon, engaging targets.

You could faintly hear in the background the bombing going on. It was a soft *boom,* and then seconds later you would hear another *boom,* then another, and another. I looked up into the night sky with my NODs on to see if I could make out anything, and all I could see was the IR spotlight coming down from the circling gunship.

Second Platoon's job was to provide security for TOC (tactical operations center). Basically park our Strykers around them and make sure they don't get attacked. A dull job, but somebody had to do it.

Once we got to where we needed to be we dismounted and pulled 360 security. By this time it was all death from above going on in Tall Afar. The C130 Specter gunship was hitting Tall Afar, and hitting it hard, with nonstop bombing. I was amazed that it was getting hit with only *one* gunship, it looked to me that there had to be at least a dozen of them up there to create this havoc. Nonstop bombing. *Boom, BOOM, boom, BOOM!!*

I removed the M240 from the tripod mount and me and my AG, Spc. Benitez, set our gun position over by this building, set the gun down, and pointed the M240 out away from the city.

I knew that this was going to be a very long night, so I set my ammo bag down and used it as a backrest as I sat down. The fireworks show that was being provided was going on behind me, and even though I was supposed to concentrate on scanning my sector, I couldn't help but turn around and watch the bombing.

It's amazing how everybody in my platoon slowly turned into professional combat photographers as this deployment went on. Everybody pulled out their digital cameras and started doing some night photography. If you want to do combat night photography, here's what you do: You take your NODs off your helmet, put your camera lens to the eyepiece of your NODs, and now your camera has night vision. (I learned this trick when I was in Kuwait and I took photos this way of the lights that would beam up at night from the oil refineries.)

Right when I got to Fort Lewis, the twenty-one-days-to-Baghdad thing was going on in Iraq. All the major news networks were showing real-time footage of the bombings. I remembered sitting at the chow hall as a cherry private, watching all this happen live on the television sets while I was trying to eat. Now, about a year later, I was witnessing the same kind of bombings with my own eyes here in Iraq.

From where we were, the explosions coming from the city looked like they were happening in slow motion, they gave off these beautiful flashes of light, magentas and reds and violets. The bombing looked extremely peaceful to me from where I was sitting. Like something out of the movie *Fantasia.* In fact in my head I had classical music going as I sat there on my ass watching all this go on. I had to remind myself that each one of those beautiful explosions that I was witnessing probably took somebody's life.

Sgt. Horrocks, a man who seemed to be increasingly in love with the experience of this war, ran to my gun position and told me, "HOLY SHIT, MAN!! This shit gives me a fucking woodie, dude!!! This is badass! *Woo Hoo! Get some!!*"

I swear to God they should have issued Horrocks a cowboy hat instead of a helmet.

At about 0400 those three Red Bulls that I slammed back in the motor pool to keep me awake all night were slowly starting to lose effect, and I was coming down hard. I should have brought some more in my cargo pocket. Even with all those explosions going off behind me, I was struggling to keep my eyes open and stay awake. One time I closed my eyes and when I opened them back up I looked down at my watch and realized that I had been asleep for more than an hour. I looked over at my AG and he was racked the fuck out as well.

"Yo! Wake the fuck up."

He woke up, looked around. "Dude, what!? What's going on?!"

"Dude you were sleeping, man!"

"No I wasn't."

"Yeah you were, man. I saw you, man!"

"No I wasn't!"

Whatever, I didn't feel like arguing with him, especially when I was also guilty of sleeping, so I just dropped it.

Finally the sun started coming up over the horizon, and the bombings slowly started to decrease, but were not over yet. About two hundred meters from my gun position was a two-story house. Beside the house were two cows, one adult and one baby cow, each with a rope tied around its neck, attached to a metal spike in the ground. I felt sorry for them and I wanted to liberate the cows and untie them and let them go, but I couldn't.

As soon as the sun came up, people in the house were running around, doing this and that, constantly going to this pickup truck that was parked outside. Finally the family mounted up onto the truck. It was an old Iraqi lady, probably the grandma, an Iraqi man, the dad, his wife, two teenage daughters, and three little kids. That's eight people, all loading up onto the truck. Then the man started up the truck and they slowly started to drive away.

If my town was getting bombed the fuck up by the United States Army, I'd probably want to evacuate the family, too.

Now that the sun was up, my squad leader initiated a rest plan for us to get sleep. Every hour one of us would walk over to the Stryker that was parked one hundred to two hundred meters away and jump in and get an hour of sleep. One hour is not enough time for rack, but it's better than nothing.

At around 0800, there was a mass exodus of people leaving the city. I was amazed that there were actually people in that city when we were bombing the hell out of it, and I was equally amazed that there were people who survived it.

Hundreds of people were evacuating the city. My platoon

sergeant was firing off warning shots to get people to not evacuate the city unless they went through the checkpoint that the INGs were doing that was located on the main street out of the city, to the left side of us, a fair distance away. These people were completely miserable. Old people, women, children. Some people who looked like they could barely walk.

Over my Icom radio, I heard my squad leader call me and Spc. Cummings over to the Stryker, so I had Benitez get behind the M240, and he handed me his M4. Once we got to the vehicle, our squad leader told us to search every single person trying to leave the city.

Cool. Kinda like a TCP. I always liked TCPs because it was a chance to mingle with the locals and practice my really bad Arabic. I looked over at Cummings, and suddenly I had a burst of motivation, and I said to him, "Hell yeah! Checkpoint Charlie dude! Hell yeah!" (Charlie being my first initial.)

There were a lot of older Iraqi people who could barely walk trying to exit the city. Some were being assisted by their sons. They would come up to me, with total exhaustion in their faces, and with my weapon slung to my back and Spc. Cummings pulling security with his M4 on the side I began searching the individuals. I made them all line up in single file, and once they got to me, I would make them put their arms up while I patted them down for RPGs and WMD.

If they had a bag with them I would search it. I didn't search any of the women though (out of respect), unless they had a bag with them, then I would search the bag, and after I searched it I would say, "*Shookran*" (thank you). The bags were either filled with clothes or rice. These people were pretty cool and understanding of the situation. Some that came to the checkpoint would break down in tears, especially the elder citizens; the walk leaving the city was physically draining for them.

I looked at Cummings and I said, "Where the fuck is the Red Cross? Shouldn't they be here for something like this?"

At first I had no idea where the hell these people were going to walk to, the nearest city was like twenty miles away, but then I was told that there was a refuge for them set up right outside the city.

The sun was out now and it was extremely hot. I wasn't even doing any walking around or anything like that and I was exhausted. The line started getting longer and longer, and people were coming out of nowhere, and we had this huge mob of people in front of us wanting to get searched so that they could exit the city.

Then my platoon sergeant gave the order for us to stop searching, that there were way too many people and we'd be there all fucking day searching them, he told us to tell them to turn around and go to the ING checkpoint that was on the street two hundred meters away.

Fuck.

I had to tell all these people to turn around? And go back in this heat? Shit. I knew only a couple phrases and words in Arabic, the only words I knew that I could use in this situation were *En-Dawl* (turn around), at least I think that means turn around, and *Sayarra,* which I knew meant car, so I yelled to them, "*En-Dawl,*" and pointed to the street and said, "*Sayarra.*" (I forgot how to say "street.")

So there I was telling all these heartbroken Iraqis to turn around and go back to the street. They all looked at me like, "Come on, give me a break, let us through, *please!*"

As much as I wanted to let them through, I couldn't, I was under a direct order to tell them to turn around and go to the street. Some slowly and reluctantly did, and some started edging forward, like, Please, *please mista!* Let us pass.

This one man who was assisting his elderly grandfather who

could barely walk came up to me, holding the old man, and he started saying shit in Arabic, probably something like, "Please mista, look at us, look at this old man, he can barely walk, please let us through."

But I couldn't, then I noticed that a lot of them were getting upset, and wouldn't move. I didn't want this situation to escalate and get out of control, so I slung my weapon back around and pointed my M4 at the crowd and charged my weapon, which is the universal language for "Turn the fuck around and get the fuck out of here and go to the fucking checkpoint over by the street!" And I motioned with my rifle to go to the checkpoint. They all understood what that meant, and without any protest they all slowly turned around and walked away.

I got no pleasure whatsoever doing this. I felt like the biggest fucking asshole on the planet, and in fact I felt like a Nazi, and for the first time ever, I felt like I was the bad guy.

I felt sorry for them and when I looked over at the old man that could barely even walk, with the Iraqi man who was probably his son holding him, I just looked at them and said the only thing that I could, which was "Sorry."

They didn't say a word; they just gave me this look of complete helplessness, turned around, and walked away.

Part Four

Leave

I was happily packing up the last of my personal belongings in my conex room, getting ready for my leave, when my squad leader banged on my door and told me not to pack up all my stuff quite yet, and to stand by because they might need me on this mission.

I slowly started losing it mentally once he told me that. Charlie and Alpha company still had Tall Afar surrounded, and at the time my company (Bravo) was hanging out at the FOB, and on the final day of Operation Black Typhoon, all the "Tommies" would go into the city and clear it. They said that it would only be a quick operation—leave in the evening and be back the next day around noon. My flight back to the States would be the day after that, and since it was so close, they were going to go ahead and let me not go with them on the mission, just in case it ended up taking a lot longer than expected, because if it did there would be no way they could get me to the airfield to catch my flight back home, and if I missed that flight, I was screwed.

So until now I was under the impression that they didn't

need me for this operation. I remember back when we were in Samarra, at first they said that operation would only last forty-eight hours, but it ended up going for almost two weeks. I didn't want to be put in a situation like that again and jeopardize my leave.

So I walked over to my squad leader's room and told him that I wanted to use the open-door policy, which was the first time I'd ever done that, and that I didn't want to go on the mission to Tall Afar. I'd already had my leave and R&R canceled once, and I didn't want go through that again.

My squad leader then took me over to my platoon sergeant's room, and when I entered his room, my squad leader told him why I wanted to speak with him, and while that was going on I looked over at Sgt. Hoerner's refrigerator and noticed that he had a Patton quote taped onto the front of it that said, "My men can eat their belts, but my tanks gotta have gas!" That wasn't a good sign.

I told Sgt. Hoerner that I didn't want to go on the mission because I'd been here in Iraq for almost eleven months now, I'd had my leave and R&R canceled, almost every single person in the company had gone home already to see their wives and family, and I didn't want to risk it by going on this mission. He then told me that he would bring it up with the First Sergeant and see what he had to say. I thanked him and then thanked my squad leader and walked to my conex room.

Underneath the concrete mortar bunker that's right outside my conex door were Spc. Callahan and Sgt. Horrocks, both of them sitting down and smoking. I took a seat by them, pulled out a smoke, and started telling them all about my dilemma, and then I told them that maybe I should go with them, because the gun teams were kinda shorthanded and they probably needed me. I asked Sgt. Horrocks if I was doing the right thing by requesting not to go out on this mission and he said,

"If I was you, I wouldn't go." Spc. Callahan told me that I shouldn't go, too. "Look man, everybody else has gone home on leave already except you. Do you think any of them gave a fuck about you when they left you hanging? No, they left you man, they didn't give a fuck about you, fuck 'em, go home on leave man, you're CBFTW, man. Fuck the war, man!"

He was right. They all went home on leave, and they didn't give two shits about me when they left, so fuck 'em.

Sgt. Hoerner then came up to our mortar bunker with a book in his hand and said, "I just talked to First Sergeant, and he said you don't have to go on the mission."

He then handed me the book and said, "The battalion commander wanted me to give this to you. He wants you to read this when you have time and give it back to him when you're done with it." He handed me a hardcover book called, *The Inner Citadel: The Meditations of Marcus Aurelius.*

Cool.

Dude, Where's My Weapon?

Everybody in my platoon told me that when they take your weapon away from you before you go home on leave you're going to feel naked and you're going to be slapped with this feeling that you were missing something. I thought to myself, "Yeah right, that's a load of shit, whatever dude, etc." But when I turned over my weapon, and for the first time in almost eleven months I was without a firearm by my side, I felt completely defenseless and vulnerable. It was the weirdest fucking feeling in the world.

I impatiently waited for the freedom bird to come pick me up and take me away. For months I'd been watching countless planes leave that airfield, and every time I'd watch one of those planes take off and leave this shithole, I'd pray to God that maybe someday soon I'd be on one of those planes, and finally it looked like that dream just might come true. Even though I'd only be away from the shithole for two and a half weeks, the war for me in Iraq was over.

In the afternoon, a sergeant from S-1 gave me and three other guys from my company a ride in the back of a Humvee to the airfield. We were all extremely excited to finally be granted "mid-tour" leave after spending almost eleven months here.

At the airfield we checked in and we were all given a brief about the flight to Kuwait, then a civilian came up to me and handed me a T-shirt that had the New York Yankees logo on it, and he said, "Here, the Yankees sent over a bunch of these T-shirts for you guys to show their support and appreciation for what you guys are doing over here."

I handed the shirt back to the guy and said, "Fuck the Yankees."

Our flight to Kuwait didn't leave till the next morning, so I decided to walk over to the little PX they had set up by the airfield to kill some time. Do some eye-shopping, maybe waste some of my combat pay on an OIF (Operation Iraqi Freedom) vet shot glass or coffee mug or something lame like that. While I was walking to the PX my entire platoon drove past me in their Strykers. Everybody in my platoon knew that today was the day that I left Iraq.

They all honked their horns and cheered as they drove past me. The guys sticking out of the hatch were yelling, "Good luck, man! Have fun!" and some swore, "You lucky fuckin' bastard! I hate you! Fuck you!" I just waved and smiled as they drove past me. One person yelled, "Baby killer!" which made me laugh. The big joke was that everybody back in the States thought of us as baby killers, and as soon as I got off that plane in the States people were going to be calling us that. Whatever.

It was sort of a heartbreaking feeling listening to the guys drive past cheering for me and me knowing that I wasn't going to be with them for the next couple of weeks.

On to Kuwait, and from Kuwait to the East Coast.

About fucking time.

Can I Go Now?

We spent a day in Kuwait. From there, we flew to Germany. If you were going to the West Coast, you flew to Texas, and if you were heading to the East Coast, you flew to Atlanta. I was flying to Atlanta, and then on to New York, where my wife lives. We had a customs brief where they told us what we could and could not bring. Believe it or not, RPGs are not allowed back in the States. They told us that an individual once actually tried to smuggle one in his duffel bag as a war trophy. Pornography of any kind was also not allowed, but they did tell us that personal sexual-gratification devices such as blow-up dolls, dildos, etc., were okay to have. All I carried with me was a backpack full of stuff. After the customs brief, they sent us over to this room where we all lined up and had to get our bags inspected by some Air Force customs guys. I dumped the contents of my backpack onto the table for the latex-rubber-glove-wearing customs inspector guy to inspect. It was kind of embarrassing, because the Air Force guy called over a bunch of his friends to check out my stuff, and laughingly he said to his friend, "Hey, check this guy out!"

Fuck.

Contents of my backpack: three issues of *High Times* magazine, Guinness beer T-shirt and Jägermeister hat (a lady sent me those in a care package), OIF shot glasses, an empty flask that I bought earlier at a gift shop, OIF beer glasses, and of course, *The Inner Citadel: The Meditations of Marcus Aurelius.*

He asked me where I was from, and I told him California. He then nodded with a smile that said, Yup, I figured you were a Californian. While him and his buddies were flipping through my issues of *High Times*, I noticed an Army officer (a major) staring at me with a look of disgust, like, What the hell is wrong with you, soldier? I just gave him a nervous smile. After the airmen chuckled at the *High Times* centerfold of some green bud, they handed me my magazines back and told me I was free to pass customs, and not to have too much fun on leave. I thanked them and repacked my backpack and got the hell out of there.

Of course the flight back to the States was overbooked, and they needed volunteers to give up their seats and wait another night in Kuwait for the flight leaving tomorrow. Of course nobody volunteered. When I joined the Army, my dad told me to never volunteer for shit, and I decided to listen to my father's advice on that one. Then some high-ranking officer came out and gave a little motivational speech about Army values and personal sacrifice, and to think about all our buddies who were not coming home and didn't make it, and how him and his men had been waiting three days to get on a flight back to the States, and for us to please step up and volunteer to go on tomorrow's flight so they could be with their wives and families. Of course after his speech a bunch of people volunteered to be bumped off this flight. I on the other hand did not consider volunteering to be bumped off. Fuck that.

First Class to Coach

Sgt. Horrocks and other people in my platoon told me that

when you go home on leave, people would sometimes give up their first-class seats to you as a thank-you gesture. I thought that was kinda cool that people (strangers) were nice enough to do that. I've never sat in first class before, and I was looking forward to the fact that maybe some nice soul would be kind enough to do this for me.

Nobody did.

When I boarded the civilian flight from Atlanta to JFK, I entered the plane, and as I was walking through the bourgeois first-class section in my DCUs to get to my seat in coach, I tried to make eye contact with everybody, to see if anybody would be nice enough to give up their seat for me. I always wanted to see what first class was like on a plane.

I have no idea what kind of response or reaction I was actually expecting to get. One overweight businessman in suspenders was reading a *Wall Street Journal*, and he just briefly looked at me, and then went right back to reading his paper.

When I finally got to my seat in coach, I sat between a white lady and a young black girl who reeked of perfume. That was weird, smelling perfume on a girl again. It'd been a while.

As soon as I sat down in my seat, my body was physically telling me that I needed a drink. Army regs say you can't drink alcoholic beverages in uniform, but right now I could give a fuck about Army regs, and if anybody has a problem with me having a couple drinks in uniform after how I've just done eleven months in Iraq, they can suck my motherfucking dick.

As soon as the flight took off and we were on our way to JFK I finally got the attention of the slender brunette flight stewardess and called her over and politely asked her for a glass of the strongest drink she could serve. The girl to the left of me chuckled as soon as I said that. I guess the way I requested the strongest drink available kinda make me look like an alcoholic or something. The stewardess then smiled and said, "How about a Jack and Coke?"

Jesus H. Christ, what kind of flight is this? That's the strongest drink they serve?

Okay, fine, whatever, I'll take one, so I told her, "That's fine."

As the stewardess walked off with a smile to get me a Jack and Coke, the girl who had the window seat next to me asked me if I was heading to Iraq. I told her that I was actually in Iraq right now, and I'd been there for almost eleven months already, and that I was just here in the States to see my wife on leave. I guess that kind of shocked her, because she then offered to pay for my drink after that, which of course I told her that it was okay and she didn't have to, but she insisted. So of course I gave in and accepted her kind offer. When the stewardess came back with my drink, the girl handed her a twenty to pay for it, but the kind stewardess refused her money, she said that soldiers don't have to pay for drinks on this flight. Fuck yeah, that's what I'm talking about!

We made some small talk, and she asked me what Iraq was like, and I honestly had no idea how to answer that one, so I just told her, "It's interesting." She then asked me if Iraq was anything like how they show it on the news, and then she said, "I'm sure Iraq is not as bad as they make it sound on the news, like it's really not that bad over there, is it?"

I stared at the ice cubes in my drink for a second and said, "I don't know, I don't watch the news," and finished my drink.

I'm a Hero, Goddammit!

As soon as I got off the plane at JFK, I made a beeline straight to the airport bar, I had like three or four Jack and Cokes in me and I was feeling pretty good. So I walked into the airport sports bar that was located conveniently near the terminal that I'd just exited, and told the bartender that I needed a Long Island iced tea, and to make it strong. He then poured the drink in a beer glass and handed it to me. With my wallet out, I asked him how much I owed him for it, and he said for me to not worry about it, that this one was on the house. Cool. So I thanked him and gave him a couple bucks for a tip.

I then slammed the Long Island as if it was tap water, which received looks of shock from the people at the bar, and I exited to the baggage-claim area where the car-service driver that my wife ordered for me would be patiently waiting for me.

When I got to the baggage-claim area, there was a man there in a *Reservoir Dogs*–looking suit with a sign that said "Buzzell."

I walked up to him, pointed at the name tape on my uniform that said "Buzzell," and said, "That's me."

I was feeling pretty warm from the drinks, and the Long Island was slowly starting to hit me, thus I was feeling pretty damn good.

Once we got in the car, I asked the driver if I could light up a smoke, and he then explained to me, in a thick European accent, that New York has some Nazi rule that you can't smoke in the back of a cab, that if you do and get caught, both the passenger and the cabbie get slapped with a fine and a ticket.

Since I was still in desert camo uniform, which probably still smelled like Iraq, he asked me if I was coming back from Iraq. My speech was starting to slur slightly, and I told him that I was actually on leave from Iraq right now, and that I was only here in N.Y.C. for a couple weeks to visit my wife, who we were now on our way to pick up. She works in Manhattan.

He then said the whole "I really appreciate what you're doing over there, thank you for serving" type of stuff, and then he called me a hero and said since I was a hero, he would look the other way and let me smoke in the back of the cab, as long as I kept it kinda hidden and inconspicuous.

Cool. So I lit up a smoke on the DL and asked him where he was from, he told me Greece. I asked him what the hell he was doing in N.Y.C. if he's from Greece, and as he was explaining to me his whole story about why he moved to New York to be a cabbie, I looked out the windows and realized how foreign New York looked to me.

I remember how New York looked to me when I first visited back in 1996, how it was like nothing I'd ever seen before, even compared to San Francisco and Los Angeles, how it was this huge metropolis with a never-ending series of skyscrapers and people and cabs.

Now that I'd been in Iraq for the last eleven months, New York just looked completely unreal to me. It'd been a while since I'd seen people wearing "normal" clothes and makeup, and the billboards and cars and buildings; it all felt like sensory overload to me again.

All these people driving on the freeway in their own vehicles, going about their everyday lives, listening to the radio, enjoying the sunshine, I was thinking to myself that this war in Iraq doesn't affect these people at all. That fucked with me a little bit.

Then without even realizing it, I extinguished my cigarette the same way that I do in Iraq. It's called field stripping. Back at FOB Marez, flicking your cigarette butt on the ground is a definite "no-go," so what you do is you roll out the cherry, and then place the butt of the cigarette in your pants pocket and throw it away in the garbage. Every soldier that smokes in theater does this, because nothing upsets a First Sergeant more than walking past a conex with hundreds of cigarette butts littered on the ground, and you're pretty much in for an ass-chewing if some NCO sees you flick a cigarette on the ground.

Finally we got to my wife's work and picked her up. My last words to her at the airport almost a year before were for her to take one last look at me because the next time she sees me there might be some parts missing. She didn't think that was too funny.

We kissed, and then she pulled away and said, "*Eww.* How much have you been drinking?" I told her that I only had a couple on the plane ride here, that the girl sitting next to me on the plane offered me a drink and I didn't want to say no, that it would have been rude or something. (I didn't tell her about the Long Island I had at the sports bar.)

It was kinda awkward seeing each other again; in fact it took a couple minutes to get adjusted to each other.

The cabdriver was now taking us to my wife's overpriced apartment, which was located in Brooklyn. By now the iced tea was hitting me hard, especially after that cigarette I just smoked which intensified its effect, and I was pretty much drunk right about now, which made the world look extremely cool to me and bearable to look at. I was also now a complete lightweight thanks to the Army's no-drinking-in-theater policy, which I've only violated a couple times.

Once we crossed the Brooklyn Bridge that goes over the East River into Brooklyn, we started coming up to a Long Island University campus when all the sudden there was a "Warning! Enemy in area!" to my ten o'clock.

There on the corner of Flatbush and Fulton was an Army recruiter dressed in his spiffy Class A uniform, talking to a couple backpack-wearing community-college students. I could tell right away by his smile and the air of friendliness he was projecting to them that this wolf in sheep's clothing was trying to recruit them.

Something had to be done.

I didn't even ask for permission to engage, I just instinctively started rolling my window down as my wife asked, "What the hell are you doing?"

I told her not to worry and to just sit back and watch this. I then yelled out as loud as I could, "DON'T FUCKING DO IT! DON'T EVEN THINK ABOUT IT! IT'S ALL A BUNCH OF LIES! LIES, I TELL YOU! FTA BABY, F-T-A!"

My wife was completely embarrassed by this and was now physically pulling me back into the cab, as I had both hands sticking out of the car window doing the middle-finger hand gesture aimed right center mass at the recruiter.

The Army recruiter and the two community-college kids that he was talking to just looked at me all confused, like, What the hell was that all about?

As I was mumbling things to myself like, "Fuck that guy, what the hell does he know about Iraq, fucking bitch-ass muthafucker, I'll kick his fucking ass," my wife was busy apologizing to the car-service driver about my moronic, juvenile drunken behavior. The car-service driver told my wife not to worry about it, that it was all okay, and that I was still a hero.

Message from Jello Biafra

I had a pretty good run with my blog for the short life it had. It lasted for about ten weeks until it got to the point where it became more of a headache. Though I posted a statement on my blog a couple weeks earlier that I was no longer writing on my blog, I thought that was kinda lame, how it just fizzled out like that, and something told me that I should go out with a bang instead, and maybe stick it to the man. Like, I thought that maybe I should finish my set with a little bit more attitude instead of just walking off the stage, maybe I should end my set the same way that a punk band might end their set to their very last show, which would be to just slam the guitars up to the amps, create as much static and feedback as possible to the point that the audience's ears just exploded, and then to smash my guitar and equipment on stage into a million fucking pieces. Basically, what I wanted to do was press the self-destruct button on my blog as an F-U to whoever higher up in the Army had a beef with it.

So I thought maybe I'd get in contact with Jello Biafra, lead singer for the legendary punk band the Dead Kennedys, known throughout both the music and activist worlds as a radical anti-hero, whose strong pro stance on the First Amendment, and whose message that people "become the media" themselves, was one that I highly respected. So I sent an e-mail to Jello's people at Alternative Tentacles Records (his record label) in San Francisco, telling them about the bullshit brought upon me by the United States Army, and asked them if Jello could write something for my blog, like a "message from Jello" kinda thing. And while in some Internet cafe in Williamsburg, Brooklyn, I posted it.

It was perfect.

The Army went ballistic.

Hey Colby,
Thanks a lot for alerting us about what's going on with you. Thanks also for the respect. Believe me, it's mutual. You have a lot of guts. No pun intended, but stick to your guns. Don't believe the hype—we are the real patriots here, not the unelected gangsters and scam artists who started this war. Real patriots care enough about our country—and the world—to speak up, stand up, and fight back when the government breaks the law, lies, steals, and gets innocent people killed. Real patriots do their buddies and the people

back home a huge favor when they bypass our censored corporate media and become the media themselves—telling us from a real person perspective what war and a grunt's life are really like. History is important. As long as people in the field speak up we have a chance of preserving the truth. Otherwise it's the bullshit gospel according to Fox News and the Bush-Croft regime and people's own memory being erased even more than we've got now. To all the troops: I and Alternative Tentacles support you. We support you by saying, "Bring the Troops Home!" as loud and as often as we can.
Stay Safe.
Don't Give Up,
JELLO BIAFRA

Posted by CBFTW at 5:47 p.m. on September 23, 2004

The next day I went back to the Internet cafe to check my e-mail.

From: Doc Haibi
Date: Mon, 27 Sep 2004 17:01:44 +0000
Subject: IMPORTANT!!!!!!!!!
Hey, it's Doc. The Lt. says that higher is pissed that you got in contact with Jello and that he e-mailed you and you posted it. It's political now and you have been ordered to STOP WRITING or face UCMJ action. This is from above Ltc. James and Brigade. Write back, Doc

What was fucking great about all this was that right after I posted Jello's message on my website, a reader posted this comment in the comment section:

I'm glad I live in a country that would allow a soldier in the

middle of a war to put this letter on the Internet. Saddam would never have allowed that, nor would just about any government in the Middle East, or in the world for that matter.

—Alice

Then I received this e-mail from my CO:

From: Robert Robinson
Date: Monday, September 27, 2004 9:42 a.m.
Subject: Blog
Buzzell,
You need to stop posting. Your last post from the Jello Biafra has gotten the entire BDE staff up in Arms. You need to stop now, before Ltc. James and or Col. Rounds presses charges. You are looking at the minimum of a Field Grade Article 15 for violation of ART 104 UCMJ (Aiding the enemy) and ART 92 (Failure to follow a lawful order). This is a direct order from Ltc. James and myself for you to cease writing. For your own sake and to make a smooth transition out of the Army you should stop writing and just wait until you publish your book. I will talk to you more about it when you get back from leave.
CO
Robert A. Robinson II
CPT, IN
Blackhawk 06 RLTW!

"The Pentagon has no specific guidelines on blogging per se," said Cheryl Irwin, a Defense Department spokeswoman. "Generally, they can do it if they are writing their blogs not on government time and not on a government computer. They have every right under the First Amendment to say any darn thing they want to say unless they reveal classified information, and then it becomes an issue as a security violation."

—Associated Press, "Soldiers' War Blogs Detail Life in Iraq," September 27, 2004

Lt. Col. Barry Venable, a Pentagon spokesman, says blogs, like other forms of communication, are tolerated so long as they don't violate operational or informational security. "We treat them the same way we would if they were writing a letter or speaking to a reporter: It's just information," he says. "If a guy is giving up secrets, it doesn't make much difference whether he's posting it on a blog or shouting it from the rooftop of a building."

—Christopher Cooper,
"Army Blogger's Tales Attract Censors' Eyes,"
Wall Street Journal, September 9, 2004, p. B1

Being almost wholly composed of dullards and intellectual sluggards, [the military] is a painful hell for anyone with an IQ over 80. Be a beachcomber, a Parisian wino, an Italian pimp, or a Danish pervert; but stay away from the Armed Forces. It is a catch-all for people who regard every tomorrow as a hammer swinging at the head of a man, and whose outstanding trait is a fearful mistrust of everything out of the ordinary.

—Hunter S. Thompson

In Service of the Queen

My battalion commander then sent me an e-mail, which I posted immediately on the blog, disobeying a lawful order. (What are they going to do, send me to Iraq?).

CBFTW,
Yours is a voice that many have heard. We have not simply heard what you have said; we have, and continue to, listen to what you are saying. Far too often we simply carry on an inner dialogue when someone else speaks to rehearse what we will say when they finish. This war on terrorism will be with us for some time, so I offer an open letter to the generation I will pass this burden on to.

I believe that we are making progress in Iraq and in Afghanistan. Despite the ravings of pundits and uninformed ambulance chasers, this fight doesn't hinge on oil or payback. It isn't about religion or race. And it damn sure is not about any innate desire to rule the world. These people will succeed or fail on their own merits. The task is daunting. You can release a person from bondage. You can remove a tyrant from power. You can create the conditions for liberty. But you cannot simply grant or proclaim freedom. Freedom without honest action is a whisper in a storm just as change without vision and purpose is the illusion of progress. For ages these people were literally beaten to the point of submission by oppression, censure, murder, torture, and rape—regardless of age or gender. I have asked myself why they let it happen. The only answer I can fathom is that evil flourished because good people refused to pay the price required to oppose it. Sure, it's easy now to pontificate and blame the poor and downtrodden for their collective indifference, but forgive my sarcasm—I think we owe them more than a couple of days to realize that their hopes and dreams have a chance to grow and one day flourish. No amount of rhetoric and no pressing agenda will change the fact that time is required to help heal these people and that ancient grievances require redress. Make no mistake: I'm no crusader—I do what I do because I am a professional soldier. For me it's been simple: protect the innocent, punish the deserving, accomplish my mission, and bring my men home, period. As Sting said, "Poets, priests, and politicians have words to thank for their positions." For a soldier it is black and white: deeds not words. If you need words to better illustrate, the Latin mottos of two Infantry Regiments I have served in will suffice: "Sua Sponte" and "Ne Desit Virtus": Of Their Own Accord and Let Valor Not Fail. Or in true cowboy fashion: Saddle your own horse, cull your own herd, and bury your own dead.

The threat we face is like nothing we've seen before. I've been in the streets with this enemy, fought him face to face, and have been lucky enough to kill him and come out alive. I have seen what he is capable of doing and the zeal with which he will do it. This threat won't fit neatly into "the box" or be governed by any paradigm. It is a cancer within our collective body as the human race. We are all threatened by this evil, and evil it is. This enemy has twisted and distorted things both sacred and profane to guide as well as justify its means and its stated end. Nothing is beyond the realm of the possible when it comes to the depths to which it will sink, the horror it is willing to commit, or the suffering it is willing to inflict. This enemy has no concept of mercy nor does it recognize combatants. Innocence is not a factor. You need only look at the headlines of the day to confirm that children, teachers, and doctors are murdered every day by these villains. What makes them evil? I submit that it is not the act that earns them the epithet of evil—it is the intent to commit and the pride they draw from the act. These animals revel in the post-act announcements that they are responsible. They feel vindicated by the proclamations that they perpetrated these horrors in the name of God and that having committed these acts somehow elevates them. Make no mistake, this enemy is formidable but by no means invincible. To defeat this cancer requires the one thing that civilized people all over the world possess in absolute abundance—the will. The will to be free can only be surrendered by the person that has it—it cannot be murdered, raped, tortured, or stolen. It's not about being a martyr or a saint, it's about being a decent human being. And the unvarnished truth is that the killing and the horror will continue until those with the will to endure prevail.

I am a simple soldier, proud to serve, but my days in the service of the Queen are drawing to a close. Soon all of the cold war junkies will also be gone and you my friends and your band of X generation anti-heroes will have the reins. Like it or not, you are now the fulcrum upon which the balance beam rests. I will tell you that the outlook is damn good. I am absolutely humbled every day to have the rare privilege to march among the young men and women who chose to give soldiering a try. None finer have ever served under the colors.

Beware the onslaught of false prophets who preach the one size fits all solution. Look beneath the facade of their self-proclaimed patriotism, peel back the shield of their dogma, and you are likely to find a charlatan malcontent who was passed over for some accolade he feels he richly deserved or a flimflam artist who knows a chance to make a buck when he sees it. They don't have the will to endure. The will to be free comes at a heavy price. For some it is more than they can bear. Divorce, estrangement, financial burdens, health problems, depression, and even suicide are very real costs. Sacrifice is rarely recognized for what it truly is because the price of recognition is guilt. Parades, giving medals, issuing promotions, and rousing speeches are simply the thin veneer that masks the desperate need of those who are kept free by our endeavors for absolution from this guilt. Adam Duritz

wrote in the song "Mrs. Potter's Lullaby" that "the price of a memory is the memory of the sorrow it brings."

I submit that it is our love of freedom, the embrace of our wives or sweethearts, the love of our children or family, and the earned respect of our brothers in arms that cast the walls that make the will to endure a fortress that can never be taken. I will be proud to stand the watch until my time is at an end, but soon you will mount the ramparts and stand the watch alone. In closing, I leave you with the words of Marcus Aurelius: "Think of yourself as dead. You have lived your life. Now, take what's left and live it properly. What doesn't transmit light creates its own darkness."

Respectfully,

"Knute Lombatton"

Nice Scar

While I was in line waiting for my flight back to Iraq at the Atlanta airport, I looked over at the guy behind me in line. I noticed he had three huge scars on his neck. I recognized the type of scars immediately. They kinda poofed out and were a bright pink and ugly as hell. I stared at the scars for a second and then looked at him and said, "Shrapnel?" With a huge smile he said, "Yeah! How'd you know?" and I told him I recognized the scars immediately because one of the sergeants in my platoon is marked for life with the same type of scars on his neck. IED, Mosul. He told me that it was from an IED on a convoy that he was on.

I got to the airport kind of early, so I took a cab to the Five Points neighborhood over by Atlanta. I got semi-trashed at some rock 'n' roll bar that had Social Distortion on the jukebox. I barely got to the airport on time.

Once I got to the airport, a sergeant who was in charge of getting people onto the plane informed me that the flight back to Iraq was overbooked, and he asked me if I wanted to give up my seat. He said that they would put the people up at the Marriott Hotel for the night, and they'd have to take a flight tomorrow.

I honestly felt kinda bad for not giving up my seat in Kuwait, so I decided to show some personal sacrifice and step up and help my fellow soldiers out, and I happily volunteered to give up my seat so that another soldier could go back to Iraq and be with his men.

So I spent the night at the Marriott with a bottle of Jäger, and the next day I took a shuttle bus to the Atlanta airport and hours later I was on a plane headed back to Iraq.

We flew from Atlanta to Frankfurt, Germany, then to Camp Doha in Kuwait. I was hoping that maybe I'd spend a couple days at Doha, but they put me on a plane that night back to Mosul. They don't fuck around on getting you back to your unit in a hurry once leave is done. They immediately put me on a C-130 and that morning I was back at the airfield on FOB Marez.

I had to wait all day for somebody to finally pick me up. I got there at 6:00 a.m. and I sat around and waited till 8:00 that night. Finally an E-4 who I'd never seen before picked me up in a Humvee and drove me back to the FOB.

He told me that my unit was no longer in Mosul, that they were now down south over by Baghdad. He didn't know anything else other than that. Once I got to FOB Marez, I was informed that I had to wait a couple days before they could put me on a plane to be back with my unit down south. No complaints there. So I just chilled out in my room for a couple days.

The only people at FOB Marez were our replacements, and they looked fat and undisciplined to me, but then again, we probably looked like that to the 101st guys when we first got here to Mosul.

Finally me and an E-6, who was in charge of the mail for my company, had a flight ready to take us to FOB Anaconda, and from there I would take a Chinook (helicopter) to Camp Cooke, where my unit was now. We then went to the airfield. Our job was to escort mail, make sure it got to our guys all right, that there was no mix-up. Mail is a huge morale booster for soldiers, especially for guys who've been out in the field for any duration of time. There's nothing cooler than coming back from a field problem to a stack of letters from friends and family. And there's nothing more depressing in the world than to come back from a field problem with no mail.

IEDs, RPGs, STDs

At the airfield there was some confusion as to who was supposed to be on the plane, and after some arguing, they kicked two guys off the flight and put us in their place. The air-crew told the guys that they kicked off that it would be at least a couple days before they could get on a plane. Before the flight took off one of the flight-crew guys told us that a plane going to the same location as us got RPG'd and took small-arms fire the day before, and that they like to hide behind this hill and engage planes coming in, so expect to take contact. I had an ear-to-ear smile when I heard this. Damn, it feels great to be back in Iraq, I thought.

One of the flight-crew guys borrowed the M4 from the E-6 sergeant that was in charge of the mail and took all his mags, said he was going to need it in case we came into contact. I felt kinda nervous, because I had no weapon or ammo. He also told us the procedures on what to do in case we received fire and crashed. Finally we took off to Anaconda. It was a cool flight, it felt like being on a boat during heavy waves, the plane kept rocking back and forth. We flew extremely low for the longest time. I was like, Why the fuck are we flying so low? No wonder Hajjis shoot at you guys. Finally they pointed the plane toward the sky and we started gaining altitude. Once we got to high level, I think like three thousand feet, they straightened out and the flight was semi-smooth.

Halfway through the flight, the guy sitting next to me grabbed one of the barf bags that's located above us and started puking like crazy. I tried not to look at or smell the barf, 'cause I knew if I did, it could start a chain reaction of barfing on my plane. I looked over at the E-4 that was barfing and he had a mustache with barf on it and puke running down his nose. I felt like barfing myself when I saw that, but I resisted. Finally the plane headed toward the ground, and again for the longest time we were flying barely above the ground. WTF? Finally we landed at the airfield.

There was some more confusion about the mail, and the sergeant had to go back to Marez, so I was in charge of making sure that the mail didn't get ganked, and for three days I chilled out by myself in this tent at FOB Anaconda until they had a ride for me to Cooke.

It was night as they drove me to the airfield. I made sure the mail got on the Chinooks. The chopper ride to Cooke would take less than thirty minutes. Cool. I sat inside and put earplugs in as we took off. My body was still trapped on East Coast time, and I was extremely tired so I went to sleep. Next thing you know I was awakened by a burst of M60. The Chinook has two M60 machine guns on it. All the sudden my adrenaline kicked in and I was like, HOLY SHIT!! ARE WE TAKING FIRE!? Then the other M60 gunner fired a burst. I looked at the gunners and they looked pretty calm, and I could tell by the way they looked that we weren't taking contact. They looked bored to death. Just a test fire. Like, fire a burst before you land type of thing. And then we landed, unloaded cargo.

There was a sergeant from headquarters there waiting for me. As soon as I got off the helicopter, he came up to me. "Are you Buzzell?" (It was at night, so you couldn't read my name tape.)

"Roger, sergeant."

"Cool, I'm here to take you to your unit."

"Awesome."

He asked me how leave was, and I told him it was cool. He also asked me if I was glad to be back and I gave him an honest answer, "Hell fucking no sergeant, fuck Iraq." He laughed. We jumped on a truck and he started to drive me back to where my guys were. I asked him about what the guys had been up to, I wanted to know. He then filled me in: They went down south to some town right outside of Baghdad, and they just got back from being out in the field a couple days ago, and right now all we were doing was turning our equipment and Strykers over to the guys that were replacing us.

Then I asked him about Camp Cooke. Like, How dangerous is it here, and does it get mortared as much as FOB Marez did? He laughed and said that it wasn't bad at all here, in fact the only thing you have to worry about at Camp Cooke is catching STDs.

I laughed, and he then gave me a serious look and said, "No, I'm serious; the number-one thing taking soldiers out here is STDs. STDs are creating more casualties here than anything else. It's like a major problem here."

I couldn't believe this, so I asked him again if he was serious, and he told me that he was dead serious and that he actually heard it himself from a medic. He explained to me that Camp Cooke was a huge post and that there were a lot of POGs (people other than grunts) here and lots of Air Force people.

The Air Force always has this reputation for having the hottest women out of all the armed forces. Finally he took me to where my guys were, and even though I fucking hated being in Iraq and couldn't wait for this deployment to end, I was extremely excited to see all the guys again and to catch up, and find out what they'd all been doing since I'd been gone.

It was kinda like I was back home again. All the guys were all excited to see me again, which of course kinda made me feel good, it's like friends for the first time in my life, like real friends. They all filled me in with what they'd been up to. I never thought I'd ever say this, but I was kind of glad to be back.

Interview with an Iraqi

One of the soldiers in my platoon has a little handheld microcassette recorder. He uses it to record messages to send his wife back home. So out of extreme boredom I borrowed it from him, and I asked the first English-speaking Iraqi person I could find a couple questions. (Note: This interview was *not* taken at gunpoint. I was completely unarmed when I interviewed this individual.)

Here is an interview I did with one of our interpreters that I posted on my blog back in August:

> **QUESTION: What do you personally think of the U.S. being here in Iraq and what seems to be the overall Iraqi feeling about that?**
> **ANSWER: I wish that American forces stay here in Iraq for a long time. As you know, until now, there is no security in Iraq, so we need American forces to stay here in Iraq with the help of police guys and the help of the ING guys. I think that**

the situation will be better. Most of the people, they like the American forces to stay here in Iraq, just to capture the bad guys, and just to get rid of the dangerous weapons. So we need American forces to stay here for a long time in order to give the Iraqis freedom and security.

QUESTION: What was it like here in Iraq before the war, when Saddam was in power?
ANSWER: The situation was very bad. Saddam Hussein prevented us to travel to any country. If you want to travel to another country, you can't travel. Because traveling is very expensive, also Saddam Hussein would collect money from you, you must pay the government 700,000 dinar. Too much expensive for a person to travel outside Iraq. We also have no freedom, we cannot speak, we cannot express our feelings towards our government. If you speak about political issues, they gonna arrest you and put you in prison. Three days ago I went to the passport office, I saw many people there, they were fighting with each other, they were shouting, and they don't stand in a line, so some of the workers that work in the passport office, they charge the people to pay, bribery, to get your passport. If you don't like to stand in a line, or like to stay with the people in the crowd, you should pay at least 100 dollars to the worker, to the employee, in order to get your passport. So this is what they did.

QUESTION: Why did all these people want to get passports?
ANSWER: They don't like to stay here. Some of them have relatives outside Iraq. There is no security here, and it's dangerous here in Iraq, so they want to go outside.

QUESTION: Do you think the U.S. did the right thing by coming over?

ANSWER: Yes, the United States did the right thing about coming here. As I told you, to give the Iraqi people freedom. Because we don't have any freedom before the war. We can't speak, we cannot talk about the government, we can't talk about the president. We are restricted here in Iraq.

QUESTION: What do you think of people that protest us being here?
ANSWER: I think some of them are crazy, because why are they protesting? They protest for nothing. Why they protest? American forces came over here in order to help them. I consider American forces a friend to the Iraqi people, not an enemy, there is no need to protest.

QUESTION: What was it like here in Iraq, when we first came over and started kicking some serious ass in the beginning of the war?
ANSWER: The situation was very bad. Most of the people they were stealing, killing each other, and the people were living in chaos. But the American forces came here and they established everything, they gave the Iraqi people the right to vote, to choose their president, to choose their mayor, they help the Iraqi to build their country. But before the war the situation was very bad. Most other people tried to kill each other, they tried to steal, they tried to fight. But after the war, when American forces came here, they established everything, they help the Iraqis, they helped by giving Iraq money to build their country. They fixed the water pipeline, they fix the power and electricity, they help the students, and they fix many schools. They paint many schools here in Iraq. So, they do a very good job.

QUESTION: Is it less dangerous here in Mosul now than it

was in the past? How dangerous is Mosul now?
ANSWER: To be honest with you the situation is still dangerous. Because many people came from Iran, and they enter inside Iraq. They use Islam and they use that banner to fight against the American forces, and what they call a jihad, and Islam doesn't say that, believe me they are far away from Islam. Islam does not say fight your brother or kill the innocent people. So I think their opinions are not true. Their ideas are not true.

QUESTION: Who seems to be the ones causing the most trouble here?
ANSWER: I think most of the people who came to fight against the American forces came from Iran, they came from Syria, they came from Yemen, they have another party, I think they belong to Al Qaeda. They came here to fight, but believe me there is no need to fight. You should start with building this country without any fighting, you should start with peace and have people live in security and peace.

QUESTION: What are some of the major improvements you've seen here in Mosul and Iraq, now that the United States is here?
ANSWER: They fixed many things here in Iraq, they paved many streets, they built many schools, they fixed the power, electricity, they fixed the water pipe.

QUESTION: What do you think of those sickos that are making the home videos of POW beheadings?
ANSWER: I think this is a very bad thing. To show the world we are brave, we want to cut off the heads of the people that want to work with the American forces, and they are far away from humanity. They don't have any sense of human being.

And Islam does not tell you to go and cut the heads off people that work with the American forces. This is not true. Islam is a religion that tells the people to work together, to live in peace. There is also a TV station here called Al Jazeera, and all they show is the bad side of the American forces. They do not show the right side or the good side of the American people, they only show the bad side. Only the negative side.

QUESTION: So you don't think these people are representing Islam at all?
ANSWER: *Nooo,* no. They are far away from Islam.

QUESTION: How good of a job do you think the INGs and ICPs are doing in Iraq?
ANSWER: They are doing a good job, they help the people, as I said the cooperation of the American forces with the ING, they are going to build this country. If there is no cooperation, there is no building. So ING with the American forces, they build this country.

QUESTION: What do you think Iraq will be like ten to twenty years from now?
ANSWER: I think Iraq, if all the Iraqi people help each other, they can build this country. And if the Iraqi people try to capture many bad guys with the helping of the police guys and American forces, they are also going to build this country.

QUESTION: What do people do for fun here in Iraq, like on a Friday night, like do you guys go to the mosque and hang out, or do you guys like go out and party? Like what's there to do here?

ANSWER: [laughs]: No, we like to go down to the river. Very peaceful there.

QUESTION: How many wives can you have here?
ANSWER: If you have enough money, you can have up to four wives here in Iraq.

QUESTION: What do you think of George W. Bush?
ANSWER: I think he's a good man.

QUESTION: If George W. Bush invited you to the White House for a cup of Chi, what would you say to him?
ANSWER: I would say "Welcome!" [Laughs.] I would go and drink a cup of tea with him. I would be glad to meet him.

QUESTION: Is the word *Hajji* offensive?
ANSWER: No. It is not offensive. People who go to Mecca and come back to Iraq, they call them Hajji, as you know the five duties in Islam, one of them is pilgrimage to Mecca. When the person come back from Mecca, that person is a Hajji.

QUESTION: What about when Americans sometimes use the word *Hajji* to refer to an Iraqi, is that bad?
ANSWER: No.

QUESTION: What do you think of Americans?
ANSWER: Each one of us have traditions. American people they have their tradition, and we have our own tradition. But I think they're friends to the Iraqi people.

QUESTION: If you had a chance to jump on a plane with your family and fly to the United States and live there hap-

pily ever after, would you do it?
ANSWER: Yes! [Huge smile.] I wish I could go there and live in the United States.

Posted by CBFTW at 9:57 p.m., August 12, 2004

The last time I saw this Iraqi interpreter that I interviewed was right before I left Mosul to go home on leave. And I haven't seen him since, and I probably never will. He was one of the coolest, most down to earth, friendliest human beings I've ever met.

When I first met him, I hung out with him as much as I possibly could, asking him a million and one questions about Iraq, the customs, history, and hit him up as many times as possible for free Arabic lessons, and it never once bothered him, and the guy not once ever didn't go out of his way to help me out.

To me, every single neighborhood in Iraq looks the same, but somebody who grew up and has lived in Mosul his entire life, he knows which neighborhoods are which, where the bad parts are and what to look out for, sees things that I can't see. And many times on missions, when we were doing a dismounted patrol (on foot) through some neighborhood, he'd sometimes come up to me and say, "Buzzell, be really careful in this neighborhood, this is a really bad neighborhood," and explain to me why the neighborhood was bad. Which helped me out, because like I said, it all looks the same to me. He truly believed that America was a friend to Iraq, and he had such a positive attitude about us being here and he knew that we were the "good guys."

He also became a very good friend to Sgt. Horrocks and I, every single day he'd stop by our room, say hello to us, and ask us if there was anything downtown that we needed that he could buy for us, and he'd also talk with us for a while about

Mosul and Iraq, or we'd sit around and joke about the other interpreters. He had a wife and kid, and when Horrocks came back from leave he got him a stuffed animal as a gift to give to his son, a bald eagle.

He loved it.

When I returned from leave, everybody in my platoon told me that right before they left Mosul, a lot of our interpreters got murdered and every single one of them quit, because somehow all their names and identities got out, and some of the mosques in Mosul were actually blasting their names on the loudspeakers.

Rumor has it that he was one of the interpreters that got murdered.

Vote? As If!

Election-themed graffiti written by soldiers tagged on a latrine wall:

- Bush keeps lying, soldiers keep dying!
- Bush pays us good though.
- The only lies that are true are the ones that you believe.
- Make a smart vote, vote to go home, vote for Kerry.
- We're committed to Iraq no matter who you vote for, dumbass.
- It doesn't matter who you vote for, you're screwed anyways. Hooah!
- Wow, you guys R gay! I can't believe you think about Bush and Kerry while holding onto your dicks.

Back in July '04, Sgt. Blough, who at the time was acting squad leader for weapons squad, wanted a list of names of everybody who wanted to vote via absentee ballot. He asked everybody in my squad to raise your hand if you wanted to vote. Surprisingly, nobody raised their hands. No, I take that back, one person did, but then realized nobody else raised theirs, and so he put his hand back down.

What the Army does best is fix problems, both big and small, or at least they try. Problem: Low absentee voter turnout. Solution: Company mass formation 0800, bring your ID cards and a pen.

So a couple days later we had an 0800 formation and an Army captain came out and said, "Men, nobody's forcing you to vote, *but* . . ." and he said a bunch of stuff like, it's un-American not to vote yadda, yadda, to get us all motivated to vote. It worked. I and a bunch of other soldiers said fuck it, let's register. He had a bunch of tables set up, divided by states, and each table had a form you filled out to register to vote.

I then overheard a noncommissioned officer say in mocking protest, "Vote?! Our job is to protect democracy, not be a part of it!"

I went to the California table and filled out the paperwork, which took about thirty seconds. I was a little confused when they asked for party affiliation, so I put down Independent, even though that's become a really trendy thing to do nowadays.

One of my friends in my platoon then asked me who I was voting for in the election. I told him Ralph Nader. His response: "Who the hell is that?"

I seriously wasn't planning on voting in this election, neither candidate excited me. I've voted in every election since I was eighteen, but I was planning on taking a break from this one, because I didn't really feel like voting for the lesser of the two evils. The first election I voted in I was still in high school, and my father (who's a lot like the dad on that TV show *The*

Wonder Years) forced me to register and vote. He said, "Look, you live in my house, you don't pay rent, all you do is hang out with all your deadbeat skateboarding buddies at the park, the least you could do for me is vote!" I was kind of shocked when my dad said that, because he hardly ever asks me to do anything for him, and he was now. So I did. On Election Day he woke my ass up and dragged me to the balloting place, which was some lady's house down the street. On the way there I asked, "Hey, Dad, how do you vote?" His answer: "Oh, voting is easy! All you do is vote for every single name that has the word *Republican* next to it." That wasn't exactly what I meant when I asked how do you vote, but whatever. I then said, "But Dad, what if the Democrat is better than the Republican?" His answer: "Impossible, there's no such thing as a Democrat that's better than a Republican, you figure the worst Republican is still ten times better than the best liberal."

That was my first lesson in voting.

I'd been gone on leave for several weeks so when I returned I had a shitload of mail waiting for me, and my absentee ballot was also in that pile of mail. As I was sitting on my Army-issued cot in my living conex, going over my absentee ballot, I heard a *ZZZOOOOOMMMMM* soar over my conex. From spending almost a year in Iraq already, I knew right away that it was one of those made-in-China rockets that the anti-Iraqi forces liked to toss at us. I waited for the explosion, but heard nothing. Either that was a dud, or I drank too much on leave and I'm just hearing shit. Confused, I continued to go over my absentee ballot. Ten minutes later, Spc. Callahan stormed into my room and said, "Dude, did you hear that rocket fly over our conexes earlier?!" Yeah, but I didn't hear it explode, I told him. He then told me that it landed nearby at the MWR center and didn't blow up. It hit the ground fifteen meters away from a soldier that I sat next to on the plane on our way home on leave.

Since I had my absentee ballot out, I asked Spc. Callahan if he was voting in the election. He told me he couldn't because he fucked up on the ballot, he sealed the envelope first without putting the ballot inside. (No, believe it or not, he's not a Florida voter, he's actually from Pennsylvania.) On the envelope it says "No Tampering," so he screwed himself on that vote. I asked him who the vote was intended for and he said Bush.

Surprisingly, I couldn't find Nader's name on my California ballot, so I ripped my ballot up and chucked it in the fucking trash can. I decided that I was going to vote in this election by not voting. Believe it or not, a lot of the other soldiers that I know in my platoon did the same thing. Reason being was because they were either like me, unimpressed with either candidate, simply didn't care, or believed that no matter who you vote for, you're screwed anyways. Hooah.

Hemingway?

The next morning, I went to the chow and got some coffee, and then I sat outside my conex, smoking and drinking coffee while talking to Sgt. Blough. He stopped talking, stood up, and said, "Group attention, good morning, sir," as he saluted. I stood up at attention, too, and then I heard, "Well look who it is, it's Hemingway reincarnated!" I turned around to see who it was and it was the battalion commander! He asked how was leave and if I read his book, and like a moron I was standing at parade rest for him. (He's an officer, you don't stand at parade rest for an officer, only NCOs.) I told him that I was excited to be back (lie) and that I was almost finished reading his book (lie, I hadn't even started it yet) and asked for permission to borrow his book for a couple more days, which he granted me. He then said, "Welcome back," and walked away. Amazing, I thought he was going to chew me out for the Jello Biafra post, but he said nothing about it.

Handoff

It came time to hand over our Stryker vehicles to the guys that were replacing us, 1st Infantry Division. Our last days here in Iraq felt like the last week of senior year in high school. There's an excitement in the air for us because this hell is about to be over. 1st ID is also from Fort Lewis, and they are the Army's second Stryker Brigade. To make the handoff easier, since both brigades are from Fort Lewis and operate on Strykers, instead of them coming out here with all their vehicles and equipment, we just handed them all our stuff, and when we got back to Fort Lewis, we'd get all their stuff. So they got our fucked-up Strykers with bullets holes and RPG impacts on them. I saw some of our guys go around and point out to them the bullet holes and RPG impacts on the armor, trying to freak them out.

I felt kinda sorry for the guys replacing us, I don't think there was a single person in my platoon that thought that Iraq was getting any safer, and a lot of people were predicting that Mosul was going to completely turn to shit after we left. We held Mosul down pretty well the entire time, but toward the end, it seemed like there was a real big insurgency going on there, and I thanked God we were getting the hell out now, because who knew what was going to happen now.

At the motor pool one day, I bumped into a couple guys who I went to basic training with. Both of them got shipped to Korea right after the graduation ceremony, and then after serving for an entire year there, they both got shipped to a unit that was headed to Iraq.

After we caught up on what the other guys we went to basic with were up to, one of them asked me, "So what's it like here? It isn't as bad as they say it is here, is it?" That put a huge smile on my face, and I said, "No, it's not as bad as they say it is, shit, I don't know man, it's hard to explain what it's like here, but you'll see, it'll be absolutely nothing like you expected it to be."

I had to go and help the guys in my platoon pack up the last of our equipment, so I told him that it was cool to bump into him again, and we said our good-byes and I wished him luck.

I See Dead People

One of the last things they had us all do before leaving theater was a medical questionnaire.

They filed us all into this room and handed all of us a PalmPilot, and with the PalmPilot toothpick thing we had to answer a couple dozen yes-or-no type of questions. The test results would be saved on a plastic credit card thing, with an Army of One logo on it, that we had to insert into the PalmPilots.

Basic questions, like, Has your sleep pattern changed? Have your eating habits changed? Do you have nightmares? That kinda stuff. But there were a couple questions on the test that really stuck out to me because it seemed to me if you answered yes to any one of these, you'd probably come up positive for being at risk for post-traumatic-stress syndrome:

1) Have you been in a situation where you felt that your life was in danger? Yes or No?

What kind of question is that? That's like asking, "Did you masturbate while you were in Iraq?" With a chuckle, I clicked yes. I then looked around the room and I could tell from the smiles on a couple other soldiers' faces that they were on this question as well.

2) Have you been in a situation where you had to discharge your weapon? Yes or No?

I clicked yes.

3) Have you seen any casualties? Yes or No?

I clicked yes.

Then it asked you to click on all that apply.

The selections were: Friendly, Enemy, and Civilian. I clicked yes to Friendly and then yes to Enemy, but I couldn't think of any civilian casualties. There were some casualties that I wasn't really sure if they were enemy or civilians, and there were times where we showed up to a car-bomb site where mass civilian casualties took place, but I didn't remember vividly having eyes on civilian casualties, so just to be on the safe side, I clicked two out of three, Friendly and Enemy.

After the test, we were released and the combat medic and I were walking back to our rooms, and I asked him what was up with that test, because if every soldier in my platoon answered that quiz truthfully, it would probably show that we were all at risk for PTSS.

He then explained to me that the test wasn't necessarily for that, but was instead just to cover the Army's six, so for example, let's say that in ten or twenty years from now you're some homeless wannabe John Rambo psycho war vet and you can't find or hold a job, and you want to blame it all on the war, the Army could pull out your test results and find out if you're bullshitting or not based on how you answered the test.

I asked the medic how he answered the "Have you seen any casualties?" question, and he told me that he checked off all three.

I then curiously asked, "You've been on every single combat mission that I've been on, and I only checked off two out of the three. What civilians did you see get whacked?"

He then reminded me of that white SUV covered in AK bullet holes, with the lifeless civilian contractor in the driver's seat, seatbelt still on, resignation letter and plane ticket to London on him. We secured the area, we placed him in a body bag.

I then said, "Holy shit, that's right! I totally forgot about that one."

Ramadan

On the first day of Ramadan, they expected heavy attacks all over Iraq, and in preparation for that, it was put out to us the night before that we all now had to wear full body armor and kit if we wanted to go anywhere on the FOB. In the morning I went to chow hall in full kit, and for breakfast I requested a double serving of the pork sausages, to celebrate the first day of Ramadan.

Army Commendation Medal

Department of the Army
This is to certify that the Army has Awarded
the Army Commendation Medal
To: Private First Class Colby C. Buzzell
1st Battalion, 23rd Infantry Regiment
For exceptionally meritorious service throughout sustained combat operations against an armed and determined enemy during Operation Iraqi Freedom. PFC Buzzell displayed

unwavering courage and endured these hardships without complaint. His exemplary dedication to duty has ensured the promise of hope for the people of Iraq and is in keeping with the honored traditions of service by all American soldiers. His exceptional service reflects great credit upon him, task force Tomahawk, the Arrowhead Brigade Combat Team, and the United States Army.
From 15 November 2003 through 1 October 2004
Signed:
Michael E Rounds
COL, IN
Commanding

At 0930 we had a blanket ARCOM platoon formation right outside our conexes at Camp Cooke. A blanket ARCOM (ARCOM: Army Commendation Medal) means everybody gets a medal, the guys that did a kick-ass job, as well as all the guys that were below standard. An ARCOM is pretty much on the bottom of the military awards totem pole and doesn't mean shit.

Great. Not that I ever would, but if I ever did decide to protest this war, I guess this meant I'd have some artillery to throw on the White House lawn. "Here you go, you assholes, take my fucking ARCOM! And while I'm at it, take my fucking Sharpshooter Badge, too! Fuck the war, man! Fuck it!"

Before the ceremony, my squad leader inspected us to make sure that we had all shaved. Of course I forgot to. I'd just woken up ten minutes earlier. The night had been pretty crazy. Spc. Callahan somehow hooked up with some POG soldier also stationed here at Camp Cooke, and he got us four bottles of cheap booze for eighty bucks. It was hard stuff, like vodka and whiskey. The guy who sold us the stuff said he could get us some hash as well, but we figured there was going to be a drug test any day now, so we passed on the hash. None of us had any niacin to flush the drugs out of our system anyway. (Niacin is this trick stoners in the Army use to pass drug tests. After you smoke pot, you take some niacin for a couple days, and supposedly it flushes it all out of your system.)

Anyway, me and a handful of other soldiers from my company (including, surprisingly, a couple NCOs) locked ourselves into one of the conexes, loaded a cheap-ass PX-bought CD player with some old-school English punk, and cracked the bottles open and passed them around and chain-smoked all night. It was pretty cool. I passed out on my cot in my room at around 0100 and I got the spins as soon as I laid down.

Getting drunk in Iraq is a trip, it makes you miss home even more.

We weren't the only ones drinking that night, it looked like a lot of us were, because in the morning someone found one of our platoon sergeants wrapped in a sleeping bag and passed out in one of the showers. Nobody asked questions about it, and we all assumed it must have been one of those nights.

Captain Robinson went around and pinned each and every one of us with an ARCOM medal on our left breast pocket. He'd come up to each soldier in the formation, pin the medal on you, say, "Good job," shake your hand, hand you a certificate for the medal, and then you'd thank him and salute him, and he'd go to the next soldier in line and pin him. I was the last soldier in my platoon to get pinned. I was kind of curious as to what the CO would say to me once it was my turn.

When it was finally my turn to get pinned, he said, "Buzzell, look, wait till you get out of the Army and then you can write as much as you want, that whole thing with Jello just got blown way out of proportion. If you ask me, I think you should get a Mickey Spillane medal for your writing.

Good job." And then I shook his hand and saluted him.

Cool.

First Sergeant Swift followed the CO as he was pinning soldiers. Both First Sergeant and our CO received Purple Hearts when shrapnel from a mortar hit them on their way to chow hall back in Mosul. After the CO would pin you, First Sergeant would shake your hand, and say "Good job."

Shit.

First Sergeant, who has a reputation as a trigger puller, has always made me nervous. I never saw him do it and I don't know if this is really true, but when I first got to the unit everybody told me that he was crazy, like he would talk to his Ranger tab when nobody was looking. When First Sergeant got to me he said, "Buzzell . . . just make me look good in your book, and get somebody tough to play me in the movie, like Arnold. None of this pussy actor playing me shit."

Everybody in the platoon cracked up when First Sergeant said that.

Relieved, I said, "Roger that, First Sergeant."

Then they released us, and the CO had us huddle around him and he gave his "Good job, men" speech, and then excused us. My squad leader called all of us over and had us read over our ARCOM awards to make sure all the info was correct and that they spelled our names right. Of course they fucking put me down as a private first class on the certificate. (I'm a specialist E-4.) God I hate that word *private*.

As I read the award I did notice a grave mistake, and I pointed it out to my squad leader. "Hey, Sergeant, they fucked up big time on this!"

He said, "Now what is it Buzzell?"

I showed him the certificate and pointed out to him the part that said: "endured these hardships without complaint."

"Sergeant, that's totally wrong, I complained the whole fucking time here."

"I know, Buzzell, I know . . ."

Don't Do It!

In the morning before the ceremony, I went to chow hall to get coffee and some breakfast eats. Up ahead of me in line entering the chow hall must have been somebody important because as soon as he entered the chow hall somebody yelled, "DEFAC!! ATTENTION!!" I tried to look and see who the guy was, and what rank he was, because I had never seen anybody call the DEFAC to attention like that, but I couldn't read his collar. He must have been some big shot. Then I found out that he was a general.

We all had a formation at the motor pool at 0900. The recruiting NCO came out and said, "All you guys that are reenlisting will be reenlisted by a general." I saw a handful of poor dumb bastards step out of formation for this. One of them was Sgt. Horrocks, a man who proudly reenlisted in theater for another four more years.

I wanted to yell out, "Don't do it!" the same way somebody might yell out "I object!" at a wedding that they knew was going to end up in disaster, but I knew Sgt. Horrocks loved the GI Joe Army shit and he loved his job, and honestly I couldn't really picture him doing anything else. All the reenlistees, a couple dozen, formed up behind the podium and the general came out. I don't think generals have to do tape tests or are required to do PT because this guy kinda had the whole potbelly look going on.

He came out and his first words to us were "Hooah, men!"

Everybody responded with an unenthusiastic "Hooah."

Unimpressed, the general said, "I said HOOAH, men!"

Then all of us a little louder said, "HOOAH!"

I fucking hate the word "Hooah," I have no idea what the fuck Hooah means. It's a word that's not even in the English fucking dictionary. It's not even a fucking word. Lame.

The general then gave his little speech, which I hardly paid any attention to, and he mentioned three things, the first two were of course officer related, about what great leaders they were, and the third thing was how disciplined he thought we were because when he visited us once he had noticed that we were all cleaning our weapons instead of playing cards before a mission. Thus, we were all well-disciplined soldiers.

After the speech, they called up all the guys that were reenlisting and the general swore in all the reenlistees. Sgt. Horrocks looked extremely proud, and I felt sad for him reenlisting, but at the same time I felt extremely proud of him, the Army needs good soldiers and he was one of them. I can picture Sgt. Horrocks making a career in the Army and someday being a crazy drill sergeant at Fort Benning, like he always wanted to be.

Then the general went around and handed each reenlisting soldier a coin. Of course right when this happened I looked over at Sgt. Horrocks and even though at the position of attention you were supposed to stay rock solid, he had a grin going. Being a lifer, coins are a big deal to him.

After that the general said some "Hooah" stuff about the Strykers, how great we were, then the battalion commander, a man who already has several combat deployments under his belt, came out with a microphone in his hand. He gave a good twenty-minute speech. First off he told us all how proud of us he was and what a great job we did, and then he told us all that now that we'd all "survived the war," our next step was to "survive the peace."

He explained to us to expect a lot of things to be entirely different when we returned home, and he stressed to all of us not to do anything stupid, like drunk drive, beat the shit out of our wives, and also to avoid getting involved in any mindless fistfights.

All throughout the BC's speech I kept on looking around at the soldiers around me and every now and then one of them would physically nod in agreement with whatever he said. At times the speech was serious and at times it was funny. It was an appropriate speech, he stressed safety and that he didn't want anybody dying the next couple days or months. Then he released us and we had a company formation for a company photo. A medic took the photo, and of course he couldn't figure out how to take the photo with a digital camera and it took him a couple seconds. One of the sergeants yelled, "Hurry up! It ain't fucking heart surgery!" Laughs. Finally he took a couple pics. When we were released, I went over to the MWR center to try to check my e-mail.

Finally I went to my room to pack my bags for the Chinook ride to Anaconda, where we'd be chilling for the next couple days till our plane took us away from this fucking shithole.

Lights, Camera, Catfish Air

In the late evening we all boarded onto buses to be escorted to the airfield at Camp Cooke, and once we got to the airfield, we'd all be waiting for the Chinooks from Catfish Air, a National Guard unit from Mississippi, to come pick us up and take us to FOB Anaconda, which wasn't too far away. Couple of days and we'd jump on a C-130 to Kuwait, and from there we'd all out-process out of theater and be handed a one-way ticket back to the U.S. of A.

We all waited at the airfield, divided by chalks, arranged by alphabetical order. I'd become very good friends with Spc. Callahan because of this type of arrangement. Whenever there was a formation or lineup or whatever that was in alphabetical order, we'd always be right next to each other.

We were all extremely excited to get the hell out of there, in fact when the first two Chinooks from Catfish Air showed up to pick up the first chalk of soldiers, everybody cheered ecstatically. Callahan was yelling out an enthusiastic, "WHOO-HOO!!! Catfish Air, baby!" He had a huge smile on his face as he yelled this. Camera flashes started going off from soldiers who pulled out their digital cameras and were taking snapshots. Soldiers who worked at the airfield then started running around yelling, "NO CAMERA FLASHES!"

After a couple runs, it was our turn to jump on a chopper. Once we got the go-ahead to jump on, we all grabbed our duffel bags and ran onto the Chinooks and took a seat. It was extremely loud inside and I'd lost my earplugs, so I got a couple expired cigarette butts out of my pants pockets and shoved them in my ears.

Everybody inside our Chinook of course had their digital cameras out taking photos. Callahan, who was sitting right next to me, leaned over to me and yelled, "I don't mean to be racist, *but* . . ."

Don't you love it when people start sentences off like that?

"You ever notice that whenever 'Joe' does anything Army he turns into a Japanese tourist?"

That made me bust up laughing.

There is so much truth in that statement. Americans, and especially Hollywood, always make fun of the Japanese for taking pictures of everything they see when they go on trips, but from what I've seen so far on this deployment,

American soldiers, when they go to war, take photos of *everything*. They even take photos during firefights.

I had even been guilty of it. At the mosque firefight, at one point I pulled out the digital camera and took some action footage of myself in the back air-guard hatch, as Pfc. Pointz was rocking the .50-cal in the background, throwing lead at the mosque.

At the beginning of the deployment, hardly any soldiers carried digital cameras, almost all used disposable cameras, but once we got to Mosul, people started buying digital cameras at the PX, and in no time, every single soldier had a digital camera on him.

At the PX they also sold this tiny digital camcorder for under $400. It was about as small as a pack of smokes, and a lot of soldiers filmed the action on raids and missions by strapping one of those things onto their helmets.

In this war, every single soldier that I knew who had a digital camera also owned a laptop computer, and almost every soldier that owned a laptop computer had that program on it that allowed you to edit and create your own home movies.

Every single line squad in my platoon had what was called a squad video. One person in each squad, usually the person most computer literate, would go around and gather up all the photos and digital footage that he could find from everybody in the squad and from the platoon, and then he'd download all of it onto his computer, and from there he'd digitally edit them all together with all sorts of cool editing techniques and special effects, and dub cool soundtrack music over it, and create a war movie.

Of course this created stiff competition between all the squads, as each squad tried to make the best squad video for bragging rights. Some of the videos that I saw produced by soldiers are about as good as anything I've seen Spike Jonze do.

Almost every single soldier in my platoon was going home with a video that stars them.

Mortar-rita-ville

We're at FOB Anaconda, which the soldiers here have nicknamed FOB "Mortar-rita-ville." We'll be staying here for the next couple days until they board us onto C-130's and we fly to Kuwait, hang out there for a couple days, and then from there fly back home.

The End of the Beginning

We had to board the buses to Kuwait Airport in full kit (body armor, weapon, helmet), which is kinda lame because the threat level there was like next to nothing. We left at around midnight for the airport. When the buses finally made it to the airport, they parked and allowed us all to exit so we could piss in this field. While I was taking a piss I stared at the Kuwaiti air tower. It'd been a year since I'd seen that thing, and hopefully I'd never have to see that or anything else in the Middle East again. When I finished pissing and smoked a couple cancer-causing Iraqi cigarettes, they made us all load back onto the buses.

Once I got to my seat I started to crash from the exhaustion. I was in and out of sleep and with my eyes closed, I heard somebody walk onto the bus and shout, "Is there a Colby Buzzell on this bus?" That woke me up. Everybody then told him that yeah, Buzzell is on this bus, and pointed at me. I was sitting kinda in the back. He then said, "Grab your shit, the Command Sergeant Major wants to see you on the plane right now." As I was making my way off the bus, wondering, What the fuck now?, people were making comments that I was busted, that the MPs were waiting for me.

I figured I was in trouble (again) and/or he wanted to chew me out for something. Who knows? When I boarded the civilian airline, a sergeant told me that the pilot wanted to meet me and that he was a big fan of my website. I thought to myself, No fucking way. I then met the pilot of the plane, he was a cool guy, he said he was a big fan and he asked me a couple questions about the blog and what my plans were once I got out. We talked for a bit, and he told me that he was from San Francisco, which was cool. He then invited me into the cockpit to meet the other pilots, and he took a photo of me in the cockpit area. I wasn't expecting this at all, so I was kinda in shock. The pilot then told me that I could sit up in first class, right in the front row. Cool! So I sat in the front row of the plane, which made me extremely nervous because I'm just an E-4 pawn in the infantry and there was nothing but top brass and officers sitting up in first class. I had the whole three-seat row to myself. In the middle section sat the major, and I tried not to look at him because I didn't want him wondering what the hell an E-4 was doing sitting up here. I started feeling uncomfortable about the whole thing, so I turned around and made eye contact with my First Sergeant, and gave him a look like, What the hell am I doing sitting here, is this okay? First Sergeant then told me to stay where I was, and that it was okay and he even joked, "You know the only reason why we're letting you sit up here is because we want you to make us look good in your book."

We had a couple-hour layover in Germany, which was freezing cold. I was hanging out in the smoking section, which was located outside, and of course everybody came up to me and asked me why the CSM wanted to see me on the plane, everybody thought I was in trouble or something again. I told them it was because the pilot of the plane was a fan of the website and wanted to meet me and show me the cockpit and take a photo of me. Horrocks then tripped out on that and said, "Wow man, that's crazy! I've never known anybody before who was famous!" I told him to cut that shit out, and then I went into kidding around about sitting up in first class and told them that I was kinda stuffed from all the Grey Poupon and fine wine they were serving up there, and I asked them how sitting in coach was. I then felt bad when they told me that it sucked back there and that they were all packed in like sardines.

Before we left Germany, I went into the bathroom stall and checked to see if the "CB11B—IRAQ—13NOV03 to ????" that I had written a year before was still tagged up on the wall. Believe it or not, it still was. I didn't have a pen on me so I couldn't fill in the exit date. Then we all loaded back onto the plane (me still sitting up in first class), and we took off for Bangor, Maine, U.S.A., our last stop before we would finally land at McCord AFB, located right next to Fort Lewis. I started feeling tired again so I fell asleep for a couple hours.

When I woke up, they were playing the new *Spider-Man* movie. I wasn't in the mood to plug in my headphones and pay attention to the movie, I'm not a big Spider-Man fan, and I was too excited to finally be going back home. I remembered the excitement I felt on the plane ride going to Iraq. That's all completely out of my system now. Like I said, I never want to go back to Iraq, ever. I'm relieved to go back home for good and never hear the sound of an RPG fly over my head again. I looked around and everybody seemed to be feeling these things as well.

Now if this was the movies, they'd have the guy sitting in the plane on his way back to the world, looking out the window, with maybe the Green Day song "Time of Your Life" playing in the background, and he's reflecting on the war, about all his buddies that he's lost, all the dead bodies he's seen, and all the life-changing experiences and epiphanies that he went through and whatnot, but for me it seemed to be the opposite. I was not really thinking about Iraq at all, in fact it actually felt like I was never there. The only things that I was thinking about was a Guinness inside a smoky bar, going to the Social Distortion show in a couple weeks in Seattle, hanging out with my wife, and just chilling out. Maybe after spending the last year in hell, I could appreciate heaven a little bit more now, but then who knows. The heaven that I'm going to could be hell for all I know, and I'll find out soon enough.

My time in the Army would be up immediately when we returned, and as soon as that plane touched ground at McChord AFB, I'd be out-processing, getting the hell out ASAP, and never looking back. At least I was crossing my trigger fingers on that one. The Army has me on inactive reserve status for six more years, which pretty much means I'm draftable, so there's that very slight possibility that I just might be called back up to fight in some other terrorist-infested cesspool someday. Especially if the North Koreans ever get crazy on the soju and start tossing nukes at us, then I'm really fucked.

If I ever get a phone call saying, "Hello, Mr. Buzzell, this is the United States Army calling to congratulate you on being called back to active duty!" I swear to God I'll say, "Dude, I'm way too stoned right now to be talking to you, hold on. Here, talk to my live-in boyfriend Stevie, and tell him exactly what you just told me, but make it quick, because me and him are about to make love to each other, now that these Ecstasy pills that we swallowed are kicking in."

The only thing that I'm really capable of doing with myself right now when I get out of the Army, at age twenty-eight, absent a college diploma, is data entry and/or fire an M240 Bravo fully automatic machine gun. Since I'm not reenlisting, and no employers that I know of are looking for M240 machine gunners, that kinda narrows my options down a bit.

But after carrying around a 27.6-pound M240 Bravo machine gun for a year in Iraq hunting down noncompliant forces, how the hell can I go back to data entry? Temp work? Valet parking? Or any "normal" job, for that matter? Like imagine having a boss yell at me for showing up to work five minutes late or tell me that I'm not smiling enough at the customers.

I'll probably end up doing what most vets do when they get out, which is to use their GI Bill to go back to school. If school doesn't work out, I guess there's always a job at the FedEx. And if that doesn't work out, I guess I can now write the word "Veteran" after the word "Homeless" on my cardboard sign.

But then again, if I ever got a call from the battalion commander saying that he was getting everyone from Second Platoon Bravo Company 1/23 INF back together, to go "Punish the Deserving" for one last tomahawk chop out there in Iraq, and that he was going to lead the way, and everyone was going, and they needed me as an M240 Bravo machine gunner again, I'd probably tell him, "That's a good copy, sir. Let's roll."

Hell yeah.

Acknowledgments

Thanks to everyone who helped make this book possible, especially my recruiter. Without your help none of this would have happened.

Permissions

The author gratefully acknowledges permission to quote from the following:

Heinrich von Treitschke, quoted in William L. Shirer, *The Rise and Fall of the Third Reich,* p. 99. Copyright © 1988 by William L. Shirer, Touchstone/Simon & Schuster. Reprinted by permission.

Black Flag (Chuck Dukowski/Gary McDaniel), "My War." Copyright © 1983 SST Records. Reprinted by permission.

Infantryman's Creed. Despite diligent research, the author has been unable to identify the source of this creed.

Carl von Clausewitz, *On War,* pages 102–3. Copyright © 1976 Princeton University Press. Reprinted by permission.

Che Guevara, *Guerrilla Warfare.* Copyright © 1961 Monthly Review

Press. Reprinted by permission of the University of Nebraska Press.

Social Distortion (Mike Ness), "Another State of Mind," in *Mommy's Little Monster.* Copyright 1983 © Wixen Music Publishing, Time Bomb label. Reprinted by permission.

George Orwell, *Homage to Catalonia,* p. 95. Copyright © renewed 1980 by Sonia Brownell Orwell (Harcourt, Inc.). Reprinted by permission.

Michael Gilbert, *News Tribune* (Tacoma, Washington). Copyright © 2005 Tacoma News, Inc., a subsidiary of the McClatchy Company. Reprinted by permission.

Christopher Cooper, "Army Blogger's Tales Attract Censors' Eyes," *Wall Street Journal,* September 9, 2004, p. B1. Copyright © 2005 Dow Jones, Inc. Reprinted by permission.

Eric Niiler, "Soldiers' Iraq Blogs Face Military Scrutiny," National Public Radio broadcast, August 24, 2004. Copyright © 2004 National Public Radio. Reprinted by permission.

Hunter S. Thompson, *The Proud Highway,* p. 48. Copyright © 1997 by Hunter S. Thompson, Villard, Ballantine Publishing Group (Random House). Reprinted by permission.

GENERATION KILL
By Evan Wright

The true story of Bravo Company in Iraq – Marines who deal in bullets, bombs and ultraviolence.

Another nameless town, another target for First Recon. It's only five in the afternoon, but a sandstorm has plunged everything into a hellish twilight of murky, red dust. On rooftops, in alleyways lurk militiamen with machine guns, AK rifles and the odd rocket-propelled grenade. Artillery bombardment has shattered the town's sewers and rubble is piled up in lagoons of human excrement. It stinks. Welcome to Iraq . . .

First Recon are the special forces of the US Marine Corps, a lean, mean fighting machine trained to perfection and spoiling for action. This is their story as they spearhead the blitzkrieg on Iraq – a story of extreme bravery, borderline lunacy, touching camaraderie and breathtaking violence on the road to Baghdad.

First Recon's thankless task is to race ahead of the main coalition forces to spring enemy ambushes, earning them the nickname 'First Suicide Battalion'. *Generation Kill* allows an intimate look at how people fighting in war actually experience it, as the voices of soldiers on the front line are heard for the first time.

'AN ADRENALINE RUSH OF INTELLIGENT PROSE. ONE OF THE BEST BOOKS TO COME OUT OF THE IRAQ WAR'
Financial Times

'EASILY THE BEST BOOK ON THE IRAQ WAR SO FAR. A DEEPLY DISTURBING, COMPULSIVELY READABLE NARRATIVE OFFERING PROFOUND INSIGHTS INTO THE LIVES OF AMERICA'S YOUNG SOLDIERS'
New Statesman

0 552 15189 0

CORGI BOOKS

BLACK HAWK DOWN
By Mark Bowden

A thrilling and visceral, no-holds-barred classic of modern war.

Late in the afternoon of Sunday, 3 October 1993, 140 elite US soldiers abseiled from helicopters into a teeming market neighbourhood in the heart of the city of Mogadishu, Somalia. Their mission was to abduct two top lieutenants of a Somali warlord and return to base. It was supposed to take them about an hour.

Instead, they were pinned down through a long and terrible night in a hostile city, fighting for their lives against thousands of heavily armed Somalis. When the unit was rescued the following morning, eighteen American soldiers were dead and more than seventy badly injured. The Somali toll was far worse – more than five hundred killed and over a thousand injured.

Authoritative, gripping, and insightful, *Black Hawk Down* is a heart-stopping, minute-by-minute account of modern war and is destined to become a classic of war reporting.

'RIP-ROARING STUFF, WITH ONE OF THE MOST GRUESOME BATTLEFIELD WOUND TREATMENTS EVER COMMITTED TO PAPER'
Maxim

'ONE OF THE MOST ELECTRIFYING, IMMEDIATE AND DETAILED ACCOUNTS OF A SINGLE BATTLE EVER TOLD . . . THE WHOLE 24-HOUR NIGHTMARE SEEMS LIKE IT'S HAPPENING TO YOU'
Later

0 552 99965 2

BRAVO TWO ZERO
By Andy McNab DCM MM

'THE BEST ACCOUNT YET OF THE SAS IN ACTION'
James Adams, *Sunday Times*

In January 1991, eight members of the SAS regiment embarked upon a top secret mission that was to infiltrate them deep behind enemy lines. Under the command of Sergeant Andy McNab, they were to sever the underground communication link between Baghdad and north-west Iraq, and to seek and destroy mobile Scud launchers. Their call sign: *Bravo Two Zero*.

Each man laden with 15 stone of equipment, they patrolled 20km across flat desert to reach their objective. Within days, their location was compromised. After a fierce firefight, they were forced to escape and evade on foot to the Syrian border. In the desperate days that followed, though stricken by hypothermia and other injuries, the patrol 'went ballistic'. Four men were captured. Three died. Only one escaped. For the survivors, however, the worst ordeals were to come. Delivered to Baghdad, they were tortured with a savagery for which not even their intensive SAS training had prepared them.

Bravo Two Zero is a breathtaking account of Special Forces soldiering: a chronicle of superhuman courage, endurance and dark humour in the face of overwhelming odds. Believed to be the most highly decorated patrol since the Boer War, *Bravo Two Zero* is already part of SAS legend.

'SUPERHUMAN ENDURANCE, HORRENDOUS TORTURE, DESPERATE ODDS – UNPARALLELED REVELATIONS'
Daily Mail

'ONE OF THE MOST EXTRAORDINARY EXAMPLES OF HUMAN COURAGE AND SURVIVAL IN MODERN WARFARE'
The Times

0 552 14127 5

CORGI BOOKS

A SELECTED LIST OF NON-FICTION TITLES AVAILABLE FROM TRANSWORLD PUBLISHERS

THE PRICES SHOWN BELOW WERE CORRECT AT THE TIME OF GOING TO PRESS. HOWEVER TRANSWORLD PUBLISHERS RESERVE THE RIGHT TO SHOW NEW RETAIL PRICES ON COVERS WHICH MAY DIFFER FROM THOSE PREVIOUSLY ADVERTISED IN THE TEXT OR ELSEWHERE.

15108 4	WITNESS TO WAR: DIARIES OF THE SECOND WORLD WAR IN EUROPE	*Richard Aldrich*	£9.99
15129 7	JIHAD vs. McWORLD	*Benjamin Barber*	£8.99
15088 6	TRACES OF GUILT	*Neil Barrett*	£6.99
99065 5	THE PAST IS MYSELF	*Christabel Bielenberg*	£8.99
99965 2	BLACK HAWK DOWN	*Mark Bowden*	£6.99
81506 7	GALLIPOLI	*L. A. Carlyon*	£9.99
14465 7	CLOSE QUARTER BATTLE	*Mike Curtis*	£7.99
81445 1	HIMMLER'S CRUSADE	*Christopher Hale*	£7.99
15022 3	INSIDE DELTA FORCE	*Eric Haney*	£6.99
14789 3	THE DREADFUL JUDGEMENT	*Neil Hanson*	£7.99
15049 5	OVERWORLD	*Larry J. Kolb*	£7.99
14965 9	YOU GOT NOTHING COMING	*Jimmy Lerner*	£7.99
77133 3	MY WAR GONE BY, I MISS IT SO	*Anthony Loyd*	£7.99
12419 2	CHICKENHAWK	*Robert C. Mason*	£8.99
13953 X	SOME OTHER RAINBOW	*John McCarthy & Jill Morrell*	£8.99
14127 5	BRAVO TWO ZERO	*Andy McNab*	£7.99
14276 X	IMMEDIATE ACTION	*Andy McNab*	£7.99
15026 6	WE WERE SOLDIERS ONCE . . . AND YOUNG	*Lt. Gen. Harold G. Moore and Joseph L. Galloway*	£7.99
81385 4	A TIME TO DIE	*Robert Moore*	£6.99
81460 5	THE WAR AND UNCLE WALTER	*Walter Musto*	£7.99
77171 6	THE FIRST HEROES	*Craig Nelson*	£7.99
14607 2	THE INFORMER	*Sean O'Callaghan*	£6.99
81657 8	ONE FOURTEENTH OF AN ELEPHANT	*Ian Denys Peek*	£9.99
99886 9	WILFUL MURDER	*Diana Preston*	£7.99
81554 7	DAD'S WAR	*Howard Reid*	£6.99
81610 1	THE LAST MISSION	*Jim Smith and Malcolm McConnell*	£7.99
81360 9	IN HARM'S WAY	*Doug Stanton*	£6.99
14984 5	WAR JUNKIE	*Jon Steele*	£6.99
81444 3	WHERE THEY LAY	*Earl Swift*	£7.99
14968 3	THE TRENCH	*Richard Van Emden*	£8.99
14788 5	COLD ZERO	*Christopher Whitcomb*	£6.99
77314 X	GERMS	*Richard Wollheim*	£7.99
15189 0	GENERATION KILL	*Evan Wright*	£6.99

All Transworld titles are available by post from:
Bookpost, PO Box 29, Douglas, Isle of Man, IM99 1BQ
Credit cards accepted. Please telephone +44 (0)1624 677237, fax +44 (0)1624 670923, Internet http://www.bookpost.co.uk or e-mail: bookshop@enterprise.net for details.
Free postage and packing in the UK. Overseas customers: allow £2 per book (paperbacks) and £3 per book (hardbacks).